Microcomputers in Accounting

Microcomputers in Accounting

Frank Blewett MA, FIS

Head of School (Accounting)
Business School
Polytechnic of North London

Robin Jarvis BA, FCCA

Principal Lecturer in Accounting and Finance
Kingston Business School
Kingston Polytechnic

Van Nostrand Reinhold (International)
The Institute of Chartered Accountants
in England and Wales

First published in 1989 by
Van Nostrand Reinhold (International) Co. Ltd
11 New Fetter Lane, London EC4P 4EE
and
The Institute of Chartered Accountants in England & Wales
Chartered Accountants' Hall,
Moorgate Place, London EC2P 2BJ

Typeset in 10/12 Cheltenham Book by
Leaper & Gard Ltd, Bristol
Printed in Great Britain by
St Edmundsbury Press, Bury St Edmunds, Suffolk

ISBN 0 7476 0033 3

British Library Cataloguing in Publication Data

Blewett, Frank
    Microcomputers in accounting.
    1. Accounting. Applications of microcomputer
    systems
    I. Title   II. Jarvis, Robin
    657'.028'5416

    ISBN 0–7476–0033–3

Contents

Acknowledgements

A considerable amount of research was required in writing this book in order to establish the developments and current usage of micro-computers by accounting practices and their clients. In this respect we have been fortunate in obtaining the co-operation of a number of practising accountants and manufacturers of software. In particular we would like to thank Alan Lindsey and a number of the members of the North London Society of Chartered Accountants, Keith Gordon and Jonathan Teller of Levy Gee, Howard Gross of Gross Klein and Co., Douglas Rose of Rose Moffat and Co., Roger Hinshelwood of Computer Services Midlands Ltd, Roy Sutcliffe of Thorn EMI Computer Software Ltd and David Blechner of Star Computer Group plc.

We would also like to thank Martin Topple and Norman Stang who have given us helpful advice in this project.

Finally we thank our wives Ros (Blewett) and Moira (Jarvis) for their encouragement and advice, and our children Tamsin, Morwenna and Kerensa (Blewett) and Philippa and Lindsay (Jarvis) for their tolerance and support during the many hours consumed in writing this book.

Preface

There has been a tendency for books on microcomputers to be written either for users of a particular microcomputer or particular computer software, or, alternatively, for the business community in general. Whilst a number of these books have made useful contributions to the development of microcomputers for business applications, they have not looked at the needs of specific users. This book is primarily aimed at one particular group of users: namely, small- to medium-sized practising firms of accountants. These firms have particular needs in relation to the provision of information to their clients and the management of their practices. For example, a large proportion of their clients tend to be sole traders and small unincorporated firms, and the accounting information requirements of these organizations have been recognized as being very different from those of larger corporations.

The emphasis of the book is on practical applications. For this reason, a number of practising firms were contacted and their experience in the application of microcomputers to their work has been taken into consideration in the text. Thus sections of the book will focus on what is being done in the field of microcomputing, examining possible applications and identifying problems experienced by firms, as well as considering likely benefits. Although the book is principally aimed at practising accountants, it should also be useful to students on accounting courses that include practical elements of microcomputing. Thus it will be relevant to undergraduate students in Accounting and Business, and to Accounting Foundation Course students, as well as to those studying for professional examinations such as ICA, ACCA, CIMA, CIPFA, ICSA and so on.

Particular computer packages will be used to illustrate applications where necessary; the packages selected are reasonable examples of their type, but this should not be taken as an endorsement. Often, there will be a number of equally good packages, and it may be that another package has facilities which make it better suited to a particular application.

Disclaimer

The authors and publishers wish to make it clear that any references to particular software packages or other computer products in this book in no way imply official endorsement by the Institute of Chartered Accountants in England and Wales (ICAEW).

Please note that where the pronouns he or she occur in the text they should be taken to mean either sex.

Glossary of computing terms

ASCII	(American Standard Code for Information Interchange) coding system which allocates numeric codes to characters, so that text can be stored in a computer.
AT	(Advanced Technology) faster microcomputer introduced by IBM in 1984 based on Intel 80286, with hard disk and 1 megabyte diskette drive.
AT-compatible	microcomputers made by other manufacturers with similar specification to IBM-AT.
Bit	(binary digit) smallest unit of capacity in a computer, storing a 0 or a 1.
Byte	most useful unit of capacity, since one byte stores one character of text. Equivalent to 8 bits.
CD-ROM	(Compact Disc, Read Only Memory) high capacity storage device, read only.
CGA	(Colour Graphics Adaptor) lowest resolution colour screen available on IBM-compatible microcomputers. Poor quality, and becoming relatively obsolete.
Chip	see Microchip
Command-driven	program which responds to a series of commands from the user, rather than providing a restricted set of choices.
Compiler	program which translates from a specified programming language into binary code.
Computer	electronic device which can perform arithmetic calculations in logical sequence and branch according to simple numeric tests.

CPU	(Central Processing Unit) see Processor.
Database	set of data files or a package which creates and updates those files: see Chapter 6.
Decision support system	(DSS) a 'user-friendly' modelling package which enables programs and reports to be easily defined, and which has powerful data-handling features. Unfortunately, there is no precise, agreed definition of a DSS.
Directory	list of files on a disk. May also contain **subdirectories**, each of which may contain files and further subdirectories.
Disk	fast, random access device for permanent storage of computer data. See also **Hard disks** and **Diskettes**.
Diskette	or floppy disk. Removable disk used on microcomputers, storing between 100 kilobytes (KB) and 1.5 megabytes (MB), depending on the type of disk drive used.
DOS	(Disk Operating System) computer program which controls the operation of a microcomputer.
EGA	(Enhanced Graphic Adaptor) high-quality colour screen available on IBM-compatible microcomputers, with a resolution of 640 × 225 pixels.
Ethernet	commonly used proprietary design of network hardware, including cabling and other communications hardware.
Field	data item on a record, e.g. the name or price of a product.
File	a set of records of similar format, e.g. a stock file will consist of stock records, each relating to one stock item.
Floppy disk	see **Diskette**.
Fourth generation language	(4GL) a high-level language with database features and facilities to easily create data entry screens and reports; however, no precise, agreed definition of a 4GL exists.
Gigabyte	1024 megabytes, or about one thousand million bytes.
Hard copy	printed output from a computer.
Hard disk	or Winchester disk, sealed fixed disk capable of storing from 10 to 500 megabytes of information.
Hardware	the physical equipment making up a computer.
IBM-compatible	microcomputer with similar specification to IBM-PC or IBM-AT microcomputers, which runs any

software written for those computers.

Interpreter translation program used in interactive mode with certain languages, especially BASIC. Similar to a compiler, an interpreter translates from the programming language into binary code.

Joystick device for moving cursor or pointer around the computer screen. Normally only used on home computers for games.

Kilobyte (KB) 1024 bytes, or about 1000 bytes.

LCD (Liquid Crystal Display) type of display used on digital watches, and commonly used on portable microcomputers.

Local area (LAN) set of microcomputers connected by cable
network and appropriate communications hardware.

Macro or macro-program, a sequence of commands activated by one single command: used to automate complex tasks.

Mainframe very large and powerful computer used for heavy batch processing, and supporting upwards of fifty simultaneous users.

Megabyte (MB) 1024 kilobytes, or about one million bytes.

Megahertz (MHz) one million cycles per second: normally used to measure the speed of a processor.

Memory fast, immediately accessible internal storage on a computer which is usually volatile, i.e it is erased when the computer is switched off. See also **RAM** and **ROM**.

Menu-driven a package which directs the user to a course of action via a series of sets of choices, or menus.

Micro-channel (MCA) internal communications hardware on the
architecture IBM PS/2 microcomputers.

Microchip small slice, usually of silicon, on which thousands of electronic circuits have been etched by a photographic process.

Microcomputer a desktop computer which can support only a few simultaneous users, and is most commonly limited to a single user.

Microprocessor microchip containing a processor, the key circuits for controlling the operations of a microcomputer and performing any necessary arithmetic calculations.

Minicomputer medium-sized computer typically supporting from ten to sixty simultaneous users.

Model	an idealized representation of reality; a computer model for planning normally contains a program or logic/rules, plus data and report/graph formats.
Modem	(modulator-demodulator) communications device used to connect computers via the telephone network.
Mouse	device used for moving a pointer around a computer screen; the mouse is moved around a flat surface, activating a roller ball or light-sensitive transistors under the mouse.
MSDOS	Microsoft operating system used on all IBM-compatible microcomputers.
Multitasking	simultaneous operation of several tasks on a computer: usually several tasks operating on one microcomputer, each using one window.
Network	set of computers connected locally, by telephone lines or by satellite communication. See also **Local Area Network**.
NLQ	(Near Letter Quality) higher quality print produced by dot matrix printer.
Operating system	program which controls all operations of a computer, and prompts the user for commands.
OS/2	Microsoft operating system adopted for the IBM PS/2 series of microcomputers.
Package	ready-written set of programs marketed to meet the requirements of a particular application.
PC	personal computer. Often refers to IBM-PC, the first microcomputer made by IBM.
PC-compatible	microcomputer with similar specification to IBM-PC or IBM-XT (relatively slow processor, 360K-disk drives) which runs any software written for the IBM-PC.
PCDOS	IBM proprietary version of Microsoft operating system.
Pixel	dot on screen used for forming characters or drawing graphs; smallest piece of screen that can be addressed. The quality of a screen operating in graphics mode is determined by the resolution, or the number of pixels in the screen.
Printer	device for producing typed output from a computer. See Chapter 2 for details of different types.
Processor	the part of the hardware containing the key circuits for controlling the operations of a computer and

	performing any necessary arithmetic calculations. On micrcomputers and on some minicomputers, the processor will be contained on a single microchip.
Program	set of instructions, written in a particular programming language, to perform a particular task. See Chapter 3.
RAM	(Random Access Memory) memory chips used for temporary internal storage of data immediately accessible to processor. Usually volatile, i.e. erased if computer is switched off.
Record	data relating to one individual in a file, e.g. a customer record containing data relating to one customer.
ROM	(Read Only Memory) non-volatile memory chips used for permanent storage of programs, most usually the programs needed to start the computer running when it is switched on.
Software	computer programs: see **Program**.
Spreadsheet	a package used for financial planning, and many other useful calculations. See Chapter 5.
Tape streamer	device for backing up hard disks, using magnetic tape cassettes.
Terminal	device connected to a computer for interactive communication by a user. May be **dumb** (as with a teletype or a simple screen and keyboard) or **intelligent** (as with a microcomputer, which can be used as a terminal, but also has its own processing capability).
Token Ring	IBM communications hardware used as a basis for many local area networks.
VGA	(Video Graphics Adaptor) high quality colour screen available on IBM PS/2 microcomputers, with a resolution of 640 × 480 pixels.
WIMP	(Window Icon Mouse Pointer) system, a 'user-friendly' type of operating system likely to become increasingly fashionable. See Chapter 3.
Winchester disk	see **Hard disk**.
Word	smallest addressable unit of storage in computer, usually 16 or 32 bits in a microcomputer.
Word processing	editing of text stored electronically. See Chapter 13.

1 Introduction to microcomputers

The nature of the work of the accountant lends itself to information technology, and in particular to microcomputer applications. A recent study, sponsored by the Chartered Association of Certified Accountants and the Department of Trade and Industry, identified the typical accountant as spending 81% of his or her time on information-related activities.

The work of an accounting practice is mainly concerned with data storage, calculation and data processing and communication; all of these are information-related activities which can be more efficiently dealt with by a computer. It is, however, only in recent years that small- to medium-sized practices have been in the position financially to invest in computers and the associated software packages. Primarily the reason for this is the dramatic decrease in the cost of hardware, which has made capital investments of this nature financially worthwhile.

A number of the clients of this size of practice have often had a longer experience with microcomputer applications. In the late 1970s the first business microcomputers were introduced, starting with Commodore PET and Apple in 1977. The marketing of these business microcomputers and their associated software packages tended to concentrate on the small business user. It was from these clients that practising accountants started to have contact with microcomputers. Since then the situation has changed radically; the majority of practices will now have quite a number of clients who are making substantial use of computers. It is therefore essential that the professional accountant has a good understanding of the problems involved. Hence the importance of understanding microcomputers and associated applications cannot be restricted to the accountant's own work; it must be extended to a working knowledge of a client's microcomputer system so that he or she can adequately service the needs of the client.

1.1 MICROCOMPUTER APPLICATIONS AND PRODUCTIVITY

A major function of the accountant is to provide information to meet regulatory requirements. There has been a tendency over the years for regulatory bodies to standardize this accounting information. Legislation has also tended towards the standardization of accounting disclosure requirements; for example, the 1985 *Companies Act* specifies a number of prescribed formats. Also, the Accounting Standards Committee has been a major force in standardizing accounting information.

It would seem that this progressive standardization will continue in the future; such standardized reporting can be coped with far more efficiently by a computer-based system than by the traditional means of accounts production. For example, the preparation of final accounts is a relatively straightforward exercise when using a microcomputer; once the balances have been established for the trial balance, these balances can automatically be transferred to the standardized format of the profit and loss account and balance sheet. These accounts do not therefore have to be manually prepared and typed for each client, as is the case in a traditional accounting system.

Legislation and Accounting Standards have also tended, over the years, to increase the information that companies, individuals and other organizations have to supply; there is no reason to believe that this trend will be reversed. These demands for more information have clearly generated more work for accountants. Much of this information can be more efficiently produced using a microcomputer with suitable accounting software.

Productivity should increase through the use of microcomputer applications in response to the regulatory bodies' move towards greater standardization and more disclosure, as well as the nature of other information-related activities performed by the accountant. Increased productivity ultimately creates important cost savings in accounting practices; the CACA/DTI study referred to at the beginning of the chapter predicted productivity gains of up to 18% when using information technology support. Many other commentators have predicted much larger savings. Some practices have also found another source of cost saving in using microcomputers: some of the work that was previously performed by qualified staff is now being performed by less costly technicians.

1.2 YOUR COMPUTER AND THE BENEFITS TO CLIENTS

For an accounting practice to expand it clearly needs to increase the number of its clients, and/or to increase the services to current clients. Obviously, clients and potential clients must be able to recognize the benefits to be gained prior to committing themselves to additional services or changing their accountant. The question arises: can microcomputers add to the services offered and make these services more attractive to clients?

There is a considerable amount of evidence to support the view that timeliness of information is critical to clients in their decision-making. In some cases, the delay in information has been cited as the main reason for the failure of firms; microcomputers can help to avoid such delays. For example, a North London sole practitioner related to us an occasion when his microcomputer solved a client's financial crisis. The client's bank refused to accept his cheques, and would not extend his overdraft facility until the bank received interim accounts and a cash budget. Happily, the sole practitioner was able to supply the information in less than a day, with the aid of his microcomputer. This, as he stressed, would not have been feasible a year or two previously when he did not have the microcomputer.

In general, the introduction of microcomputers to accounting practices has substantially reduced the time taken to produce information for clients. This time-saving can be passed on to clients and their businesses will clearly benefit from more timely decision-making that should translate itself into financial benefits.

Experience has shown that the services that accountants offer, in terms of information, can also be extended when microcomputers are used. In the past, information that was relevant to clients for their internal management control purposes was often too costly to produce. Thus accountants found that there was a very limited market for such information. Today, by employing microcomputers, accountants can offer such a service at a relatively low cost. In the current competitive environment, services of this nature are extremely helpful to clients in controlling their business activities.

Clients have also benefited from the improved quality of presentation of information when their accountants use microcomputers; by using word processing facilities, it is possible to produce much more 'tailored' reports for clients. Presentation of information is not always seen as one of the more important characteristics of an information service; however, users of accounting information are often strongly affected in their attitudes by the quality of presentation. For example, bank managers tend to be more inclined to accept the credibility of a customer if the information that he supplies with a loan application is well presented.

Lastly, the productivity gains, resulting in cost savings as mentioned earlier, can be passed on to the client, making the practice more cost competitive.

The increase in the number of practising firms of accountants and other institutions (e.g. banks) offering accounting services has resulted in clients and potential clients being more aware of the range of services available. A number of benefits have been identified in this section when accountants use microcomputers — there are more! It is generally recognized that if accounting practices do not keep up to date in applying computers, then it is likely that their business will decline. In contrast, there are a number of accounting practices which are well advanced in the field of microcomputer applications and have consequently experienced an expansion in the demand for their services.

It is also the case in recent years that medium-sized practices using microcomputers have been able to compete much more effectively with the top accounting firms for large-client accounts. Prior to the introduction of microcomputers there was a very noticeable move towards market concentration. In 1968 the top ten accounting firms had one-third of the listed companies as clients; in 1983 the respective figure was two-thirds. It would appear that this trend is now declining as the medium-sized practices can often now offer at least compatible services at competitive prices to clients.

1.3 DEVELOPMENT OF MICROCOMPUTERS

Until the mid 1970s, computers required massive investment in hardware, air-conditioned rooms to operate in, and vast numbers of staff to make them work. Most small- to medium-sized businesses, if they used a computer at all, used time on a machine belonging to a computer bureau.

In the mid 1970s, minicomputers appeared: these were desk-sized computers, not requiring air-conditioning or too much in the way of attention from special staff. Minicomputers were acquired by thousands of medium-sized businesses, and by many larger accounting practices. Nevertheless, they still represented a fairly large investment, and were not that easy to use for a small business without the time to get to know their quirks.

The microcomputer revolution began quietly around 1977, with the launch of the Apple II and the Commodore Pet. At first, microcomputers were seen just as something of interest to computer freaks, but gradually they developed into serious business machines. Partly, this was a question of developing the equipment to cope adequately with business applications, but mainly it was a question of software development. The programs needed to perform business applications had to be written in a way that was sufficiently 'user-friendly' for a small business.

By the early 1980s, microcomputers were available with good software for most of the common business applications. Since then, growth has been extremely rapid, although a key factor was the launch by IBM of the PC in 1983. Many companies started to consider microcomputers seriously for the first time, and UK sales of business microcomputers began to be measured in hundreds of thousands rather than thousands. Another key factor has been the reducing costs of microcomputers, due to improving technology and to a highly competitive market. The net result is that business microcomputers currently available are more powerful and much cheaper than they were only two or three years ago.

The photographs in this chapter show some typical current business microcomputers. Figure 1.1 shows an IBM Personal System/2 Model 30, one of the series of business microcomputers launched by IBM in 1987. There seems no reason to doubt that eventual sales will reach several million; like the original IBM-PC and the later IBM-AT models, the PS/2 series will undoubtedly have many imitators. The PS/2 Model 30 is typical of current desk-top microcomputers; they all look fairly similar, although their detailed characteristics may vary slightly.

Many accountants find it convenient to have a computer that they can take home, or to a client's office where it can be used to record data on an audit, and can communicate with the main office computer via a telephone line. A number of computer companies now offer genuinely portable microcomputers, and Figure 1.2 shows the Toshiba 3100 portable which weighs just under 15 lb (about 7 kg), and fits into a briefcase. This has a flat supertwisted LCD screen built in to the lid, and includes a 20 MB hard disk which can store both software and huge amounts of data. Because of the special technology used, it is slightly more expensive than a standard business microcomputer, but for many users requiring a highly portable machine, the extra cost is well worthwhile.

Finally, Figure 1.3 shows a multi-user system, such as used by many accounting offices for general work. The computer shown here is the Star Auditor 1000, which allows up to eight simultaneous users where a single processor is used, and up to 128 users where multiple processors are used.

Figure 1.1 IBM Personal System/2 Model 30. Reproduced courtesy of IBM.

1.4 MICROCOMPUTER APPLICATIONS

Internal management applications

The internal management of a practice will be concerned with the planning and control function, producing the partnership accounts, and the routine office administration functions. It is of course a fact that investment in computer hardware and software for these functions will not translate itself into precise measurable benefits (i.e. fee income) as in the case of work directly related to the needs of clients. However, accountants do not need to be told about the importance of these functions in business organizations. It is a fact that small- to medium-sized practices in particular are constantly subject to financial pressures brought about by the long wait for fee income. Investment

Figure 1.2 Toshiba T3100/20 portable microcomputer. Reproduced courtesy of Toshiba Information Systems (UK) Ltd.

in computer hardware and software can improve the financial controls of the practice as well as making cost savings.

The question as to whether or not it is appropriate to use such applications for these internal management functions is clearly a cost-benefit question, which will be considered later. It should, however, be said that all practices, whether a sole practitioner or a 'large' medium-sized firm, in our experience have gained from using these microcomputer applications.

Applications for clients

The demand for microcomputer applications from clients will depend upon whether or not the clients have their own computer systems.

Figure 1.3 Star Auditor 1000 multi-user system. Reproduced courtesy of Star Computer Group PLC.

Often in the case of smaller clients a number of practices offer bureau facilities, which may include, for example, a comprehensive integrated accounting system.

The following briefly describes some of the applications available and used by practices for their own internal management and applications for clients; a number of these applications will be dealt with in more detail later in the book.

Time recording

The recording of time spent on work for clients is one of the most important controls necessary for an efficiently run practice. A database package can be used to keep records in the way that any particular practice requires, although a specialist time recording and fees ledger is often used.

Maintaining ledger accounts

Software packages relating to the bookkeeping and the accounting function may include:

1. nominal ledger
2. purchase ledger
3. sales ledger
4. invoicing
5. credit control
6. VAT computations and returns.

These packages are ongoing in the sense that entries are made throughout the year and ledgers are updated. This updating process distinguishes them from incomplete record packages which normally ascertain balances for ledgers for the whole of an accounting period.

Packages covering these functions could be integrated, or they could be stand-alone programs. The use of these packages will clearly depend upon the client and the practice. For example, a retailer with a large range of purchases from a number of suppliers who offer varying credit terms would probably find a purchase ledger package extremely useful. The same retailer, assuming all his sales are for cash, would hardly find a sales ledger package useful. In contrast, a wholesaler may use both sales and purchase ledger packages, but the sales ledger is likely to be far more critical.

In general, the software available is well tested and reliable. Standardized off-the-shelf packages will normally satisfy the requirements of both clients and professional firms.

Accounts production and incomplete records

Accounts production packages can vary considerably in coverage and in the information they generate, and the packages used will depend to a large extent on the client's requirements. For many clients, the first stage in accounts production will be reconciliations of incomplete records kept by the client; for other clients who maintain their own ledger accounts it may merely be a matter of making suitable adjustments to produce the final accounts.

A typical accounts production package would generate the following items of information:

1. nominal ledger
2. bank and cash reconciliation
3. trial balance
4. VAT returns
5. final accounts, including notes to the accounts and the directors' report.

Stock control
Stock control packages can relate to stock purchased and/or sold. In the case of a wholesaler, for example, stocks purchased and sold are clearly closely related and the software may extend to both forms of stock control. The packages can be of an individual nature or integrated with the purchase and/or sales ledgers. A typical stock control package will generate the following information:

1. stock movements over defined periods by description and value
2. the identification of slow moving stock
3. stock prices/costs: a package will give options for differing valuation models, e.g. LIFO
4. outstanding orders, detailing customers/suppliers, dates of the orders and values
5. lead times
6. location of stock.

Office Administration
There are three main applications for microcomputers in this area: payroll, general records and mailing lists, and word processing. These applications are relevant to both the accountant and to his clients.

Payroll is often a very obvious application for a microcomputer, because it can be time-consuming and tedious to do otherwise, particularly remembering all the reports that are needed relating to tax, national insurance, pension contributions and so on. Some accountants run a bureau service for their smaller clients, as well as running their own payroll on their microcomputer.

Records may be kept on either employees or clients for reference purposes, and this is often done by using a database package, which allows complete flexibility in defining how the records are to be kept. This can be especially useful where regular reports are needed, or where address labels are needed for mailing purposes.

Word processing has been by far the most popular application for microcomputers, and can be invaluable in an accounting office. Where reports need several drafts before being sent to clients, considerable retyping can be avoided, at a significant cost saving. It is also useful where a standard letter needs to be sent out to different clients, or where standard contracts (with minor revisions) are to be issued to different clients. Word processing software is often linked into mailing list software, enabling the same standard letter to be addressed to a number of different clients.

Financial planning and budgets

The applications that have been developed in this area are becoming very sophisticated and very marketable. The majority of these applications use a spreadsheet modelling concept.

The most popular applications include:

1. investment appraisal
2. budgeting: sales, production and cash budgets
3. long-term forecasting
4. sensitivity analysis
5. monitoring of actual performance with budgets.

The reports generated can be very useful for presentation to outside parties, e.g. cash budgets included in the application for a bank loan.

Tax packages

Although a number of software suppliers have experienced teething problems, there has been a considerable amount of investment in the development of these applications. By far the majority of the packages on the market produce tax returns. There are a number of packages that are designed to do a number of different things, for example from full tax computations to capital gains computations.

1.5 MICROCOMPUTERS AND THEIR IMPACT ON PEOPLE

It was pointed out earlier that the introduction of microcomputers to accounting practices can bring about greater productivity and cost savings. The experience to date suggests that these savings will be spent developing and expanding the range of services offered by the practice. This expansion, to a degree, is reflected in employment patterns.

The division of staff between qualified and support staff over the last few years shows a marginal increase in the employment of qualified staff and a marginal decrease in support staff. It is anticipated with the expansion of microcomputers that this trend will continue. This trend is not surprising when one considers how the use of word processing has evolved in a number of accounting practices. Partners and senior staff often now carry out text creation and edit their own texts on word processors, thereby removing one of the main functions of secretaries.

Observers and commentators alike agree upon one aspect in the development of microcomputers in accounting practices: that the work of the accountant in the profession will change radically due to developments in information technology. It is the case at present that a large proportion of qualified staff have yet to obtain the experience and skills to cope with information technology and, in particular, with microcomputers. This is not surprising as the skills required to cope with this change are inadequately covered at present in professional education schemes, which mainly consist of professional examinations and continuing professional education courses. It is, however, true to say that all the professional bodies are investing considerable amounts of time and money in an attempt to alleviate this problem. For example, the Chartered Association of Certified Accountants, the Institute of Chartered Accountants in England and Wales and the Chartered Institute of Management Accountants have completed or are in the process of completing research projects on the effect of information technology on their members. All three bodies are also keenly organizing and sponsoring courses related to information technology. Thus it is clear that they recognize the importance of information technology and in particular its impact upon their members.

Some years ago, commentators saw the advent of computers in business as bringing tedium to people's working lives. Experience has shown that this need not be the case. Often the introduction of computers to businesses has enriched the quality of work previously performed manually. Computers can give greater responsibility to individuals in their work, as well as giving flexibility to practices in terms of working hours and job sharing where this is appropriate. In some cases it is possible for staff to work at home using microcomputers or accessing the firm's computer via a telephone line. Many people see the environment and the function of the office dramatically changing, from a place where once work was carried out, to a meeting place to discuss work that has been completed in the home environment.

2 Hardware

Hardware is the physical equipment which makes up a computer, as opposed to **software**, which is the set of programs (or instructions) that make the hardware operate. For convenience, this chapter relates to hardware and the next chapter to software, but they are totally interdependent in reality, and the two chapters are therefore inter-related. The aim of this chapter is to provide an understanding of basic hardware concepts, as far as is relevant to the professional accountant, without going too deeply into technical details. A detailed knowledge of technicalities is not necessary to run a computer, any more than it is needed to drive a motor car, but a certain degree of understanding can still be extremely useful at times.

The first section of this chapter discusses the main types of computer, followed by a description of the various pieces of hardware that form part of a microcomputer system. The later sections consider communications facilities relevant to an accountant, as well as networks and multi-user systems, which are likely to be of particular relevance to accounting practices and their clients.

The chapter relates principally to microcomputers, but many of the descriptions apply equally to hardware used on larger computers. The hardware used on larger computers will be faster and more expensive, but in principle very similar. Even medium-sized practices are likely to find a need for computers more powerful than the standard single-user microcomputers.

2.1 TYPES OF COMPUTER

Computers are usually classified into three main types, according to size: mainframes, minicomputers and microcomputers. However, the distinctions have become very blurred, and the descriptions given here are only very approximate.

Mainframe computers are very large machines costing upwards of £500000, and usually require air-conditioned rooms. They will support upwards of 50 users simultaneously, and will also have massive processing power. Mainframes are used only by very large companies, and often then only to take over the heavier processing from smaller computers when they get overloaded. The dominant mainframe manufacturer in the UK (as in most other countries) is undoubtedly IBM; other well-known names include Honeywell, ICL, Digital and Unisys. Even the largest accounting practices are unlikely to use mainframe computers, although many of their clients will use them.

Minicomputers (or minis) are medium-sized machines, costing from £15000 up to about £500000. A typical business minicomputer will support about 20 users simultaneously, but larger minis such as the Digital Vax 7650 can support 60 users or more. Well-known suppliers of minicomputers in the UK include IBM, Digital, Data General and Olivetti; there are also many smaller companies active in selling minicomputer systems, who buy in all the necessary major components and merely do a limited amount of final assembly work. There are also smaller companies, such as Star Computers, who have specialized in supplying small minicomputers to professional accountants.

Microcomputers are typically single-user systems (i.e. just one screen and keyboard), but they can support several users. A microcomputer system for eight users costs about £20000 (at 1988 prices), but larger microcomputer systems are available. Originally, microcomputers were manufactured by companies not previously active in computers; some companies, such as Apple, are still very successful but many others have gone out of business. The major development since 1982 has been that the more established computer manufacturers have all brought out microcomputers, most notably IBM for whom the PC and AT have been remarkably successful, though more recently IBM microcomputer sales have been badly hit by cheap 'clones' from companies such as Amstrad. In 1987, IBM introduced the Personal System/2 series in order to regain a strong position in the business market.

As mentioned above, the distinction between the different types is not all that clear; one also sometimes sees references to other types such as 'superminis' or 'supermicros', the definition of which varies from year to year. The distinction between multi-user micros and small minis is particularly unclear, and the term **small business computer (SBC)** is often used instead to refer to any machine up to the size of a small mini. This is a useful term, especially as it covers the type of computer likely to be used by most accounting practices.

Some very large practices will have large minis, but most will not need so much processing power.

2.2 PARTS OF THE COMPUTER

The **peripheral** parts of a microcomputer are usually fairly obvious at a casual glance, as in the photograph of an IBM PS/2 in Figure 1.1: a **screen** and **keyboard** to enable the user to communicate with the computer, and a **disk drive** to enable programs to be loaded and data to be permanently stored (the disk slot is on the left at the front). A **printer** for output will usually also be attached.

The main part of the computer, the **central processing unit (CPU)** or **processor**, is much less obvious to see. On cheap home micros, the processor is usually contained in the same box as the keyboard; on small business computers, the processor is usually contained in the same box as the disk drives. The processor box has sockets at the back for attaching screens and printers. For a single-user system, the screen is often placed on top of the processor box, with the keyboard in front; on a multi-user system, there will be several screens and keyboards (one for each user), each connected to the processor box. Some of these may be in different offices and connected by long cables.

2.3 MEASURING THE CAPACITY OF A COMPUTER

The basic unit of capacity in a computer is a **bit**, which can store one binary digit; computers operate in binary arithmetic, but sensible human beings do not need to. The most useful unit in referring to computer storage is a **byte**; a byte consists of eight bits, which can store any number from 0 to 255 ($= 2^8 - 1$). This means that a byte can be used to store a two-digit number, but perhaps more importantly it can be used to store one character in suitably coded form; most micro-computers allow up to 256 different characters, which are stored internally as numbers by the computer, having been coded according to a standard coding system. The usual system of coding used is known as ASCII, and Table 2.1 shows some examples of ASCII codes.

Other useful units of capacity are **kilobytes** and **megabytes**. A kilobyte (usually written as K or KB) is approximately 1000 bytes (actually 1024 bytes) and a megabyte (M or MB) is approximately 1000000 bytes. Disk capacities for small business computers are measured in kilobytes or megabytes, but for larger computers disk

Table 2.1 Examples of ASCII codes

Character	Code	Character	Code
F	70	(	40
f	102	)	41
X	88	&	38

capacities are often quoted in **gigabytes**, being approximately 1000000000 bytes.

Even experts sometimes find it difficult to predict whether a particular computer has enough capacity for certain applications, but there are broadly three points to consider:

1. *Memory* this is the temporary storage space in the computer, used to store programs and data while an application is running;
2. *Disk* the permanent storage space for programs and data files;
3. *Performance* how fast the computer carries out operations.

Because a byte stores one character, crude calculation of disk requirements becomes relatively straightforward: for example, a name and address which can be a maximum of 100 characters will require 100 bytes of disk storage; 2000 records would then require 200K of disk. In practice, allowance does need to be made for various overheads in these calculations, but at least it does give a rough guide. Allowance also has to be made for any software to be stored on the disk, but a competent dealer could tell you what space to allow for this. Disk capacity is not usually a major problem, since it has become relatively cheap, and disks of between 20 and 80MB are now standard.

Calculation of memory requirements is more complex, and an exact calculation needs intelligent guesswork, plus considerable knowledge as to how the operating system and other programs work. Fortunately, a minimum of at least 512K is now standard, and this is easily enough for most accounting applications.

There remains the question of performance, and even this is not important for many users; for a simple application, any commercially available business microcomputer will usually be quite fast enough. Performance needs to be considered where there is heavy processing (searching through a database of 1000 records or more) or in a multi-user system, where several users are sharing the same processor. Performance can be related to a number of factors: speed of the processor, access time on disks, and so on. Some microcomputer magazines run benchmark tests, which provide a useful guide of over-all performance, for single-user systems. For multi-user accounting systems, the only sensible guide is to visit current users of similar systems to see whether the total system can really cope with your workload.

2.4 CENTRAL PROCESSING UNIT (CPU)

The **central processing unit** consists of a number of microchips and other components mounted on printed circuit boards (PCBs). The key component is the microprocessor chip itself (sometimes referred to as the microprocessor unit, or MPU). The processor has two main functions: to control the sequence of operations within the computer (**logical function**) and to perform calculations (**arithmetic function**). In addition to the processor, there will be a number of memory chips, which allow temporary storage of programs and data while a program is being processed; these are discussed further in the next section. Most single-user microcomputers use one of the Intel chips, whereas multi-user accounting machines have tended to be based on the Motorola 68010 or 68020 processors; this has caused compatibility problems, because different software has been required for the different machines. In the near future, it is likely that many multi-user systems will be based on the Intel 80386 processor.

Emphasis tends to be given to the performance of the processor by manufacturers, but for many business applications this is of little importance. Most business applications involve frequent input/output operations via disk or printer; these are so vastly slower than the processor, that having a faster processor may contribute virtually nothing to overall performance. The performance of the processor in a single-user micro is only important in applications involving heavy processing, such as database applications or financial simulations, and especially graphics. However, having a powerful enough processor is important in a multi-user system, in order to ensure that the system is capable of responding quickly enough to all its users.

Memory

The memory for a microcomputer is contained in microchips either on the processor board or on a memory extension board. Its function is to provide immediate access storage for data and programs, enabling very fast retrieval by the processor.

The microchips used in microcomputers contain a tiny silicon wafer, in which it is possible to create a very large number of electronic circuits by etching (the Intel 80386 processor chip contains about 300 000 transistors); the silicon is enclosed in a block of epoxy resin and metal for protection. It was the cheap availability of microchips in very large numbers which led to the very rapid development of microcomputers. Manufacturing a microcomputer has become a relatively simple assembly operation, and this has led to a profusion of manufacturers — in the UK alone, there were over 100 different makes of microcomputer on sale in 1988.

Nevertheless, assessing the relative performance of different business microcomputers is not as difficult as one might initially think, because they can be classified according to which processor chip they are based on; virtually all business micros are based on one or another of a few standard chips.

Discussions of processors often also refer to **words**, the number of bits that can be processed at a time by a computer. This is important, because a processor with a longer word length will be faster as it will process more bits in a given period of time. Most microcomputers now sold have a word length of 16 bits (or 2 bytes). Some have a word length of 32 bits, to enable faster processing, while larger number-crunching mainframe computers may have a word length of 64 bits or more.

A useful comparison between different processor chips is the speed of operation, usually quoted in megahertz (MHz); 1 MHz is 1 000 000 cycles (or operations) per second.

Table 2.2 lists the standard processor chips currently in use for accounting applications, together with some of the microcomputers currently using those chips.

There are two types of memory chip, each with a specific function:

1. **RAM** (random access memory) is immediately erasable, and volatile, i.e. the contents are lost if the machine is switched off or if there is an accidental power cut. RAM is used to store the program currently being processed and any data that it requires.
2. **ROM** (read-only memory) is non-erasable and used for permanent storage of some operating system programs. The main function of this is to enable the computer to set itself into operation when it is switched on.

Microcomputers tend to have a relatively small ROM, typically about 60 K on a business micro. IBM-PC and AT microcomputers have a part of their operating system contained in ROM in a copyright BIOS chip; the purpose of this is to make it difficult for competitors to emulate precisely an IBM microcomputer. Sometimes, applications

Table 2.2 Standard processor chips

Processor chip	Word length	Speed (MHz)	Microcomputers using this processor
Intel 8086	16-bit	8	IBM PC-compatibles (e.g. Amstrad PC1640) IBM PS/2 Model 30
Intel 80286	16-bit	10	IBM AT and compatibles IBM PS/2 Models 50 and 60
Intel 80386	32-bit	16-20	IBM PS/2 Model 80 Compaq 386 Other high-performance micros
Motorola 68000 series	16/32 bits	Various (up to 12.5)	Apple Macintosh Various graphics workstations Multi-user accounting systems (e.g. Star Auditor 1000)

software is also supplied with an essential part of the program etched into a ROM chip; the purpose of this is to prevent software theft by copying of program disks. Programs supplied on ROM chips are referred to as **firmware** (being a combination of hardware and software).

RAM is relatively cheap, so a large memory is now standard on business micros, even though it is underutilized on many applications. It is no longer sensible to have less than 640K, particularly as this is the minimum requirement for some accounting software; 'AT-compatible' business micros often have 1MB or more. For most accounting applications, 640K RAM is totally adequate, but certain applications may require more; large spreadsheet models (Chapter 5) often need 1 or 2MB of RAM, and multi-tasking (where several programs are running simultaneously) can be very expensive on memory. Indeed, IBM recommend a minimum of 3MB of RAM for their larger PS/2 microcomputers, while multi-user computers will require substantially more memory.

Open architecture: 'add-ons'

A major factor in the success of the IBM-PC and AT series has undoubtedly been the **open architecture** adopted: the design of these microcomputers provides spare slots, so that additional circuit boards (usually referred to as 'add-on cards') can be added very simply. These have enabled users to develop their microcomputers for purposes not originally conceived by them (and perhaps not even by the original designers). At a time of rapid development, this has allowed considerable flexibility for progressive change. Many add-on cards are available for IBM-compatible microcomputers, some of the more common being:

1.   enhanced graphics adaptor (EGA) card for high-quality colour graphics
2.   mathematical card containing 8087 or 80287 mathematical co-processor for statistical and scientific applications
3.   memory enhancement card, containing additional RAM
4.   hard disk card (see section 2.5 below).

Other examples of add-on cards will be given later in this chapter.

The IBM PS/2 series offers features as standard which had previously only been available with add-on cards. The PS/2 is based on a new **micro-channel architecture** (MCA), the micro-channel taking the internal communications between the different parts of the micro-computer. While possibly being an improvement on previous designs, the micro-channel also has the advantage for IBM of making it more difficult for other manufacturers to supply add-ons without specific IBM approval. However, ways will doubtless be found around this, and add-on cards will undoubtedly continue to be important, offering a convenient way to upgrade microcomputers as new developments are introduced.

2.5 MAGNETIC DISK

Memory is unsuitable for permanent storage of programs or data, partly because it is limited in size, and also because of its volatility: data in RAM is erased when the computer is switched off, or even when there is a temporary loss of power. Permanent storage is provided on microcomputers by magnetic disk.

There are various types of disk, but the principles of operation are similar in each case. The disk itself consists of a circular piece of strong plastic, coated with a magnetic surface; the disk drive has a magnetic read/write head similar to that of a cassette recorder. Data is written on the disk in a series of concentric circles, referred to as **tracks**; the disk spins around fast, enabling any data stored on the disk to be very rapidly accessed by the read/write head. The disk drive has a controller which is a complex piece of electronic equipment, incorporating its own microprocessor, and using very sophisticated electromechanical equipment to move the head to access a specified track.

There are two main types of disk in use on microcomputers: **hard disks (Winchester disks)** and **diskettes** (or **floppy disks**). Their main characteristics are summarized in Table 2.3.

Hard disks are sealed units with capacities of 10 MB or more. They are manufactured in a completely dust-free environment, and hence can operate to a far higher packing density for data than a diskette. They are also usually faster than diskette drives.

Diskettes (usually referred to as disks) are removable flexible disks, contained in a paper or plastic envelope which is designed to protect the surface of the disk when it is removed from the disk drive. A small section of the disk is exposed when it is inserted in the disk drive, enabling the surface to be accessed by the disk head. The main types of floppy disks in current use are 5.25 inch and 3.5 inch disks, where the size is the diameter of the disk. A diskette drive is an essential part of any business microcomputer which enables new software or data to be loaded. Diskettes are also useful for making 'back-up' copies of data files, and sometimes important files are kept only on diskette, to guarantee that access is restricted.

Up until 1987, the type of disk most commonly used had been 5.25 in.; as used on the IBM-PC, the disk holds only 360 K, which is inadequate for many applications. The disks on the IBM PC/AT hold 1.2 MB, and this is much more satisfactory for most users.

Table 2.3 Comparison of different types of disk drive

Type	Capacity (bytes)	Access time (milliseconds)
5.25 in. floppy (IBM-PC format)	360 K	90-100
5.25 in. floppy (IBM-AT format)	1.2 MB	90-100
3.5 in. microdisk	720 K or 1.44 MB	90-100
Hard disk (slow)	10-20 MB	70-90
Hard disk (fast)	20-300 MB	30-60

The alternative 'microdisk', which is 3.5 in. in diameter, stores either 720 K or 1.44 MB. This is used in the Apple Macintosh and in most portable microcomputers, as well as the IBM PS/2. This type of disk is encased in a stiff plastic envelope, which enables the disk to be carried unprotected in a jacket pocket.

As a design, the 3.5 in. disk is superior to the older 5.25 in. and is likely to become the new standard, but the process of transition from the 5.25 in. standard will be slow, because companies have huge financial investments in hardware and software which they do not want to write off. The design is superior because 5.25 in. disks are easily damaged by mistreatment: they can be rendered unreadable by bending them, pouring tea over them, or simply by holding them by the exposed reading surface. Although 3.5 in. disks can also be damaged by determined vandals, they are much less likely to be damaged by simple human error.

The cheaper microcomputers suitable for business use have two diskette drives: one for a program disk, and one for a data disk. The disks themselves are not expensive, with prices ranging from about £1 to £8 depending on size and quality. A diskette drive costs £100.

Most business users prefer to have a hard disk instead of one diskette drive. A 20 MB hard disk adds about £300 to the cost of the computer, but makes the computer much more convenient to use. Indeed, many users have upgraded their microcomputers by inserting hard disk cards: add-on cards containing a hard disk unit and its controller.

The main advantage of having a hard disk is that it enables all programs and data to be immediately accessible, rather than spread over a series of diskettes. For a major accounting application, a hard disk is essential to enable all the data files to be kept together. The minimum size of hard disk is 10 MB, but 20 or 30 MB hard disks are now common. On multi-user systems, hard disks of 80 MB and upwards are now standard. The access times quoted in Table 2.3 indicate the average time taken to read a record; they require careful technical interpretation, and are useful mainly as a means of comparison between different makes of hard disk. In general, larger capacity (and more expensive) hard disks are faster, because they are designed for heavy usage.

2.6 BACKING UP DISKS

Some form of back-up is essential on any business micro; floppy disks wear out, or can get damaged or overwritten by a malfunctioning disk drive. Hard disks occasionally go wrong, and when they do their entire contents will probably be lost. Copies of programs are easily replaced, even if this does entail expenditure, but lost data files are extremely difficult to reconstruct and may even be irreplaceable. This applies especially to accounting systems: a sales ledger system may have been built up over several years, and it would be quite an awesome task to have to re-create all the customer accounts records because the hard disk had been lost.

With a well-run computer system this is unnecessary. It is simply a question of taking regular back-up copies of all data files (or at least keeping a record of changes), so that, if the file is damaged or over-written, it can then be restored from the back-up copy.

If the computer has twin diskette drives, then a back-up copy will be made from the original data disk on to a second disk. Even for a small hard disk, the diskette may provide an adequate back-up facility when one remembers that only the data files (or possibly only the day's updates) need to be copied regularly. For larger files (perhaps upwards of 10MB), the back-up files are likely to occupy several diskettes, and at this stage the process becomes quite unwieldy; a better solution is to use special back-up software, or to purchase suitable hardware.

Of these two options, back-up software provides the cheaper solution: there are a number of packages on the market which provide such a facility. They vary in their degree of sophistication, but essentially operate by keeping a record of any changes made to data files. It is then only necessary to copy these changes to a diskette each day (or each week), making the process relatively fast, rather than the slow process of copying the entire data file.

The second option is to use a **fast tape streamer**. This writes to a large tape cassette, and will copy a 20MB hard disk in about twenty minutes or so, the device costing about £850 at 1988 prices. A fast tape streamer is an expensive option where only one microcomputer is in use, but it is generally much more convenient to use than back-up software, which needs to be set up carefully. It is especially appropriate where several microcomputers are used, as it may be shared between the different machines. For large data files, as in a multi-user accounting system, this is the only viable option.

Finally, it should be remembered that one major reason for keeping back-up copies is the possibility of disasters such as fire or flood. It is important that copies are stored elsewhere than in the original office. If this is done, then in the event of fire, a computerized accounting system can be put back into operation on a different computer in a matter of hours. Restoring a manual accounting system in the event of fire is often nothing like as straightforward.

2.7 OPTICAL DISKS: CD-ROM AND WORM

An optical disk is a disk with a reflective surface into which tiny indentations are burned, the patterns representing data in coded form. These are then read by a laser device, the technology being similar to a home compact disc player. The advantage of an optical disk is the very high capacity: one disk can hold 500 MB or more. The disadvantage is that an optical disk can only be written once, unlike a conventional magnetic disk which can be overwritten many times.

There are two types of optical disk: **CD-ROM** (compact disc, read-only memory) and **WORM** (write once, read many). CD-ROM would be used for externally supplied databases, whereas WORM technology would be necessary for a user setting up a database.

CD-ROM players cost about £1000; they would be purchased by users of very large databases. For example, the UK Post Office has published all 23 million UK addresses on CD-ROM, and Lotus Development markets a very large financial database (including daily stock price history) on CD-ROM, which is of considerable relevance to medium or large accounting firms. Perhaps most remarkable is the BBC Domesday project (based on a BBC micro) which contains a vast range of detailed facts and pictures about the economy, social structure and geography of Great Britain.

2.8 VISUAL DISPLAY UNITS (VDUs)

A visual display unit is the usual form of communication between a user and a computer, and consists of a screen and a keyboard, which is usually detachable. The keyboard itself usually has the standard QWERTY layout as used on most typewriters, with a number of additional keys; these include a numeric keypad, cursor movement keys, and special function keys which can be programmed to carry out various tasks in conjunction with applications programs. Apart from the standard 'shift' key used as on typewriters to type capital letters, there are usually two other keys marked 'ctrl' (or 'control') and 'alt' which are used for generating special command characters.

The screen is usually 24 rows by 80 columns, although sometimes larger screens are used, especially for word processing. It takes a matter of a couple of seconds for a screenful of characters to be displayed. If the microcomputer has a graphics board, then the screen may also be addressed as a set of dots (known as **pixels**); a standard EGA (enhanced graphics adaptor) board with a high resolution monitor has a resolution of 640×225 pixels. Higher resolution screens are available, the VGA (video graphics adaptor) board on the IBM PS/2 allowing a resolution of up to 640 × 480 pixels, and even higher resolution is available on some microcomputers designed for graphics applications. For most business applications, an EGA or VGA system offers extremely good colour quality. Only users such as architects and designers are likely to need higher resolution screens.

For accounting applications, a monochrome screen is often adequate, monochrome being green or amber on a black background. A good quality monochrome screen is considerably cheaper than a similar colour screen. On the other hand, many recent packages do rely on colour for effective presentation, and colour is valuable for programs that use graphics (such as Lotus 1-2-3).

2.9 OTHER INPUT DEVICES

Much attention has been paid recently to avoiding the use of keyboards, and making things easier for new (or occasional) users to overcome their fear of computers. It is certainly useful to provide such users with a more direct means of communication than a keyboard; ideally, this would be by speech, but unfortunately voice communication with computers is still at a very rudimentary level. Home micros often have **joysticks** for moving things around on the screen, and this is ideal for games. However, for business applications, a joystick is rather unstable, and a device known as a **mouse** is used.

A mouse is a plastic object, designed to be held in the palm of the hand. It has a couple of buttons on top, and usually a roller ball underneath. It is also necessary to install a mouse interface card in your microcomputer, which has a socket for the mouse cable to plug into. There are various makes, of which the best-known is the Microsoft mouse, shown in Figure 2.1, which uses a roller ball. An alternative design, the PC-Mouse, operates by optically detecting its movements around a special flat pad. The basic idea is that the mouse can be moved along the desk in order to move an arrow on the screen; decisions can be signalled by pressing one or both buttons. It is ideal for situations where the user needs to select his next action from one of a series of choices.

Mouse-based systems are becoming increasingly popular, and are discussed at greater length in the next chapter. However, for accounting offices, such systems are likely to remain a side issue; the main concern in accounting is usually to get large amounts of data into the computer in the shortest time possible. Much the same consideration applies with word processing, and hence there is unlikely to be any

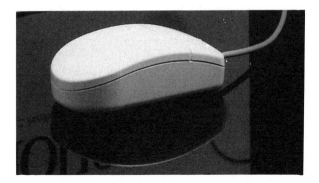

Figure 2.1 Microsoft mouse. Reproduced courtesy of Microsoft Ltd.

real substitute for a keyboard in the near future. The most that can be said for mice is that they may make computers slightly more user-friendly.

2.10 PRINTERS

A suitable printer is essential with any microcomputer for business use. Although it is sometimes claimed that computers are leading to paperless systems, experience shows that in reality computer systems generate vast amounts of paper. There are four main kinds of printers in common use: laser printers, dot matrix printers, daisywheel printers and inkjet printers. The characteristics of these printers are compared in Table 2.4.

Laser printers resemble photocopiers, and indeed use similar technology. They are easier to use than other types of printer, simply requiring paper to be loaded as for a photocopier and very occasional other maintenance. They are expensive (£2000 to £3000), but are quiet and generally ideal for an office environment; they provide very high quality printing, suitable for letters and for professional documents. Laser printers will not accept continuous computer paper, and will not usually accept special stationery, such as label stationery. Because of high running costs and slowish speeds, laser printers are unsuitable for general accounting applications, but would normally be used where high quality print is necessary. Laser printers are essentially graphics page printers: they print a page at a time consisting of a large number of dots in the form of text, but the dots can equally form pictures or graphs. Lasers are therefore also extremely useful for printing graphs,

Table 2.4 Comparison of different printers

Type	Speed (cps)	Cost (£)	General comments
Laser	8 pages per minute	2000-3000	Silent, high quality
Daisywheel	40-60	1200-1600	High quality, extremely noisy
Dot matrix	150-400 40-100 (NLQ)	150-600	Cheap, robust, adequate for most documents
Inkjet	Various	500-2000	Cheap, silent printer (some inkjet printers print in three or more colours)

and are an essential part of a desk-top publishing system (see Chapter 13).

Daisywheel printers were the standard letter quality office printers until about 1985. The name refers to the print-wheel, which is reminiscent of the head of a daisy. Daisywheels are character printers (they print one character at a stroke), and can produce very high quality print but are useless for graphics or desk-top publishing applications. Fast daisywheel printers cost from £1200 upwards. To be effective in an office environment, sheet feeders and acoustic covers are necessary, and the cost is then comparable to a laser printer. The running costs for daisywheels are theoretically lower than for lasers, but they require more maintenance and are noisier; for most purposes, a laser would be a better choice. However, daisywheels can cut stencils and print multiple copies or use label stationery, whereas lasers cannot. Not surprisingly, the market for daisywheel printers has been rapidly eroded by laser printers for high quality work. It has also been eroded by cheap competition from dot matrix printers producing near letter quality (NLQ) print.

Dot matrix printers are the standard 'workhorse' printers of any accounting office: speeds of up to about 400 characters per second (cps) are possible. Standard dot matrix printers print 150 cps, or about 2 pages per minute, and cost up to £300; they form characters by printing from a matrix of dots, as shown in Figure 2.2. A dot matrix has a standard character set, but usually offers about 50 to 100 alternative character sets, including boldface and large print for headings. A printer with a width of 80 characters will also produce 96 characters

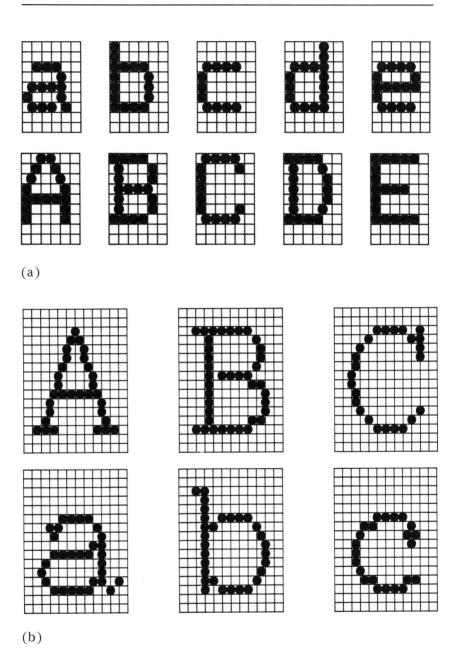

(a)

(b)

Figure 2.2 Formation of dot matrix characters: (a) draft print; (b) near letter quality (NLQ). Note the much greater number of dots in NLQ mode (achieved by over-printing). Reproduced courtesy of Taxan.

per line, or 132 by using a smaller typeface. These various character sets are activated by software sending special characters to the printer.

Examples of various printer's output are shown in Figure 2.3. For most users, the most useful character set is the dot matrix near letter quality. NLQ on a cheap dot matrix printer is adequate for most correspondence. The quality of NLQ print on a good dot matrix printer (cost about £600), however, is difficult to distinguish from the output of a laser printer. NLQ print is usually available by pressing a switch on the printer; it is much slower than normal print, and manufacturers usually quote two speeds for their printers (standard and NLQ speeds). Dot matrix printers may also be used for printing graphs (as in Figure 10.5). Good quality is possible but it is a slow process because the graphs are printed as a series of dots, and it may take twenty minutes to print a page in graphics mode.

Inkjet printers operate by squirting ink through a print-head; they are quieter than dot matrix printers, but the character quality is relatively poor. Monochrome inkjet printers are sometimes used for draft printing in an office where a very quiet printer is necessary. However, the major application is as a colour printer to print graphs.

Thus, the average accounting office is likely to have several dot matrix printers for general use, with laser printers for word processing. Other types of printers will be encountered less frequently, although older daisywheel printers may remain in use.

2.11 MICROCOMPUTER CONFIGURATIONS

As has already been mentioned, a typical single-user microcomputer consists of a processor unit, a screen and keyboard and a printer. Such a system is perfectly adequate for a small accounting practice, or for one of the smaller clients, and is capable of large amounts of data processing for a relatively small outlay.

A larger office will find it more convenient to have several computers, and this leads to problems: inevitably, data on one computer will be needed by another. There are several possible solutions to this problem.

The first possibility is to transfer the data on diskette from one microcomputer to another (assuming that the two machines are totally compatible). This is certainly the cheapest way of transferring data, and often this approach is perfectly satisfactory. For example, an accountant on a visit to a client may record data on a portable microcomputer, which he later transfers to a computer at his office for further analysis.

This is an example of printing from a Taxan Kaga KP-810 printer in draft mode, showing **bold type,** underlining and *use of italics*

In Enlarged Mode

Same printer in condensed mode

This is an example of printing from the same printer in Near Letter Quality (NLQ) mode.

(a)

This **is an example of printing** from a Hewlett Packard Laser Jet printer.

(b)

This is an example of print from an Aptec Flowriter RP1600Q daisywheel, showing **bold type** and underlining

(c)

Figure 2.3 Examples of printer output: (a) dot matrix; (b) laser; (c) daisywheel.

However, that would not be satisfactory where several users require frequent access to the same data, and where they all need to update the database. It then becomes necessary for the data to be kept on a central hard disk, to which all users are connected by direct cabling or by a telephone line. There are two possible systems available: multi-user systems and local area networks.

Multi-user systems have been used for accounting for many years; a typical system is illustrated in Figure 2.4. Each user has a screen and keyboard connected to a shared central processor and hard disk. Alternatively, he may have a microcomputer which can carry out 'local' processing for applications such as word processing, as well as acting as a **terminal** to the main processor (i.e. as a screen and keyboard, without any processing capability). Originally, multi-user systems would have required expensive minicomputers to support them, but now 'supermicros' based on processors such as the Motorola 68020 commonly support eight to sixteen users, and can support far more users provided that the applications do not involve

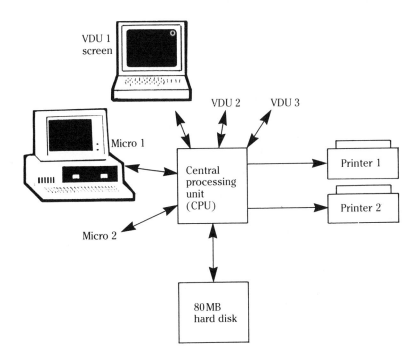

Figure 2.4 Multi-user system: typical configuration. All messages pass via the CPU.

too much number-crunching and complex processing. One such 'supermicro' used by many accounting firms is the Star Auditor 1000 series, shown in Figure 1.3. Because multi-user systems have been in use since the late 1960s, the technology is well-developed — the major problem lies in designing suitable operating software to schedule operations between different users. Multi-user systems are generally the best solution where several users need frequently to access and update a central filebase, as is often the case in an accounting office.

Local area networks (or LANs) of microcomputers are a more recent development than multi-user systems. 'Local' implies that microcomputers in the network are in close proximity, usually in the same office block, as opposed to networks where computers are connected over longer distances, and possibly by telephone. Figure 2.5 shows a typical configuration for a local area network: the heart of the network is the file server where all the shared data files and software are stored, while the various printers may be accessed by any of the users. Alternatively, the network may be controlled by one of the microcomputers in the network, with the hard disk in that microcomputer used to store shared files.

The technology required to control a network and pass messages rapidly between various microcomputers is complex and beyond the scope of this book. For most users, it is only the software interface that they will be aware of, and this is discussed in more detail in the next chapter. The hardware required, apart from a file server, will be

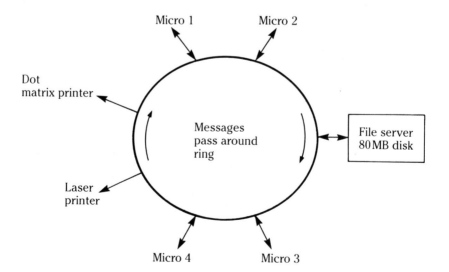

Figure 2.5 Local area network: typical configuration.

cabling and add-on interface cards for each microcomputer. There are a number of different standards for network hardware, the two most common being Ethernet and IBM Token Ring.

A LAN may be used for general accounting work, but it is probably most suitable in a situation where several users are running independent applications, but need sometimes to access common data. A LAN also has the advantage, relative to a stand-alone microcomputer, of allowing expensive facilities such as software and laser printers to be shared between users. However, the cost per user of connecting to a LAN can easily be higher than the cost of buying a microcomputer. Therefore, many users have chosen not to network their microcomputers, deciding that for them the benefits were not enough to justify the costs.

A small- to medium-sized accounting firm may find that stand-alone microcomputers are adequate for their needs, at least initially. As they develop experience, they are likely to find a need to share data files or pass files from one user to another; if they wish to set up a central database for the practice, then this is essential. Hence, many practices will graduate to multi-user systems or local area networks, even if they start off with single-user systems.

2.12 COMMUNICATIONS

Apart from in local area networks, there are a number of situations in which it is desirable that one microcomputer should communicate with another computer, either a large computer on the same site, or a computer elsewhere.

Communication with a minicomputer or mainframe computer

This is a common requirement in large offices; it is often useful to extract raw data from the sales ledger on the main central computer and then to analyse it using microcomputer software. Conversely, it is often useful to transfer files to the main computer, for example a memo may be typed by word processing on a microcomputer, and then sent to other offices via the message system on the mainframe. In many offices, dedicated mainframe terminals no longer exist, and microcomputers are used in a dual role.

To operate a microcomputer as a terminal to a larger computer simply requires a communications board and appropriate terminal emulation software to be installed. Unfortunately, different mainframe manufacturers adopt totally different standards for computer terminals; however, software is available that will emulate most currently existing terminals using an IBM-compatible microcomputer. Once the emulation software is loaded, the microcomputer will then operate more or less exactly like the specified terminal. In addition, the software will offer the option of transferring files between the disks on the microcomputer and on the mainframe computer.

Probably the best known such communications facility is IRMA from DCA, which emulates an IBM 3278 mainframe terminal; this consists of an add-on board, together with emulation software. Other makes are available, including emulations of most computer terminals from well-known computer manufacturers.

External communications

The simplest means of communication is to connect directly to the other computer via a telephone line. This requires a suitable communications board and software to be installed in the microcomputer, with the connection from computer to telephone via a **modem** (modulator/demodulator). Modems code the outgoing signal by modulating a high frequency carrier wave, and demodulate (or decode) the incoming signal. Modems have to be approved by British Telecom, and the software usually includes auto-dial facilities. The typical transfer speed is 1200 bits per second, or about 75 characters per second; it is possible to get much higher speeds where necessary by renting a special line from British Telecom.

Such a system does assume that the modem and computer at the other end of the telephone operate in a way which is totally compatible with your own system. This may be true of other computers within your own company, but will not be true in general of other computers. Until recently, there has been little compatibility between different makes of modems in the UK, but increasingly, Hayes-compatibility is becoming the *de facto* standard. In the USA, Hayes have been the most successful manufacturer of modems, and other manufacturers have aimed to be compatible. Hayes modems are now selling well in the UK, since they adapted their designs to meet the requirements of the British Telecommunications Approvals Board (BTAB).

Where modems are incompatible, such as when they operate at different transmission rates, then one cannot use direct interactive communication, and it is necessary to send messages via an 'electronic mailbox' system. The best-known such system in the UK is Telecom Gold, but similar systems operate world-wide. Such systems are referred to as packet switching systems (PSS), because they divide messages into small 'packets' which are transmitted separately and then finally reassembled.

External communication can be extremely useful to professional accountants at various times: for sending data from an audit site back to a computer in the office, and for sending urgent memos from one office to another.

2.13 HARDWARE STANDARDS: PROBLEMS OF COMPATIBILITY

A major problem with microcomputers is that different pieces of equipment often refuse to communicate with one another. In one example, a printer refused to work with a newly purchased microcomputer. A telephone call to the computer dealer produced the advice that the printer was faulty, while a telephone call to the supplier of the printer produced similar advice about the microcomputer. In fact, a replacement printer cable was all that was needed, and the printer and computer then worked happily together.

Where possible, it is sensible to buy all equipment from the same dealer, and leave him to sort out any problems. However, this is not always possible, especially if equipment is acquired over a period of time. Fortunately, there are certain generally accepted standards which lessen compatibility problems.

IBM-compatible microcomputers

Until the original IBM-PC was launched, different makes of microcomputer used different disk formats and totally different screen control characters. The net result was that data files could only be transferred with difficulty, and software written for one microcomputer would refuse to work on another. Although the IBM-PC could have achieved more, nevertheless it did at least create a *de facto* standard for a 360K 5.25in. disk format and a standard set of screen control characters. Thus, any PC-compatible microcomputer (including cheap clones such as the Amstrad) should now be capable of running any standard IBM software. IBM microcomputers include a BIOS chip (a part of the operating system in a ROM chip). For a long time, competitors found it difficult to emulate precisely the operations of this BIOS chip without infringing IBM copyright; however, such problems have now been overcome, and even cheap clones can usually emulate IBM microcomputers. However, it is wise if buying a cheap clone to check that it does have a legal BIOS, and that it does run all the business software that you intend to use.

Many current computers are referred to as AT-compatible: this means that they are similar in design to an IBM-AT microcomputer, with an Intel 80286 processor, 1.2MB 5.25in. disks and a similar keyboard. Standard AT-type disk drives will read disks written in 360K format, but it is not recommended to write to 360K disks using an AT drive because there is a danger of corrupting files. Most software for the IBM-PC will run on the IBM-AT and AT-compatibles, although occasionally there are problems due to the different keyboards.

Undoubtedly, a third standard will develop based on the IBM PS/2 series. For most established users, a change to 3.5in. disks will involve considerable inconvenience and cost; there will be several years of change-over when users will have different microcomputers with incompatible disks. Also, the graphics characteristics of the new microcomputers are superior to previous IBM microcomputers, but the screens are not entirely compatible with PC and AT machines. This means that certain graphics software for the PC and AT may not run on the PS/2, without being adapted. Initially, other manufacturers will find it difficult to emulate the PS/2, but will doubtless manage to do so before too long.

For computers larger than single-user microcomputers, compatibility is extremely limited; the only safe assumptions are that different makes of equipment will be totally incompatible, and that software written for one computer will not run on another. If you are buying a multi-user system, unless you have considerable expertise, then it is essential to buy all hardware and software from the same dealer. It is also well worth employing a computer consultant to get independent advice as to what is really appropriate to your needs.

Printers

A major problem for users can be communicating with printers — either the printer refuses to print the output sent to it, or it produces random paper-throws and unsatisfactory output. This is particularly a problem where one is trying to print graphics output. The answer is to make absolutely certain before you buy a printer that all the software that you intend to use will operate with that printer.

Printers usually have a wide range of character sets, and a program can switch character sets by sending a special character to the printer. This is especially useful for printing in bold or condensed print, or printing in large characters for headings. A special character also needs to be sent to the printer to generate a paper-throw for a new page. Unfortunately, printers vary in the precise facilities offered, and also in the special characters required; this is especially true where the printer is used in graphics mode.

Epson, the Japanese manufacturers, have undoubtedly been the most successful manufacturers of dot matrix printers, and a number of other manufacturers make Epson-compatible printers, which use the same special control characters as Epson printers. This is a useful standard to aim at, although you do need to be careful that the printer you are buying is really Epson-compatible, especially if you want to print graphs. There are also a number of good dot matrix printers on the market which are not Epson-compatible. All business software, including Lotus 1-2-3, will drive a number of different printers, including Epson printers; however, the unwary user may end up buying a printer that is totally non-standard.

Laser printers are similar to dot matrix printers in most of their characteristics; indeed, a number of laser printers do claim to be Epson-compatible. However, the page size is slightly different, and different character sets can often only be obtained by changing the print cartridge.

Daisywheel printers will not, of course, print graphs; in general, they will be compatible with dot matrix printers in printing text, but will ignore most control characters. On the other hand, daisywheel printers will respond to certain characters which a dot matrix printer will ignore; for example, one can usually vary the line height on a daisywheel to get non-standard line spacing.

Other equipment

Any other equipment, such as graph plotters, tends to be totally lacking in standardization. Great care, and preferably specialist advice, is essential. As with printers, the general rule is to go for a well-known make, rather than look for bargains. One can rely, for example, on any reasonable graphics software working with a Hewlett-Packard graph plotter because otherwise the software would be unsaleable; the same confidence does not always apply to more obscure makes of plotters.

Software problems

Finally, remember that the only function of hardware is as a vehicle for running software. For convenience, hardware and software have been separated as topics in this book, but in reality they are inseparable. Make sure that whatever software you intend using does actually run on the hardware you have chosen. If not, make a different choice.

3 Software

Computer software is the set of computer programs, or instructions, which enables the computer hardware to carry out various tasks. Human beings cannot function at the speed of computers, so it has always been necessary to develop such programs for specific tasks in order to use computers effectively. Also, computers are intrinsically rather 'unfriendly', thinking in binary code and insisting on working in short, pedantic, logical steps. If modern computers give the impression of being 'user-friendly', it is only because of the software which provides the interface between the human user and the computer hardware.

Thus, it is with software that a microcomputer user communicates, and an understanding of what software does is crucial to being able to use a microcomputer effectively. This chapter is therefore not just a theoretical one, but one of strong practical value to the professional accountant who intends to use a microcomputer.

3.1 TYPES OF SOFTWARE

Computer software fits broadly into two categories: system software and applications software. Software for microcomputers is invariably supplied on diskettes, and may be run from the diskette or loaded on to the hard disk.

System software consists of those programs necessary to enable a computer to function: the operating system and utility programs (to copy disks, and so on), as well as compilers and interpreters to translate from high-level languages to binary machine code.

Applications software is designed to carry out the tasks associated with specific applications: such as payroll, word processing, and so on. A set of programs designed to process a specific application is usually referred to as a **computer package**. There are several thousand packages on sale in the UK of relevance to accountants — the remaining chapters of this book aim to provide a guide to some of the most useful packages on the market, but inevitably some equally good software will not get the attention it merits.

Some system software is usually an automatic purchase with a microcomputer (and may be included in the price of the micro-computer), although users may find it useful to buy additional utility software for specific tasks. The cost of such software tends to reflect what it does; basic systems software can be relatively cheap (£30 to £100), although even the most sophisticated systems software tends to cost only about £300 or so.

On the other hand, applications software is purchased as required by users for specific tasks, and is generally more expensive. A good accounting package is likely to cost more than a microcomputer, and specialist software for applications such as vehicle scheduling can cost as much as £30 000 — to run on a microcomputer costing £4000. More expensive software tends to be 'copy-protected' in order to preserve copyright; this typically means that the original diskettes cannot be copied on to other diskettes, and can only be copied once on to a hard disk.

This chapter has two main aims: first, to explain the function of system software, and in particular the type of packages on the market of relevance to the accountant; and secondly, to discuss the character-istics to be looked for in good applications software. Detailed discus-sion of the actual applications is left to later chapters.

3.2 SYSTEM SOFTWARE: OPERATING SYSTEM

Any microcomputer has a program permanently stored in ROM (i.e. in memory) to 'boot' (or start up) the microcomputer. It is this program which automatically sets the computer into action when it is switched on, and calls up the operating system from disk.

The **operating system** is the program which controls all the basic operations of the microcomputer; computer specialists often refer to the microcomputer operating system as DOS, which is short for disk operating system. The following are examples of simple tasks which the operating system would initiate:

1. copy from hard disk to floppy disk
2. print some text
3. display text on screen
4. calculate how much space is left on a disk

5. start an application program running.

The average accounting user will make very limited direct use of the operating system, although he may frequently access the operating system from an application program without being aware of going so. Similarly, the user may not even be aware of using the operating system when the microcomputer is switched on because the accounting program may be set up to start running automatically.

Nevertheless, some knowledge of operating systems is often useful in order to avoid problems that arise from time to time, for example programs may run slower or hang (get caught in an endless repetition of program steps) for no apparent reason. For professional accountants, a working knowledge of operating systems is essential, since they need to be able to audit clients' systems as well as to control systems in their own practice.

There are two main operating systems in use on current business microcomputers: MSDOS and OS/2, both from Microsoft. **MSDOS** runs on 'IBM-compatible' microcomputers, which are those that have the same characteristics as the IBM-PC and AT models. **OS/2** has many similarities to MSDOS, but runs on IBM PS/2 and compatible microcomputers.

Because MSDOS was the standard operating system up until 1987, this meant that standard applications software could be immediately transferred from one make of microcomputer to another; this was undoubtedly very beneficial for users in inducing a strong degree of competition between suppliers. OS/2 will almost certainly take over from MSDOS as the standard operating system as the market becomes progressively more dominated by IBM PS/2 microcomputers and compatibles.

However, other operating systems may be encountered. Some older microcomputers, and current machines designed for hobby use, have their own special operating systems; they cannot run any of the standard business packages. The Apple Macintosh, which is popular for desk-top publishing (see Chapter 13), has its own unique and very user-friendly operating system. Larger multi-user computers have a variety of operating systems, so that applications software cannot usually be easily transferred from one computer to another. The most common such operating system is UNIX, together with its variants, which is discussed briefly at the end of this section. Multi-user operating systems require much more sophisticated programs, because they need to cope with simultaneous demands from the various users, while maintaining adequate security for each individual user from other users of the system.

Directories, subdirectories and files

As the name DOS implies, the major task of a microcomputer operating system is to control disk operations; this is particularly critical
where a hard disk is used with a considerable amount of data to be
located. On a disk will be stored a large number of **files**: A file is any
block of data or text stored on the disk; this may be used to store a
set of accounting records, or a report typed by word processing, or a
computer program. The file may be retrieved as necessary by the
operating system, modified by an applications program and then
saved in the new form. The operating system cannot generally
perform operations within a file, but can only carry out global operations on the entire file.


```
C> dir/w

Volume in C has no label
Directory of \ACCOUNTS\SALES

.                ..              SALES    EXE    SALES    DAT
SALESCAL BAS     SDISCNT  BAS    MENU     BAT    LETTER   TXT
README   TXT     SALESMAN DBF    SALESMAN NDX    SALESMAN PRG

     10 File(s)    7309321 bytes free
```

Figure 3.1 MS-DOS directory listing. This is a typical (/w) directory listing;
only the files in the current subdirectory are listed, but the free space of 7.3 MB
is for the entire hard disk. (. Represents the current directory; .. the parent
directory of this subdirectory.)

The conventions described here are those used by MSDOS and OS/
2, but similar conventions apply to other operating systems such as
UNIX. Any file is referred to by a filename of up to eight characters
and an extension of up to three characters; where necessary, the filename may be prefaced by the disk drive, so that a typical complete
name for a file on disk drive A would be A:ACCTSFIL.DAT. The list of
files contained on a disk is referred to as a **directory**, and Figure 3.1
shows a typical directory listing. The filenames should be chosen by
the user to be as meaningful as possible, while the extension usually
indicates the type of file, as in the following examples:

1. .BAS   BASIC program
2. .DAT   BASIC data file
3. .WK1   Lotus 1-2-3 file

4. .DBF   dBASE3 database file
5. .COM and .EXE   files which initiate running of programs, such as **LOTUS.EXE** to start Lotus 1-2-3 running
6. .BAT   batch command file (see below).

On a diskette, it is usual to keep all the files on the same directory, but this is not generally feasible where a hard disk is used for several different applications. The hard disk may well contain several hundred files, making it difficult to identify the file that one is looking for. The problem can be overcome by splitting the files into groups relating to a particular application and setting up subdirectories. This should be done so as to ensure that there are no more than about a hundred files on any subdirectory. This simplifies matters, because by default the operating system restricts operations to files on the subdirectory currently being accessed.

For example, if one were using dBASE3 (a database package), one might well create a subdirectory **\DBASE** on which the various dBASE3 program files could be loaded (\ indicates that this is a subdirectory of the main, or root, directory). Various subdirectories of **\DBASE** could then be set up with different types of records on them; thus the subdirectory **OURS** might contain various records relating to the practice, while the subdirectory **CLIENT** contains records relating to clients. Assuming that drive C contained the hard disk, the complete file specification of a database file **SMITH.DBF**, referring to a client, Smith Bros Ltd, would then be:

C:\DBASE\CLIENT\SMITH.DBF

The complete specification would only be used where it was necessary to refer to a file on a different subdirectory from the one currently being accessed.

MSDOS

MSDOS was the standard operating system on IBM PC-compatible and AT-compatible microcomputers from 1982 to 1987, and will continue to be in common use as long as such microcomputers remain popular. It costs about £60 per copy. MSDOS has owed its popularity to being adopted originally for the IBM-PC, in a variant known as PCDOS. Although it has some faults, its continued use has been guaranteed, at least until 1987, by the fact that most popular microcomputer software would only work in conjunction with MSDOS or OS/2.

Figure 3.2 shows some typical simple MSDOS commands, corresponding to the tasks mentioned previously, which are required of an

dir	List current directory
dir *.acb	List all files with extension .ACB
copy sales.dat a:salescop.dat	Copy file from current directory to disk drive A, renamed as SALESCOP.DAT
del sales.dat	Delete the file SALES.DAT
chkdsk a:	Calculates the amount of disk space in drive A, and checks for bad areas
type readme.txt	List the text file README.TXT
mkdir accounts	Create subdirectory ACCOUNTS
chdir accounts	Change to subdirectory ACCOUNTS
WS	Run the Wordstar program WS.EXE
menu	Run the file MENU.BAT to display a menu of options on the screen

Figure 3.2 Examples of MSDOS commands.

operating system. Inevitably, most of these commands refer to tasks associated with disk operations, since that is the main function of an operating system on a single-user microcomputer. To the user, MSDOS presents the prompt C> when it is awaiting a command, where the letter indicates the disk drive currently in use (in this case, drive C); in some versions of MSDOS, the prompt also indicates the subdirectory in use, so that from the subdirectory \DBASE on drive C, the prompt will be:

C:\DBASE>

The following two types of files, mentioned briefly above, are of interest because in effect they extend the range of commands available in MSDOS:

1. **Executable files** (extension .EXE or .COM). A file with either of these extensions is assumed to be a program in a compiled format (.EXE is the more efficient, and hence more usual); the program may be activated simply by typing the filename as a command (see example in Figure 3.2).
2. **Batch files** (extension .BAT). Any file with this extension is assumed to contain a set of MSDOS commands, and typing the filename is equivalent to typing the whole series of commands. Batch files are particularly useful where a number of different applications are run on the same microcomputer, and one wants to set up user-friendly procedures to guide the user through. Figure 3.3 gives examples of this.

MENU.BAT

```
echo off
cls
echo              Blewett/Jarvis - Demonstration Menu
echo
echo
echo         BUSMAIL    -    BUS placement mailing system
echo         DB         -    dBASE3
echo         FCS        -    Micro-FCS
echo         LOTUS      -    LOTUS 1-2-3
echo         PEG        -    PEGASUS
echo         REF        -    REFLEX
echo         WS         -    WORDSTAR
```

LOTUS.BAT

```
chdir 123      ... change to subdirectory 123
lotus          ... run LOTUS.EXE
chdir\         ... change to main directory
menu           ... run MENU.BAT
```

Screen display when running the batch files

```
              Blewett/Jarvis - Demonstration Menu

CACHE         -     Cache system for printing
DB            -     dBASE3
FCS           -     Micro-FCS
LOTUS         -     LOTUS 1-2-3
PEG           -     PEGASUS
REF           -     REFLEX
WS            -     WORDSTAR

C> lotus
```

Figure 3.3 MSDOS batch files. The first file **MENU.BAT** displays a menu on the screen, and the second file **LOTUS.BAT** is activated by the command **LOTUS**; this runs Lotus 1-2-3, and returns to the main directory and redisplays the menu when the run has been completed. Note that the command **CLS** clears the screen, while any message following the **ECHO** command is displayed on the screen.

If there is a file called **AUTOEXEC.BAT**, MSDOS will automatically run that batch file when the system is started up. This is useful for running initialization routines, and it is often used as a convenient way of bypassing MSDOS, and taking the user directly into an applications program.

MSDOS has proved to be a very robust system, which perhaps takes a little understanding, but which has nevertheless done most of what has been required by millions of users. However, as technology has progressed, problems have become more apparent:

1. *Memory limitation.* Only 640K of RAM can be used by MSDOS. This is often inadequate for large spreadsheets, or for multi-tasking (running several programs simultaneously).
2. *Disk limitation.* Only 32MB of disk can be addressed by MSDOS. Larger hard disks are now common, and disk manufacturers have had to devise complex methods to overcome this problem.
3. *User-unfriendliness.* Many users find MSDOS difficult to cope with, at least initially. Good software packages, such as Lotus 1-2-3, have taken over many tasks which might be more sensibly handled by the operating system.

Microsoft OS/2

OS/2 is the standard operating system for the IBM PS/2 series, but versions are likely to become available on other microcomputers based on the Intel 80286 or 80386 processors. OS/2, Version 1.0, looks very similar to MSDOS, and the prompt lines and commands are much the same. The hardware requirements for OS/2 are much greater; IBM recommend at least 3MB of RAM, and a hard disk is essential.

OS/2 works in **native** and **compatibility** modes; in compatibility mode, OS/2 is designed to emulate MSDOS, so that most current applications software will also run under OS/2, but only 640K of RAM may be accessed; in native mode, OS/2 accesses up to 16MB of RAM, and virtually unlimited disk space (although only one 32MB disk partition may be accessed at a time). It also has numerous other features of interest to the professional software programmer, which are beyond the scope of this book; the implications for accounting users are likely to include substantially faster processing when specific OS/2 applications software appears on the market, at a cost to users for upgrading existing software.

One development of interest to accounting users is that in native mode, OS/2 allows true multi-tasking, i.e. several programs running simultaneously. This means that while the microcomputer is busy doing a long payroll or accounts run in 'background' mode, it can be used to do word processing or financial planning calculations in 'foreground' mode. The foreground user is then completely unaware of what is happening in the background, and may feel that he has sole use of the microcomputer. In an accounting office, this can be tremendously useful, because under MSDOS a microcomputer will often be tied down for long periods, performing major tasks.

Perhaps the most interesting development will be Presentation Manager, scheduled for release in OS/2, Version 1.1, in late 1988. This will change OS/2 into a **window icon mouse pointer** (WIMP) operating system. This is designed to be extremely user-friendly, and follows the lines of the operating system pioneered by Apple for their Macintosh microcomputer. The components of a WIMP system are as follows:

1. *Window.* The screen can be divided in to two or more sections, each displaying a different application, and thus providing 'windows' on to the different applications. This is useful where one wants to produce a combined report, for example from a graphics package and a financial planning package.
2. *Icons.* These are symbols that represent the options from which one can select; for example there might be a picture of a disk to represent the command for copying a file, and a waste paper basket to represent deleting a file.
3. *Mouse.* This device has been described in Chapter 2. A mouse is not strictly necessary with OS/2 Presentation Manager, although it is preferable to have one to move the pointer and make selections.
4. *Pointer.* This is an arrow that one can move around on the screen to point to the option to be selected. It can be moved by the mouse or by using the cursor control keys.

Precise details of Presentation Manager have not been released at the time of writing, but it will be very similar to the package Microsoft Windows, which is available currently to run with MSDOS. Figure 3.4 shows a typical screen display from Windows.

WIMP systems such as OS/2 Presentation Manager and the Macintosh operating system are a very impressive development, but their impact on professional accountants may be limited. As already mentioned, almost all computing in an accounting office involves interfacing with applications software, rather than with the operating system, so that the benefits derived from a user-friendly operating system will not be very great. The net result is that many accounting practices may decide that it is not worth buying Presentation Manager because of the additional cost.

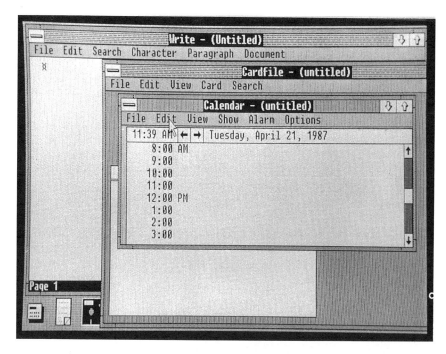

Figure 3.4 Screen display from Microsoft Windows showing two tables currently running. Reproduced courtesy of Microsoft Ltd.

Networking

The hardware implications of using a local area network have already been discussed in Chapter 2. A special operating system is also necessary, since MSDOS and OS/2 both lack the commands and facilities to communicate around a network. There is a variety of network software for MSDOS on the market from companies such as 3Com, Novell, Interquadram and Torus; they are similar to one another in the facilities offered, but each system has its own set of commands. 3Com and Microsoft have also produced Lan Manager, to run in conjunction with OS/2.

Broadly, the facilities offered are as follows:

1. To run each microcomputer as a 'stand-alone' system with its own set of files, using MSDOS or OS/2.
2. To set up accounts and passwords for logging in to the network, no access to the network being allowed without logging in.
3. To access shared files on the hard disk in a central file server. It

should be possible to lock records (or files), so that a second user cannot access the record while the first user is in the process of amending it.

4.   To print on any printer attached to the network, with a queue of work being kept by the network operating system if several users wish to print at the same time.

Many accounting practices will find that a network fits their needs. Although slightly more complex to use than a single-user system, networks are by no means difficult. Designers of network software tend to make strong efforts to develop user-friendly interfaces in order to reduce the problems that might otherwise be experienced by non-technical users. For example, Figure 3.5 shows a screen display from Torus Icon network software, which makes selection of the correct options relatively straightforward. Even this is of a complexity that most users would not face, because once they have logged into the network, they would simply run the applications software;

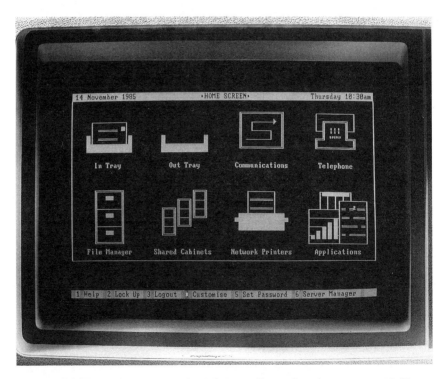

Figure 3.5 Torus Icon network software. Reproduced courtesy of Torus Systems Ltd.

however, the person controlling the network would need a good understanding of the network operating system, in order to be able to install software initially, and in order to be able to carry out regular security back-ups of data files.

Finally, it should be noted that although some suppliers offer both hardware and software, many users have chosen not to buy a complete system from the same supplier; for example, many network users in the City of London have opted to use Novell or Torus software with IBM Token Ring hardware. Indeed, some suppliers of network software do not manufacture hardware themselves, but merely emphasize the compatibility of their software with various makes of network hardware.

Multi-user systems

Almost every large computer has a different operating system, although the facilities offered to the user are much the same as those already described for MSDOS together with those offered by a network. Even different models of computers from the same manufacturer have different operating systems with quite different commands to perform the same tasks. The only objective appears to be to confuse the user as much as possible.

The only multi-user operating system worth mentioning here is UNIX, because it is commonly used in the type of 'supermicros' often purchased by accounting practices. UNIX was developed originally by AT&T, although Microsoft wrote their own version entitled XENIX for the IBM-AT. IBM have also used UNIX as the basis of their AIX multi-user operating system, which is being developed for the IBM PS/2 series, and for some other larger IBM computers.

In itself, UNIX is an unfriendly but very powerful operating system; its great attraction to software developers is that it is easily extendible. The net effect is that by writing suitable program extensions to the operating system, it is possible to write a friendly interface, and thus to design applications software to run under UNIX that is user-friendly. The other attraction of UNIX to software developers is that it is available on a wide range of computers from microcomputers to mainframes; they can therefore produce software which is *portable* between different computers, and this enormously reduces development costs.

External communications

Just as with a local area network, external communications requires the hardware (in this case, to interface with a telephone) together with suitable software to implement an appropriate set of commands. It is no coincidence that several companies that are involved in network software are also investing heavily in developing communications software. For an accounting practice, it is useful to have external communications so that staff on audit can send in data from portable microcomputers direct to the internal practice network. It is often useful also to be able to dial up external financial databases.

3.3 UTILITY SOFTWARE

There are many packages on the market designed to carry out useful tasks which do not relate to any specific application. These are often classified as utility software, although the borderline between this type of software and applications software is often difficult to draw. A few examples are given here, but perusing the advertisements in any microcomputer magazine will yield a long list of similar packages.

Sidekick

Sidekick (from Borland) sells for about £40, and is probably the best-selling utility package in the UK. It is RAM-resident, i.e. it should be loaded into memory before loading an applications package, and can be called up at any time without disrupting the main application. Sidekick has the following options:

1. *Notepad.* This is an editor designed for typing brief notes, which has many of the facilities of a word-processing package, and can create documents up to 25 pages in length.
2. *Calendar.* This provides a week-by-week perpetual calendar into which appointments can be entered.
3. *Calculator.* This simulates a pocket calculator.
4. *Dialer.* This keeps a list of teleiphone numbers, and will automatically dial any chosen number.

The attraction of Sidekick is that it provides a range of useful facilities at a very low price, although the last option is probably the one which is most useful. Many accounting practices now use microcomputers to communicate with computers at other branches, or to access large financial databases, and find Sidekick very useful.

Sideways

Another useful package for accountants is Sideways from Borland. Accountants often use financial tables for future projections, which are much too wide for a normal printer. Sideways gets over this problem by printing the table sideways on a dot matrix printer.

Microcache

A further package (which has also been most helpful in writing this book) is the Microcache suite of programs from Microcosm Research Ltd which is designed to speed up certain operations in a micro-computer. This performs two main operations:

1. *Print buffering.* Printing a long document or set of results can occupy the microcomputer for a long period, stopping the user from doing anything else. Buffering the printer means that the print output is stored temporarily in RAM before printing, a process which takes about a minute for a document that takes twenty minutes to print. Once this is over, the microcomputer can be used for other tasks.
2. *Disk cacheing.* Even a fast hard disk is still significantly slower than memory. Disk cacheing means that disk output is stored temporarily in RAM, and actual disk writing is done in the background. This can provide significant gains in speeds where there is a lot of disk writing.

Finally, there are also a number of useful packages which are designed to provide greater security. The need for this is discussed in a later section of this chapter.

3.4 COMPUTER LANGUAGES

Computer languages are used for writing computer programs (or sets of instructions). A **high-level language** usually bears a passing resemblance to English or algebra, but in fact has a very rigid syntax, and statements in a computer language correspond exactly to computer operations. Alternatively, some packages are written in assembler code, which translates directly into binary; this produces efficient programs, but takes an inordinate amount of programming time. Developing commercial software is very expensive, and therefore it is usually important to make the programming time as short as possible.

To use any computer language, it is necessary to buy a **compiler**, which is a computer package that translates from the language into binary computer instructions. The exception is BASIC, which may instead have an **interpreter** that translates interactively line by line. For most accounting users, knowledge of computer languages will not be relevant, but for reference the high-level languages available on mirocomputers include the following:

1. **BASIC** is the most common microcomputer language, and a version (GWBASIC) is available free as part of MSDOS. Most microcomputer accounting software is written in BASIC. It is relatively easy to write short programs in BASIC, but it is disliked by computer professionals because it is ill structured and unstandardized.

2. **COBOL** has been, for many years, the standard commercial programming language on larger computers, and accounting software on minicomputers and supermicros is often written in COBOL. It is sometimes used for microcomputer accounting software, but less often than BASIC, perhaps because of the higher cost of buying a COBOL compiler.

3. **FORTRAN** is essentially designed for scientific programming. It is rarely used for accounting work, although it is used in some specialist software, which has usually been written originally for a mainframe computer and transferred to a microcomputer.

4. **PASCAL**, like FORTRAN, is essentially a scientific programming language, but compilers for microcomputers are readily available. Moreover, it is well structured as a language and tends to produce efficient computer code; it has therefore been used by a number of suppliers to write accounting software.

5. **C**, despite its rather terse name, is a very powerful language which is becoming increasingly popular with professional software programmers. Although a relatively high-level language, C can carry out the same tasks as assembler code, and produce fairly efficient programs. For this reason, a number of well-known packages such as Wordstar and Micro-FCS are written in C, as is most of the UNIX operating system.

Figure 3.6 gives examples of programs in various of these languages. In the main, they simply provide different statements for doing the same task, although there are some differences in what can be achieved.

In recent years, there has been a major development of considerable consequence to many professional accountants. This is the

BASIC

```
100 AMTDUE = HRS * HRATE
110 IF AMTDUE <= MAXA THEN AMTBILL = AMTDUE
                     ELSE AMTBILL = MAXA
120 LPRINT "Amount to be billed is "; AMTBILL
```

COBOL

```
MULTIPLY HRS BY HRATE, GIVING AMTDUE.
IF AMTDUE <= MAXA THEN MOVE AMTDUE TO AMTBILL
                  ELSE MOVE MAXA TO AMTBILL.
WRITE BILL-LINE, AFTER ADVANCING 2 LINES.
```

C

```
amtdue = hrs * hrate;
if amtdue <= maxa {
         amtbill = amtdue;
   }else{
         amtbill = maxa;}
printf("Amount to be billed is %8.2f\n", amtbill)
```

Figure 3.6 Sample computer programs. This shows sections of program in BASIC, COBOL and C to calculate the amount owed by a client from the hours worked and the hourly rate, with a maximum amount MAXA to be billed; the amount to be billed AMTBILL being finally printed out.

increasing use of so-called **fourth generation languages** (4GL), based on database packages. Their use is discussed further in Chapter 6. Immense savings can be made in programming development time, and large companies are increasingly reluctant to use traditional languages such as COBOL. The benefit to accountants is that where there is no package that fits their specific application, it is often possible to write bespoke software at a reasonable price using a package such as dBASE3.

3.5 APPLICATIONS SOFTWARE

The remaining chapters of this book discuss applications relevant to the professional accountant, and give examples of software suitable for those applications. In fact, the term 'applications software' embraces a very wide range: on the one hand, there are packages such as spreadsheet (Chapter 5) and database (Chapter 6) which merely provide a convenient facility for writing certain types of applications; on the other hand, most accounting software is written for very specific applications.

Popular microcomputer software has been through a very hard process of acceptance testing. Microcomputers tend to be used by non-technical, impatient users with no interest in the mystique of computing. Any software which was not sufficiently fool-proof and user-friendly disappeared fairly rapidly from the market. The packages which survive and have a strong user base usually deserve to do so. Any accounting software will need to be updated periodically as government legislation changes, and it is therefore essential to find a supplier who can be relied on to continue in operation.

Applications software is essentially presented in two styles: menu-driven and command-driven. Specialist applications such as accounting tend to be menu-driven, as are spreadsheets and simple database packages designed for non-technical users. On the other hand, dBASE3 (Chapter 6) and the financial modelling package, Micro-FCS (Chapter 4), are both command-driven.

In a **menu-driven** package, the user is presented with a menu of options at each stage from which an option must be selected. In an accounting package, the options are usually numbered, and the user selects an option by typing the appropriate number, perhaps going rapidly through three or four levels of menus before arriving at the task that is to be performed.

An alternative approach is used by most spreadsheet packages (Chapter 5). The options are expressed by a single word on a 'command line', one of which is highlighted; the user moves the cursor to highlight the required option, and then presses the 'enter' key. Often, there are several levels of menu to go through, and the process can be speeded up by using a mouse.

Another refinement is the use of pop-up menus which appear when a selection is being made, and disappear when not required. Figure 3.4 showed a pop-up menu displayed by Microsoft Windows being used to select a file view. Recent applications software has made very effective use of pop-up menus which can provide a very friendly interface, particularly where a mouse is used to make selections from the menu. A good example of such software is Reflex from Borland, a database package which is used as an example in Chapter 6.

In a **command-driven** package, the user is presented with a prompt, to which he responds with various commands. In general, this requires rather more knowledge from the user, and such software is not normally appropriate for the occasional user. However, a command-driven package can be a very powerful tool when used by experienced operators, who will probably find that they can achieve much faster and more effective results than by using a menu-driven package. The great strength of command-driven systems is that one can set up files containing a long series of commands, referred to as macro-programs or just macros. Macros can be designed which, for example, set up a particular database in dBASE3 and present the user with a menu of options to carry out various tasks on that database. The net effect is that a command-driven package can be used to set up customized systems which are extremely simple to use. Macros are also available in some menu-driven packages such as Lotus 1-2-3, but tend to be more difficult to set up than with a command-driven package.

The other important facility to look for in good software is the quality of **help** available. This is particularly essential with a command-driven package, where no list of options is available. With good software, there should be no need to look at the manual, except perhaps when one is starting, though, admittedly, with complex accounting software a manual may sometimes be necessary. Originally, packages tended to produce many screenfuls of help information, and it was a matter of paging through until one found what one was looking for. Increasingly, the emphasis now is on context-related help messages, where the help message given relates to the option or command currently about to be used.

In general, the quality of presentation of microcomputer software is now very high. Often, it is much better than one can expect from very expensive software on minicomputers and mainframes.

3.6 SECURITY AND CONTROL ASPECTS OF MICROCOMPUTERS

Security in accounting systems is concerned with ensuring that access to data is restricted to those individuals who need it in order to perform their jobs efficiently. Sometimes, the objective is to maintain privacy; for example, individuals on a company payroll may want their salaries to be confidential, and hence restricted to payroll staff and senior management. Indeed, clients often have their payroll processed by their accountant's office in order to maintain confidentiality.

Security is also important as a means of preventing fraud in accounting systems, and of maintaining adequate control. This can be achieved by setting precise limits to what each individual member of staff is allowed to access or change.

Control of an accounting system is concerned with ensuring that the information contained in the system is accurate, up to date and complete. This implies, for example, that staff have clearly defined responsibilities for updating different parts of the system. Since mistakes are certain to be made, it is also essential that procedures exist for tracing errors and identifying responsibility for them.

Security and control are therefore both very much matters of concern for the professional accountant; they are interlinked, and it is usually convenient to consider the two aspects together. Maintaining adequate control of computer-based systems is primarily a question of maintaining control of staff and ensuring that strict procedures are adhered to. Computer-based systems usually malfunction because of what people do to them; nevertheless, well-designed software can minimize the chances of things going wrong.

A third consideration is that of **privacy**, which is central to the 1984 *Data Protection Act* concerned with the storing of data relating to private citizens on a computer. The Act applies to employee data kept for payroll purposes, and to mailing lists kept for marketing purposes. The Act requires the company to register their system, to demonstrate that adequate controls exist to ensure that data is correct and kept confidential, and to show that all the data kept is essential for the specific application. The Act also lays down that individuals should have the right to inspect their own record on payment of a nominal fee.

It is often not realized that the Act covers any data kept on a computer: not just databases, but also any data typed on a word processor. Because of the Act, the various professional accounting bodies have been forced to publish exam marks to students (these being processed by computer), something that they have always previously refused to do.

Later in this book, we shall discuss the broader issues involved with maintaining security and control in accounts systems. For the moment, we shall concentrate on the implications for good software design, and the potential dangers in using certain types of software in the wrong situations.

Operating systems and utility software

In the past, microcomputer operating systems have had little in the way of security features incorporated. Originally, microcomputers were single-user devices with diskettes. A high degree of control was not needed if only one or two individuals were using the system, and security could be ensured by locking diskettes away when not in use.

Unfortunately, this is no longer the case. Microcomputers now tend to have hard disks which contain a very large amount of data, freely accessible to anybody who wanders into the office. Copies of confidential letters can easily be typed out, and even accounting records may be accessed by those with sufficient knowledge. Most microcomputers have 'ignition' locks which lock out the keyboard, but unfortunately most users tend not to use them, perhaps for fear of losing the key. Network operating systems usually have a satisfactory system of accounts and passwords, but these controls only apply to shared files; any files saved on a personal account may still have no security protection.

Moreover, most users assume that files which have been 'deleted' by the operating system are unreadable; unfortunately, this is not so. A **DELETE** command in most operating systems merely deletes the directory reference, and makes the file difficult to locate; it is still possible for a skilled assembler programmer to rebuild the file. In a major UK trial in 1987, a drugs smuggler was convicted because of the detailed appointment diary he kept on a Psion Organiser pocket computer; he deleted his files when he realized the police were closing in, but computer experts working for the prosecution managed to rebuild the files with the aid of a mainframe computer. The moral is that if the costs of a security loss are high, then it is worth investing seriously in preventive measures.

The best solution is to purchase a suitable security package, of which PS3 (from Protection Systems) and Fortress Plus are good examples; significantly, Fortress Plus is marketed by a major professional accounting firm, Deloitte Haskins and Sells. The features in Fortress Plus are fairly typical of such packages, and include the following:

1. Control over users:
   (a) Users required to give passwords
   (b) Time slices can be defined — automatic logoff at end of time slice
   (c) No access to hard disk if you boot from a floppy disk.
2. Security on files:
   (a) Passwords on individual files
   (b) Encryption of files to make them unreadable
   (c) Total deletion, i.e. over-writing with zeros.
3. Operational controls:
   (a) Full audit control facilities.

Other points on security

Security depends on factors other than good software; it depends on organizations taking it seriously. Hackers have found their way into supposedly secure mainframe computers by trying obvious passwords such as GOD, MASTER, FRED, PASSWORD or HERO.

Hardware can also be at fault: an unsheathed VDU lead can transmit radio waves which can be picked up 100 metres away and amplified by suitable equipment. Thus an unscrupulous competitor could reproduce your VDU screen in his office, and presumably gain sensitive marketing data from you.

3.7 CONCLUSIONS

For most users, the performance of their microcomputer will depend far more on the software than on the hardware; factors such as ease of use, security and efficiency of procedures are likely to be far more important than the number-crunching ability of the system. Choice of software such as spreadsheet and database packages is not difficult, because there is so much good software of that type on the market. On the other hand, accounting software, especially software designed for use in a practice, is much more specialist; most dealers have only a very limited understanding of accounting. It is essential to look carefully for a dealer with a real understanding of the problems. Finally, it is important where possible to buy software and hardware from the same dealer, otherwise it may be difficult to locate responsibility if anything does go wrong.

4 Financial modelling

4.1 WHAT IS A FINANCIAL MODEL?

Computing books often define a model rather grandly as 'a mathematical representation of a real-world phenomenon'. This definition has tended to discourage a number of potential users, including accountants, from applying computer modelling techniques to their work. Although accountants do not generally use the term 'model' (or the structure formats used by computing personnel in building models), they have in fact a vast experience of models. For example, accountants for a number of years have used modelling for planning, in particular in the construction of budgets. However, these models have invariably been constructed manually with the aid of a calculator rather than by using a computer.

Perhaps a more easily digestible definition of a financial model in the context of accounting is 'a set of logically linked accounting relationships used to solve financial problems'. A typical accounting relationship that is frequently used by accountants in constructing financial models is:

$$\text{Sales revenue} = \text{Sales volume} \times \text{Unit price}$$

This accounting relationship would then normally be linked with other relationships to construct a model. For example, another relationship which is often linked is:

$$\text{Cost of sales} = \text{A \% of sales revenue}$$

The conversion from manually constructed models to those using a computer is in our experience not such a large step as is often perceived; useful computer-based financial models are often quite simple in concept. In this chapter we hope to persuade those who are currently using manual financial models to apply their skills to computer modelling, and to encourage present users to expand their repertoire.

An example of a simple model

In computing, models are divided into two important elements:

1. the *logic*: the sequence of steps to solve a problem
2. the *data*: the input variables.

Figure 4.1 shows the construction of a profit plan for a five-year period. (This model is not an example of any particular computer language or package; it is shown to emphasize the separate elements of the model: the logic, the data and the subsequent results.) In Figure 4.1, the logic is the first element of the model shown. In this type of construction, the accounting relationships are expressed in steps within the logic — the steps in this example are referred to as row numbers. The logic is derived from a number of assumptions, e.g. the cost of sales being 45% of sales value. To be able to effectively make reasonable assumptions regarding the logic, the model builder must have a good insight into the logical nature of the business and the problem under consideration.

The only data required for this model are the sales figures; once these have been input to the model, all the other steps in the logic can be calculated without reference to any other input variable, and the profit plan can then be prepared. Sales are assumed to be £1m in the first year growing by £100 000 each year, i.e. arithmetic growth. Data is similarly derived as a result of certain assumptions. In this example, there is the assumption that sales will grow arithmetically over 5 years. This may be derived from market surveys or estimates from sales staff.

Finally, the result is shown.

Types of model

In accounting a model is normally used to:

1. construct plans such as cash budgets
2. produce optimizing models, e,g. a model to determine a sales mix that would maximize profits subject to certain production constraints.

Although optimizing models can be found in academic and profes-

Logic

```
ROW Nos.                    DESCRIPTION
    1    SALES
    2    COST OF SALES = 45% OF SALES
    3    GROSS MARGIN = SALES-COST OF SALES
    4    OTHER OPERATING EXPENSES = £200,000 + 12.5% OF SALES
    5    PROFIT = GROSS MARGIN-OPERATING EXPENSES
```

Data

```
ROW Nos.                    AMOUNT
    1    £1.0M,£1.1M,£1.2M,£1.3M,£1.4M.
```

Result (all amounts in £000s)

	1989	1990	1991	1992	1993
	£	£	£	£	£
SALES [Input Variable]	1,000.0	1,100.0	1,200.0	1,300.0	1,400.0
COST OF SALES [£1M*45%]	450.0	495.0	540.0	585.0	630.0
GROSS MARGIN [£1M-£450,000]	550.0	605.0	660.0	715.0	770.0
OPERATING EXPENSES [£200,000+12.5%*£1M]	325.0	337.5	350.0	362.5	375.0
PROFIT [£550,000-£325,000]	225.0	267.5	310.0	352.5	395.0

[1989 calculations in brackets]

Figure 4.1 Simple financial model – construction of a five-year profit plan.

sional accounting course curricula, we recognize their limited application in practice. Therefore we will concentrate on the first type of model, in particular such models used for planning. These types of model are frequently referred to in computing texts as deterministic simulation models.

4.2 COMPUTER APPLICATIONS AND FINANCIAL MODELLING

In this chapter, we shall be considering applications of microcomputer financial modelling packages. This term is generally used to refer to a specific type of package — financial models can, however, also be written using a general purpose language such as BASIC, or constructed by the use of spreadsheet packages (although spreadsheets also have other uses). Although most financial models on microcomputers are actually based on spreadsheet packages, the process of model building can be more clearly illustrated using a financial modelling package rather than a spreadsheet package.

Spreadsheets are considered in detail in the next chapter. Spreadsheets tend to be easy to understand when they are demonstrated, but not easy to follow from a description in a book. They have therefore been left to the next chapter, even though for many users they are more relevant than financial modelling packages. Also, as a number of the basic principles of financial modelling are important to the understanding of spreadsheets it is appropriate to consider financial modelling before looking at spreadsheet packages. A separate section at the end of the next chapter compares some of the main financial modelling and spreadsheet packages, and discusses where different types of packages are likely to be most suitable.

The original microcomputer financial modelling package was Micromodeller. Most of the current packages have been developed by companies with substantial experience of financial modelling on mainframes — some of the better known ones are Micro-FCS, MicroFinar and IFPS-Personal. Here, we shall be using Micro-FCS to illustrate a number of the features of computer-based financial modelling. Micro-FCS is marketed by Thorn-EMI Computer Software, who also sell the mainframe/minicomputer package known as FCS, the UK market leader used by many major companies. Micro-FCS embodies the same principles as the mainframe version, and is totally upwards compatible, so that models developed on a microcomputer may be transferred easily to a larger computer if required. The system is very user-friendly, which is one of the main reasons for its popularity.

Figure 4.2 illustrates the key features of a financial modelling package; the diagram refers specifically to Micro-FCS, but any financial modelling package will have similar features. The most important point is the ability to define the rules for calculations (the logic) separately from the data and the output report specifications; this is totally different from the way a model is set up using a spread sheet.

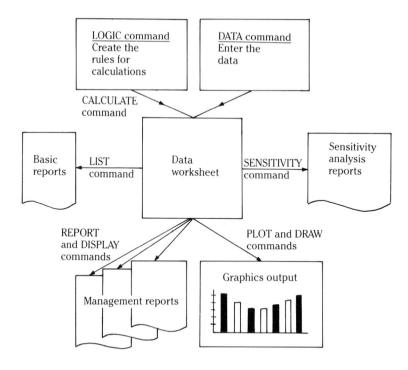

Figure 4.2 Micro-FCS: structure of a typical financial modelling system. Once the data and logic have been separately entered the worksheet is calculated and used as a basis for various reports.

This leads to a number of advantages: it makes it much simpler to re-run the same model with different data sets, and it also means that a range of reports can be produced more easily from the same model. It also makes it easier to present the accounting logic to a financial director or a client in a form that is easy for them to understand.

The other major point is that Micro-FCS, like most financial model-ling packages, is command-driven, i.e. the user is given a standard prompt of **System**> to which he responds by a series of commands. This implies a certain degree of knowledge on his part, although a **HELP** command is available. For a beginner, this may not be as easy as a menu-driven system (where one selects from a menu of choices), but a command-driven system has considerable advantages in deve-loping larger accounting models when one wishes to automate the model and make it more manageable.

4.3 A SIMPLE MODEL — USING MICRO-FCS

The process of setting up the logic, data and the reporting of the results using Micro-FCS is shown in Figure 4.3, for the same five-year profit plan as was illustrated earlier in Figure 4.1. It can be seen that after entering Micro-FCS, the user will be confronted with a standard prompt of **System>**. On all occasions, the first command to be entered by the user after the standard prompt is **Set columns**, which defines the number of columns in the model, that is the horizontal dimensions of the model. In this example, five columns are required, one for each of the years of the plan. The system is then ready to accept input in the form of the logic and data from the user; in Micro-FCS, **Logic** and **Data** are the commands which initiate these two processes. Once set up, the logic and data may be saved as separate files. There are many more user commands available, some of which are illustrated in this example. To obtain a comprehensive list of these user commands, the user just has to type **Help** after the **System>** prompt.

The following details the sequence of operations in setting up the model:

1. Enter logic

The command **Logic** allows the user to edit his logic. Here, the command is being invoked for the first time to enter a new set of logic; on a subsequent occasion, the **Logic** command can be used to re-edit existing logic if changes are necessary.

The prompt **+** is given to remind the user that he is editing his logic; the user simply enters lines of logic, followed by the 'return' key. Any mistyped lines can be either retyped, or can be 'screen-edited' (as in word processing): this means that the user can move the cursor around the screen and insert or delete characters as he wishes. Each row is given a number and a name by the user, and where appropriate an instruction for a calculation. (Notice that row names are enclosed in primes (single inverted commas). The function of the primes is to allow the user the flexibility to enter a name within the primes made up of any characters from the keyboard, whether alpha, numeric or any other sign, without the system registering a syntax error. This is useful for names such as 'Cost/Unit', but a one-word name such as 'Sales' where there is no danger of ambiguity may be entered without primes if you wish. However, these row names will be shown in the report, so it is also important that the names should be precise, as well as concise.)

```
System>Set columns 5
System>Logic
+1 'Sales'
+2 'Cost of Sales'='Sales'* 45./100.
+3 'Gross Margin'='Sales'-'Cost of Sales'
+4 'Other Operating Costs'='Sales'*12.5/100.+200000.
+5 'Profit'='Gross Margin'-'Other Operating Costs'
+end
System>Data
*1,A,1000000,100000
```

(£1,000,000 in the first year growing by £100,000
each year; i.e. arithmetic growth)


```
*end
System>Calculate
System>Title
Title:5 Year Profit Plan
System>Heading
Option:Nu 1989,1
Option:end
System>List
Columns?1-5
Rows?1-5
```

```
                        5 Year Profit Plan
                   1989    1990    1991    1992    1993
1 Sales         1000.00 1100.00 1200.00 1300.00 1400.00 K
2 Cost of Sales  450.00  495.00  540.00  585.00  630.00 K
3 Gross Margin   550.00  605.00  660.00  715.00  770.00 K
4 Other Operating
Costs            325.00  337.50  350.00  362.50  375.00 K
5 Profit         225.00  267.50  310.00  352.50  395.00 K
```

```
System>Report
Specifications
10 supr               (suppress row numbers)
20 sname 0 priname 18 (start names from left of page, width 18)
30 width 9            (column width 9- default is 8)
```

```
40 Text 8, 'All Amounts in £000'  (a comment)
50 Decimal 2             (output values to 2 decimal places)
60 rows 1,2
70 udata                 (after rows 1 and 2 underline data)
80 row 4
90 udata                 (after row 4 underline data)
100 row 5 udash '='      (row 5, followed by a line of '=')
110 end
System>Display
```

5 Year Profit Plan

	1989	1990	1991	1992	1993
[All Amounts in £000]					
Sales	1000.00	1100.00	1200.00	1300.00	1400.00
Cost of Sales	450.00	495.00	540.00	585.00	630.00
Gross Margin	550.00	605.00	660.00	715.00	770.00
Other Operating Costs	325.00	337.50	350.00	362.50	375.00
Profit	225.00	267.50	310.00	352.50	395.00

```
System>Save Logic/Planlog
System>Save Data/Plandat
System>Save Report/Planrep
System>Exit
```

Figure 4.3 Micro-FCS solution for the simple example given in Figure 4.1. The Micro-FCS prompts are given here in light type, the user's responses are underlined.

In this example, row 1 shows purely a name: +1 'Sales' as this is a data entry. Row 2 shows a name plus an instruction for a calculation: +2 'Cost of Sales' = 'Sales' * 45./100., i.e. 45% of 'Sales'. (Note that if a row name is to be used within an instruction the primes usually need to be inserted to avoid ambiguity, although the primes around 'Sales' could have been omitted.)

Logic instructions can refer to row names as here, but often it is more convenient to refer to row numbers. Thus the logic for row 3 could be written: +3 'Gross Margin' = 1-2 Clearly, the use of row numbers in this context can save time, especially when there are numerous logic instructions to be typed. Real numbers can also be used in the instructions, for example row 4 shows a fixed cost of £200 000:

+4'Other Operating Costs' = 'Sales'*12.5/100.+200000.

Real numbers are distinguished from row numbers in logic by the use of decimal points; the user must also disregard commas relating to thousands and millions.

The logic therefore, as previously mentioned, is built through accounting relationships to eventually obtain the desired result, that is the profit for each of the five years.

Finally, the command **end** returns the user from editing logic to the **System** > prompt.

2. Enter data

In response to the standard prompt **System**> the user types in the command **Data**, and this will be followed by the data prompt *. Each row of data is entered separately, first indicating the applicable row number (the row numbers must be compatible with those used in the logic).

In this simple example, the only data required is for row 1 (Sales); the other rows are instructions for calculations. Data may be entered directly into the data matrix in 'on-screen' mode, or, if preferred, the data options facility may be used. The data options are specified by a single letter entered after the row number but before any numbers are input; in this example, **A** indicates arithmetic growth. There are many other data options available which make the process of entering the data easier; these can be time saving, especially when the data to be entered is increasing by a fixed amount (or percentage) each period, or the data is in large numbers such as millions.

Typing **end** again returns us to the **System**> prompt.

3. Calculate results

This is achieved by the command **Calculate**.

4. Define title and headings

These are defined by the commands **Title** and **Heading**. Notice that where an output extends over several printed pages, the title and heading will be repeated on each page of output. The **Heading** command has several options: in this case, a numerically increasing value is chosen to give calendar years as headings.

5. Output results

In this first instance, this is done by typing the command **List**: the user has the option of what rows and columns are to be listed; this is useful if the user only wants to look at part of a large data matrix.

The report is in a fixed and not very ideal format; the **K** at the end of a line indicates that the values are in thousands. However, the standard report produced via the **List** command can still be very useful. In particular, at this stage, it is often prudent to check calculations as well as to appraise how the information should be best presented.

In this case, output is to the screen, but the output can be printed simply by typing the command **List printer** instead of **List**.

6. Producing neat reports

List is often convenient to use, and the quality of report may be good enough for internal use, but it is not really satisfactory for presentation to senior management or to one's bankers. The alternative is to specify completely your own report format using the **Report** command, the final output being produced by the command **Display** or **Display Printer**.

The reporting facility within Micro-FCS is one of its strongest features, and is vastly more flexible than most spreadsheet packages. Micro-FCS gives the user a large number of specifications with which the user can define the format of the report. The example, although limited due to the size of the model, illustrates a number of the options available to the user, together with comments to explain their meaning. The row numbers by the side of each specification do not relate to the rows defined in the logic or data, but are simply generated by Micro-FCS to allow re-editing of the report specification.

Finally, the command **Display**, after the creation of the report file, displays the report on the screen.

7. Saving the files

Lastly, Figure 4.3 shows the method by which the files are saved. For each file the user must type after the **System >** prompt **Save** and the relevant file, followed by the user's unique identification for the file, e.g. in the case of the logic file /**Planlog**. Clearly, the ability to save the file for further use is essential in financial modelling. (Note that file names in Micro-FCS are always preceded by a /.)

4.4 OTHER FEATURES IN MICRO-FCS

So far we have considered only a very simple model in order to explain how a financial model is constructed in Micro-FCS. In practice, it is more likely to be used for relatively complex models, where the user will gain in understanding by being able to consider his logic more explicitly than he could if he used a spreadsheet.

One key feature is the ability to create **job files**. A job file consists of a whole series of commands, which may be activated and then run automatically. Using our previous example, the job file in Figure 4.4 could be set up.

The commands in the job file will automatically call up the logic, data and report files which were previously saved. Responses to questions may also be included in the job file, such as the questions **Columns to list?** and **Rows?** which will follow the command **List Printer**.

Often accountants need the capability to run large jobs on a regular basis. These types of job are invariably complex and the logic, data and report files tend to be extremely long; a good example of this type of job is the consolidation of monthly accounting reports. The use of job files for such work can be very cost effective. Setting up job files for such procedures is a relatively easy exercise, once the various files have been created, and Micro-FCS has its own text editor which can be used to create the job file.

```
Set Columns 5
Logic using /Planlog          .... recall saved logic
Data using /Plandat           .... recall saved data
Calculate
Title
5 Year Profit Plan            .... response to 'Title:' prompt
Heading
Nu 1989,1                     .... response to 'Option:'
                              prompt
End                           .... ditto - return to 'System>'
List Printer
1-5                           .... Columns to list?
1-5                           .... Rows to list?
Report using /Planrep         .... recall saved report spec
Display Printer
```

Figure 4.4 Example of a job file.

Micro-FCS also has a useful feature for doing consolidations, the **Read** command. This enables a specified section of any data file to be read into any part of the current matrix. This makes it extremely easy to consolidate data for several departments or subsidiaries, even where the data kept for one subsidiary is in a slightly different form from the data kept for others.

The creation of job files is also very helpful in accounting when producing monthly reports. The logic and the report specification files would normally be the same each month. The only file that would change from month to month would be the data file, detailing each month's input. Using the job file facility and the **Read** command, it is easy to create a data file and add the new data to the existing model each month.

Micro-FCS links in easily with other packages such as word processing or database, because any output produced by Micro-FCS can be written to a text file, rather than being output to screen or printer. The text file can then be read in as input data by a database or statistical package, or it can be edited using a word processing package. In the context of accounting information this facility can be very advantageous when there is a need to add explanations to the report, such as information regarding the assumptions underlying the elements of the model

Lastly, Micro-FCS does have powerful graphics features, which are important for many users. The use of graphics by professional accountants is discussed in Chapter 10.

4.5 CORPORATE PLANNING

A corporate plan is a quantitative statement of the long-term policies and strategies of an organization as a whole. These policies and strategies will take account of the courses of action necessary to achieve the objectives of the organization in respect of such items as investment, growth, product development and market share.

Corporate planning is the process by which the plan is established. In the planning process a number of different policies are considered, and run through a computer model which reflects the organization's financial structure. The process is concluded by management deciding which policies should be adopted in the corporate plan.

The model of the organization is usually referred to as a corporate model, and it will normally be based on the financial information framework embodied in the final accounts, that is the profit and loss account, balance sheet, and sources and applications of funds statement. The model is constructed in a very similar way to the model shown in Figure 4.3.

A corporate model built using Micro-FCS for A&B PLC, a retail company, is illustrated below. The results, given in Figure 4.5, are in the form of a balance sheet, income statement, a sources and applications of funds statement and a selective number of financial ratios for a four-year period.

Corporate Planning Example
A&B PLC started trading in 1988. The first balance sheet was at 31.12.88, and the following is a summary of that balance sheet:

		£000
Fixed assets		800
Net working capital		200
		£1000

	£000	
Owners equity	500	
Retained earnings	100	600
Loan		400
		£1000

Management forecasts for the four year period (all amounts in £000):

	1989	1990	1991	1992
Sales	2808	increasing by 15% p.a.		
Investment into fixed assets	300	300	200	200
Average borrowings during the year	500	555	610	665

The following were the assumptions upon which the model was built:

1. Cost of goods sold represent 90% of sales during the year;
2. The cost of borrowings is anticipated to be 9% p.a. based on the average borrowings during the year;
3. The company's depreciation policy is 10% p.a. based on the value of the fixed assets at the end of the year;
4. The company's dividend policy is to pay dividends of 60% of each year's net income;
5. The working capital requirement at any time during the four year period will be 9.3% of sales revenue for the year in question;
6. No additional shares will be issued during any of the four years;

Figure 4.5 Results of a simple corporate planning model on A&B PLC using Micro-FCS (all amounts in £000).

Income Statement.

Year:	1989 £	1990 £	1991 £	1992 £
REVENUE	2808	3229	3714	4271
COST OF GOODS SOLD	2527	2906	3342	3844
	281	323	371	427
LESS: DEPRECIATION	110	129	136	142
INTEREST	45	50	55	60
NET INCOME	126	144	180	225

Source and Application of Funds Statement

Year:	1989 £	1990 £	1991 £	1992 £
SOURCES:				
NET INCOME	126	144	180	225
DEPRECIATION	110	129	136	142
	236	273	316	367
BORROWINGS	201	153	37	19
	437	426	353	387
APPLICATIONS:	£	£	£	£
INVESTMENT	300	300	200	200
DIVIDEND	75	86	108	135
CHANGE IN NET WORKING CAPITAL	61	39	45	52
	437	426	353	387

Balance Sheet

Years:	1989 £	1990 £	1991 £	1992 £
FIXED ASSETS	990	1161	1225	1282
NET WORKING CAPITAL	261	300	345	397
TOTAL ASSETS	1251	1461	1570	1680

	£	£	£	£
EQUITY	650	708	780	870
DEBT	601	753	790	810
CAPITAL EMPLOYED	1251	1461	1570	1680

Financial Ratios

	1989	1990	1991	1992
NET PROFIT MARGIN [%]	4.5	4.5	4.9	5.3
RETURN ON EQUITY [%]	19.3	20.3	23.1	25.8
RETURN ON ASSETS [%]	10.1	9.9	11.5	13.4
ASSET TURNOVER [times]	2.2	2.2	2.4	2.5
GEARING [%]	48.0	51.6	50.3	48.2
WORKING CAPITAL TURNOVER [times]	10.8	10.8	10.8	10.8

The following are the definitions of each of the Financial Ratios listed above:

* Net Profit Margin : Net Income/ Revenue * 100

* Return on Equity : Net Income/ Equity * 100 [Equity= Share Capital + Retained Earnings]

* Asset Turnover : Revenue/ Total Assets *100

* Gearing : Debt/ Capital Employed * 100

* Working Capital Turnover : Revenue/ Net Working Capital.

7. Any additional finance will be funded through borrowings from the company's bank.

It is often implied in texts that corporate planning is only relevant to large corporations. This is clearly a myth; it could be argued that medium and small firms, with their inherent cashflow and financing problems, are more in need of long-term planning. The development of microcomputer-based financial modelling applications by a number of accounting practices who service smaller firms — and by the firms themselves — has resulted in these smaller companies being able to get substantial benefits from long-term planning activities.

Finally a word of caution: although the advertisements of some companies selling financial modelling packages would suggest the opposite, the process of corporate modelling can be extremely complex. This, of course, is not surprising, for two reasons. First, corporations themselves tend to be extremely complex structures, certainly at the multinational end of the scale. Secondly, the nature of long-term planning itself is also complex in that a successful plan is partially dependent upon the quality of the forecasting. Forecasting takes energy and a lot of time. The complexity of modelling, however, has not stopped the rapid growth of companies applying the technique to their long-term planning.

The points to remember are: initially, do not be too ambitious, and as experience is gained the modelling process will be easier and more successful — keep persevering.

4.6 SENSITIVITY ANALYSIS — 'WHAT IF ...?' QUESTIONS

One of the major advantages with financial modelling packages applied to planning and decision-making problems in accounting is the facility to change data input by brief commands; this is usually referred to as sensitivity analysis. In the planning and decision-making process there are numerous occasions when the planner wishes to consider the outcome of a percentage increase or decrease of one of the more sensitive input variables of a model, for example an increase in selling prices. The question 'What if ...?' is often used to describe this process: 'What if the selling price were increased by 5%?' In the case of Micro-FCS there are two such facilities for calculating the outcomes of proposed scenarios in the form of system commands: the **Sensitivity** and **Target** commands.

The **Sensitivity** command is the most convenient way of making a single percentage change to an input variable, or making a series of different percentage changes to a whole set of input variables. Successive **Sensitivity** commands may also be used to change an input variable by a range of percentages, e.g. selling prices to be changed in steps of 5% from −5% to +10%. The **Target** command will inform the user what the input variables will have to be to meet a certain defined target, e.g. what the selling price has to be to obtain a return on investment of 20%. These facilities are particularly useful for corporate planning as there tends to be greater uncertainty in respect of the assumptions and input variables because the time horizon is longer.

To illustrate the use of this facility consider the corporate model developed for A&B PLC in the previous section. It can be seen from the income statement in Figure 4.5 that an important cost element in the model is interest payments on borrowings. The company has made the assumption that the rate for borrowing will be 9% per annum. Interest rates, as we all know, are somewhat difficult to predict, and are effectively outside the control of the company. This being the case, the management of A&B PLC may wish to consider the effect if there was an increase in these rates, e.g. from 9%, in steps of 4%, up to 17%. Using Micro-FCS facilities the user can also operate management by exception, and in the example of A&B PLC the management may only wish to consider the effect on their financial position as reflected in the financial ratios.

Figure 4.6 shows the output in the form of financial ratios generated from the Micro-FCS **Sensitivity** command for interest rates of 13% and 17% (the asset turnover ratio and the working capital turnover ratio have been excluded as they are not affected by the change in interest rates). The net profit margin, return on equity and return on assets ratios in this figure for interest rates of 13% and 17% all show a decrease in percentage terms as compared to the ratios shown in the original corporate plan in Figure 4.5. These decreases are the result of the drop in net income, reflecting the higher interest costs. The gearing ratio, on the other hand, has increased, which means that the assets of the company are being financed by a higher proportion of debt capital (borrowings) as compared to the position in the original corporate plan. This is due to the reduction in retained earnings, resulting once again from the increase in interest charges.

The financial ratios in Figure 4.6 clearly reflect a weaker financial position than the same ratios shown in the original plan. How critical these changes may be on A&B PLC would depend upon the judgement of the management of the company. The important point to recognize is that the information generated from the sensitivity analysis will give management the opportunity to consider the potential effects of changes in interest rates. This may result in the company making contingency plans, such as reducing the level of activities or seeking cheaper sources of finance to lessen the effect of a possible increase in interest charges.

4.7 FINANCIAL MODELLING PACKAGES: THE BENEFITS

The application of financial modelling packages to the work of the accounting practice has made a dramatic impact on time saving and fee income. Practices have become more efficient in their own management control, whilst being in a better position to give clients a

Interest Rates at 13%

	1989 %	1990 %	1991 %	1992 %
NET PROFIT MARGIN	3.77	3.77	4.20	4.64
RETURN ON EQUITY	16.47	17.62	20.70	23.79
RETURN ON ASSETS	8.46	8.33	9.93	11.80
GEARING	48.66	52.71	52.02	50.45

Interest Rates at 17%

	1989 %	1990 %	1991 %	1992 %
NET PROFIT MARGIN	3.60	3.08	3.54	4.02
RETURN ON EQUITY	13.53	14.77	18.10	21.56
RETURN ON ASSETS	6.86	6.81	8.38	10.21
GEARING	49.30	53.87	53.72	52.64

Figure 4.6 Financial ratios at different interest rates.

wider and more cost effective service.

The following summarizes the main benefits which have been earlier identified in the text of this chapter:

1. The nature of the modelling process requires the model builder to analyse all the aspects of the financial problem under consideration. This will help in understanding the problem as well as ensuring that the model builder develops a good insight into the business and the logical accounting relationships.
2. The data entry facilities makes it easy and quick to input data.
3. The system will automatically calculate the results, by means of a simple instruction.
4. The model can easily be edited, by changing either the logic or the data.
5. These packages produce excellent reports that can be presented to clients and other users of the information. This reporting facility also saves the time involved in typing a good copy.
6. The logic, data and the report can easily be saved and retrieved for updating, amending, etc.
7. Job files can be created, which facility enables large complex jobs to be run on a regular basis; this is especially the case where the logic and report specification remains the same each month, and the only input is the new data to be entered each month.

8. Job files are also extremely useful when it is required to consolidate large and complex divisional, departmental or group accounts.
9. Sensitivity analysis can easily be performed.
10. The experience of accounting practices using computers has shown that accuracy is considerably enhanced, as transaction errors are eliminated.

A cautionary note: there is a learning process involved in the introduction of financial modelling packages. The evidence is that to be successful this will include senior staff involvement in the development of the application. Although this may be a heavy cost to bear initially, the majority of users have found it to be a very worthwhile investment.

5 Spreadsheets: financial planning and reporting

Spreadsheets were referred to in the last chapter as packages that are very suitable for building financial models. However it was also stressed that the spreadsheets are not solely used for this function, but are also used for other accounting applications. In this chapter, we will concentrate purely on spreadsheets, considering their development in the accounting context and their versatility in the provision of information. In particular, we shall show how to develop a model using Lotus 1-2-3 and draw a comparison between the most popular spreadsheet packages currently being marketed. The chapters to follow will focus on specific accounting applications, where spreadsheet packages often have an important role. This chapter will therefore make an essential contribution to the appreciation and understanding of spreadsheets to specific accounting applications which will be considered later.

Spreadsheet packages have undoubtedly been by far the most successful of all business computer packages in terms of the number of copies sold. The first such package was Visicalc, of which several hundred thousand copies were sold on the Apple II. Supercalc and Multiplan have since been very successful, but the most successful such package has undoubtedly been Lotus 1-2-3 on IBM-compatible microcomputers. Lotus 1-2-3 is rather more than a spreadsheet, because it also includes graphics and database features; however, although Lotus 1-2-3 was the first spreadsheet to include these features, most spreadsheet packages now include similar facilities.

The name 'spreadsheet' derives from the traditional accountant's approach to drawing up a financial plan for a small business, using a large spread sheet of accounting paper to calculate the income and net cash flow for a project, with the columns representing months or years, and the rows representing the revenues and costs of various kinds. The name worksheet is often used instead of spreadsheet (especially by American sources); for convenience, we shall use the name spreadsheet to refer to the type of computer package, and worksheet to refer to the table which is being set up.

Figure 5.1 shows a typical but simplified financial plan for Macho Cycles Ltd, a small company specializing in building high-quality racing bicycles. Macho make two models, the FB Racer and the RJ Tourer; the revenues and the gross and net profits are calculated in a fairly obvious way, and the percentage margin for gross and net profits are calculated by taking the profits as a percentage of total revenue.

The next section describes some of the features of Lotus 1-2-3, and how to set up a spreadsheet model using Macho Cycles Ltd as an example; the actual results are shown later in Figure 5.5. As well as having all the features necessary to set up such a spreadsheet, 1-2-3 has a number of other powerful features which could be useful to professional accounting firms, and some practices have developed very sophisticated financial reporting systems using 1-2-3. There are also limited word processing facilities, and the printout of the plan

```
                        Macho Cycles Ltd
                        ----------------

                   1989      1990      1991      1992      1993

FB Racer - Quantity  100       110       120       130       140
         - Price     300       310       325       340       350
         - Revenue        Quantity x Price

RJ Tourer - Quantity 150       165       180       195       210
          - Price    350       360       370       385       400
          - Revenue       Quantity x Price

   Total Revenue         Revenue(FB) + Revenue(RJ)

Material Cost per FB  130       135       140       145       150
Material Cost per RJ  150       155       160       165       170
Total Material Cost   Cost(FB) x Qty(FB)  +  Cost(RJ) x Qty(RJ)
Labour Cost           £25,000 in 1989 and increasing by 5% each year

   Gross Profit       Revenue - Material Cost - Labour Cost

Other Costs           £12,000 in 1989 and increasing by 6% each year

   Net Profit         Gross Profit - Other Costs

Gr Profit % Margin    Gross Profit as percentage of Revenue
Net Profit % Margin   Net Profit as percentage of Revenue
```

Figure 5.1 Spreadsheet plan for Macho Cycles Ltd.

shown in Figure 5.1 was produced using Lotus 1-2-3. Other features of 1-2-3 are discussed in later sections of this chapter.

The one reservation about spreadsheet packages is the ability of the human user to cope with large and complicated models where only a small section can be viewed at a time. It can be particularly difficult if large amounts of data have to be drawn together and processed on a weekly or monthly basis. In that situation, it may be worth using a financial modelling package such as Micro-FCS or Finar. Where a large consolidation is to be carried out, a financial modelling package will certainly be a better option than a spreadsheet package.

5.1 SETTING UP A MODEL USING LOTUS 1-2-3

Lotus 1-2-3 sets up what is referred to either as a **computer model** or as a **spreadsheet model**. A model is simply a set of instructions to the computer as to how everything is to be defined. A standard spreadsheet model will require the following definitions:

1. text for titles and headings
2. layout for tables: column widths
3. data for input values
4. formulae for doing calculations.

Lotus 1-2-3 has additional facilities apart from just defining a spreadsheet, hence a 1-2-3 model may also contain:

5. layouts for graphs
6. macros, i.e. predetermined tasks.

When you enter 1-2-3, you are presented with a blank table, the rows being referred to by numbers and the columns by letters. This provides a means of referencing different cells: C1 is the cell in Column C Row 1, while D5 refers to Column D Row 5. In theory, up to 8192 rows and 256 columns are possible in 1-2-3 (assuming enough memory is available); in practice, that is likely to be far more than a human can cope with, given that only about 20 rows and 7 columns can be viewed on screen at any time.

Figure 5.2 shows the Macho computer model in the process of being edited; here, the main Lotus menu is shown above the worksheet on line 2 of the screen, but initially lines 2 and 3 of the screen would be blank. To create such a model simply involves making an entry into each cell of the model, there being three possible types of entry:

C8: (FB) + C6*C7

Worksheet Range Copy Move File Print Graph Data Quit
Global Insert Delete Column-Width Erase Titles Window Status

	A	B	C	D	E	F
1						
2				Macho Cycles Ltd		
3				---------------		
4		1989	1990	1991	1992	1993
5						
6	FB Racer - Quantity	100	110	120	130	140
7	- Price	300	310	325	340	350
8	- Revenue	30000	34100	39000	44200	49000
9						
10	RJ Tourer - Quantity	150	165	180	195	210
11	- Price	350	360	370	385	400
12	- Revenue	52500	59400	66600	75075	84000
13						
14	Total Revenue	82500	93500	105600	119275	133000
15						
16	Material Cost per FB	130	135	140	145	150
17	Material Cost per RJ	150	155	160	165	170
18	Total Material Cost	35500	40425	45600	51025	56700
19	Labour Cost	25000	26250	27563	28941	30388
20						

Figure 5.2: Screen display: editing in Lotus 1.2.3. Cursor is currently on cell C8, and the formula for that cell is displayed above the worksheet. The second row of the screen shows the main 1-2-3 menu, and the third row shows the options on the worksheet menu (the current option highlighted).

Enter Text

This is necessary for titles and column headings, as well as for specifying variables at the beginning of each row. It is also often useful to put in comments or lines of dashes in the middle of the calculations to improve the legibility of the eventual printed report.

To enter text in 1-2-3, you simply move the cursor to the relevant cell using the cursor control keys, and then type in the text, followed by the return key. The text will then appear in the cell; if the text is too wide for that cell, it will run on into any empty cells to the right. This is especially useful for typing titles or long comments.

Enter Data

Data values can be entered in a similar way to entering text, i.e. you position the cursor on the appropriate cell, and then type in the required value, followed by a 'return'. The data values to be entered in the Macho model are the quantities, prices and unit costs, together with the labour cost.

Enter Formulae

These are necessary for any entries which are to be calculated. For example:

$$\text{Revenue} = \text{Quantity} \times \text{Price}$$

Formulae in 1-2-3 start with + (or − or ') and use the cell references described above, together with the operators:

+   add   −   subtract   *   multiply   /   divide

Thus, the 1-2-3 formula (equivalent to the revenue formula above) for the **Revenue for FB Racers** in 1987 (in cell B8) is:

$$+B6*B7$$

and the **Total Revenue** (in cell B14) will be given by:

$$+B8+B12$$

(Revenue for FB Racers + Revenue for RJ Tourers)

A formula can be entered in a similar way to entering text, provided that you type a + at the beginning of the formula. The full list of formulae needed for the year 1988 of the Macho model is shown in Figure 5.3; the printout gives data or text where these are used rather than a formula for that cell.

Once you have mastered these ideas, it is very easy to create financial

```
C4:  1990
C6:  (F0)  110
C7:  (F0)  310
C8:  (F0)  +C6*C7
C10: (F0)  165
C11: (F0)  360
C12: (F0)  +C10*C11
C14: (F0)  +C8+C12
C16: (F0)  135
C17: (F0)  155
C18: (F0)  +C6*C16+C10*C17
C19: (F0)  +B19*1.05
C21: (F0)  +C14-C18-C19
C23: (F0)  +B23*1.06
C25: (F0)  +C21-C23
C27: (F1)  +C21/C14*100
C28: (F1)  +C25/C14*100
```

Figure 5.3 Formulae for Macho model, year 1990. The formulae for other years are similar.

planning models using 1-2-3. Not only can you set things up quickly, but it is also possible to repeat your calculations very rapidly with different input data. All that you need to do is to enter a new data value into a cell, and 1-2-3 will automatically redo all the calculations for you.

Creating a formula on screen

This is often easier than typing a formula, as it saves needing to remember which cells you are referring to; it is also usually quicker. The process for setting up the formula for **Revenue in 1987 for FB Racers** (Price × Quantity, i.e. +B6*B7) is as follows:

1. With cursor at B8 (1987 Revenue), type +
2. Move cursor to B6; we now have displayed: +B6
3. Type *; cursor returns to B8, display: +B6*
4. Move cursor to B7 to display: +B6*B7
5. Press 'return' to store formula for cell B8.

This method of setting up cell references on screen is often used for other purposes in 1-2-3, such as for setting up ranges of cells to be printed or graphed, and is quite powerful.

Menus and Commands

1-2-3 has a wide range of commands available, which, for example, allow you to redesign the layout of the display, or to print out the results, or to draw a graph on the screen. All commands in 1-2-3 start with a /, for example:

/WCS   Change width of current column
/C   Copy a section of the worksheet
/PPG   Print results

However, people cannot normally remember such a wide range of commands as are possible; 1-2-3 therefore presents the commands to you as a series of 'step-by-step' menus (or lists of options). The main menu appears when you type / and is shown in Figures 5.2 and 5.4. The first line in a menu is a list of up to eight options; the first option is highlighted initially, but you can move to a different option by using the cursor movement keys. You select an option either by typing the first letter of the option (e.g. C for **Copy**) or by pressing return when the option is highlighted. The second line in the menu gives a more detailed description of the option which is currently highlighted, and is particularly useful where the option leads into another menu.

Figure 5.4 also shows the use of a series of menus to arrive at a final command: **/WCS** (**/Worksheet Column-width Set**) to be prompted by 1-2-3 for a new column-width, involves options from three menus as shown to arrive at the prompt.

If you get into a secondary menu that you did not intend, then pressing the 'escape' key will normally return you to the level above.

Figure 5.5 shows the final results from the computer model that has been discussed for Macho Cycles Ltd. The printout for Biggs Tricycles Ltd is omitted here, but is identical in format to the Macho output. The consolidated results for the whole group are also given. The three sets of calculations are all contained within the same model and the outputs were obtained by printing out different parts of the worksheet.

Further points on setting up a model

The /C (/Copy) command is often useful in setting up a model, as the same formula often applies across a row or column. Thus having created a formula in row B8, it can be copied into rows C8 to F8 simply by using the /Copy command; the formula +B6*B7 will automatically change into +C6*C7, +D6*D7, etc., when it is copied.

The command /WCS (/Worksheet Column-width Set) will almost always be used to change the width of the column that contains the row-headings, as the default column width of 9 characters will not usually be adequate. The data columns may also need widening, especially if large sums of money are involved in the report.

The other feature of 1-2-3 which is used in the Macho model is the

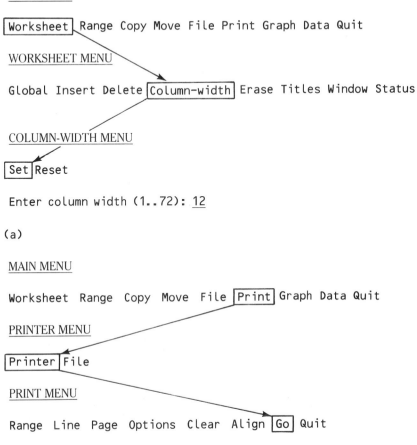

MAIN MENU

Worksheet Range Copy Move File Print Graph Data Quit

WORKSHEET MENU

Global Insert Delete Column-width Erase Titles Window Status

COLUMN-WIDTH MENU

Set Reset

Enter column width (1..72): 12

(a)

MAIN MENU

Worksheet Range Copy Move File Print Graph Data Quit

PRINTER MENU

Printer File

PRINT MENU

Range Line Page Options Clear Align Go Quit

(b)

Figure 5.4 Use of menus for Lotus 1-2-3 commands: (a) sequence for /WCS command; (b) sequence for /PPG command.

ability to format parts of the worksheet using the /RF command (Range Format). In the case of Macho, some of the rows have been formatted so that the percentages are displayed with one or more decimal places. It is also possible to display numbers with $ before or % after the number, as well as showing financial losses in brackets (according to the standard accounting terminology); thus (145.25) would mean a loss of £145.25.

There are many other commands in 1-2-3 which are helpful but not essential to the beginner, for example to insert or delete rows and

Macho Cycles Ltd

	1989	1990	1991	1992	1993
FB Racer - Quantity	100	110	120	130	140
- Price	300	310	325	340	350
- Revenue	30000	34100	39000	44200	49000
RJ Tourer - Quantity	150	165	180	195	210
- Price	350	360	370	385	400
- Revenue	52500	59400	66600	75075	84000
Total Revenue	82500	93500	105600	119275	133000
Material Cost per FB	130	135	140	145	150
Material Cost per RJ	150	155	160	165	170
Total Material Cost	35500	40425	45600	51025	56700
Labour Cost	25000	26250	27563	28941	30388
Gross Profit	22000	26825	32438	39309	45912
Other Costs	12000	12720	13483	14292	15150
Net Profit	10000	14105	18954	25017	30763
Gr Profit % Margin	26.7	28.7	30.7	33.0	34.5
Net Profit % Margin	12.1	15.1	17.9	21.0	23.1

Macho-Biggs Consolidated Results

	1989	1990	1991	1992	1993
Total Revenue	156500	177100	204900	227075	252550
Total Material Cost	65000	75625	89900	99625	111850
Labour Cost	43000	45150	47408	49778	52267
Gross Profit	48500	56325	67593	77672	88433
Other Costs	21000	22260	23596	25011	26512
Net Profit	27500	34065	43997	52661	61921
Gr Profit % Margin	31.0	31.8	33.0	34.2	35.0
Net Profit % Margin	17.6	19.2	21.5	23.2	24.5

Figure 5.5 Output from Lotus 1-2-3: results from Macho Cycles Ltd and consolidated accounts for the Macho-Biggs group.

columns, or to move sections of the model from one point to another. 1-2-3 also has a wide range of mathematical and statistical functions, and financial functions for internal rate of return and annuities.

Lastly, it is essential to be able to save the model on disk to avoid having to start from scratch each time. The relevant commands in 1-2-3 are:

/FS (/File Save)   to save the file
/FR (/File Retrieve)   to reload the file on a subsequent run.

5.2 OTHER USES OF SPREADSHEETS

One tends to think of spreadsheets as being used exclusively for financial planning, but this does not totally explain why they have been so popular. 1-2-3 has easily been the most popular package sold on the IBM-PC, and well over two million of these machines have now been sold. In fact, there are many applications where a table needs to be set up with a few simple calculations to be made from the data, and some explanatory text added. These may relate to reporting of management accounts, or may be quite different 'one-off' applications. As an example, Figure 5.6 shows a monthly statement (broken down to weekly cost reports) for the client of an accounting firm; the consultancy project concerns the setting up of a computerized accounting system. Having set up the model initially, all that is necessary is to enter the hours worked each week; 1-2-3 will automatically calculate the results, which can then be printed out.

There are many such applications and indeed many users just see a spreadsheet package as a means of performing a few calculations and then producing a neatly typed output. Often, the original data will come from the main accounts ledgers, which have been processed on a larger computer. All that needs to be done is to connect the micro to the minicomputer or mainframe, and persuade them to communicate by using the appropriate software. If the original data has been written to an ASCII (text) file, it is then easy to copy it down to the micro's disk so that it can be read into a 1-2-3 model for whatever further analysis is necessary.

There are two advantages of doing things this way. First, the user has complete independence in what he is doing, and does not have to fight with other users for computer time or worry about restrictions imposed by the computer manager. Secondly, and more importantly, the software on micros is specifically designed for non-technical users, and a package such as Lotus 1-2-3 is much easier and quicker to use

```
SCRAPHAM JINKS LTD              For: Balbec Metals Ltd
33 DIDHAM RD                          29 Mexham St
SUDBURY                               Sudbury

                    Weekly Cost Report for February 1988
                    =======================================

                     W/E       W/E       W/E       W/E       W/E
                     Feb 5     Feb 12    Feb 19    Feb 26    May 30
                     ------    ------    ------    ------    ------

Employee             Hours Worked
--------             ------------
Senior Consultant      4         6        12         2         4
  (£45 per hour)
Financial Analyst     25        35        30        25        20
  (£35 per hour)
Programmers           75        65        70        68        80
  (£30 per hour)


                     Cost (£)                                          TOTAL
                     --------                                          -----
Senior Consultant    180.00    270.00    540.00     90.00    180.00   1,260.00

Financial Analyst    875.00  1,225.00  1,050.00    875.00    700.00   4,725.00

Programmers        2,250.00  1,950.00  2,100.00  2,040.00  2,400.00  10,740.00
                   --------  --------  --------  --------  --------  ---------


            TOTAL  3,305.00  3,445.00  3,690.00  3,005.00  3,280.00  16,725.00


TOTAL DUE FOR MARCH 1988
         (Exc VAT)              16,725.00

         VAT at 15%             2,508.75
                                --------

TOTAL DUE FOR March 1988        19,233.75
         (Incl VAT)             =========
```

Figure 5.6 Monthly statement printed by Lotus 1-2-3.

than the equivalent mainframe software. It is noticeable now that many executives are using micro-based spreadsheets, whereas they would not have considered using a mainframe terminal because of the complications involved. Indeed, micros are becoming common even in boardrooms.

1-2-3 has been used by a number of firms of professional accountants to prepare final accounts for clients which satisfy the requirements of the 1985 *Companies Act*. This typically involves doing relatively standard calculations, with slight modifications for each individual client, and explanatory comments added where necessary. Using 1-2-3 saves time for both the accounts clerk and for the typist; also, the macros in 1-2-3 (see section 5.4) can be used to create a very user-friendly system, customized to the particular application.

1-2-3 is also ideally suited to producing regular management accounts for clients, to measure their performance against various budget headings. Standard accounting software will produce such reports, and indeed usually have scope for designing one-off reports. The advantages of using 1-2-3 to produce such one-off reports are the sheer flexibility that it offers in terms of performing additional analyses, and the facility to design the report on screen before printing it out. Figure 5.7 shows a management accounting report produced by Levy-Gee, in their accounts production package which is based on Lotus 1-2-3.

5.3 OTHER FACILITIES IN LOTUS 1-2-3

Lotus 1-2-3 was the first spreadsheet package to include graphics, and many users find this a very useful additional feature; this is discussed further in Chapter 14. There are also limited facilities for word processing, suitable mainly for adding text to tables (as in Figure 5.1) rather than for major applications. Finally, Lotus 1-2-3 has commands for database-handling which can be useful at times.

None of these facilities fit naturally into the context of financial planning; on the other hand, they do fit conveniently with the idea of a spreadsheet package as a sort of general workhorse. There are many small jobs involving the analysis of a small set of records which can be done quickly with 1-2-3, thus saving the expense of buying a database package. The data can easily be imported into 1-2-3 from another program, as 1-2-3 will happily read data from an ASCII (text) file or even from a data file produced by packages such as dBASE3 or Wordstar.

5.4 DESIGNING CUSTOMIZED APPLICATIONS

Spreadsheets are excellent for relatively simple applications, such as the Macho model mentioned earlier, but they do have limitations. A problem often encountered with very large models is running out of memory; 1-2-3 is quite wasteful in its use of RAM, and large models can easily use up 640 K or more of memory. Power of computation is usually less of a limitation, as 1-2-3 will cope with large models without slowing down greatly. However, the main problem is with the human operator: whether he can remember where everything is with a large model since only about 20 rows and 7 columns can be viewed at a time.

The difficulty lies in the nature of accounting data, which tends to be multi-dimensional rather than just two-dimensional. A typical accounts system will have a series of cost and revenue account headings which need to be aggregated into totals; department totals may then need to be consolidated into company data, and company

```
                                        DEMONSTRATOR - SALES ANALYSIS
                                        ================================

                                        1ST MARCH 1988 TO 28TH FEBRUARY 1989
                                        ====================================

                                Total       Mar      Apr      May      Jun      Jul
                                -----       ---      ---      ---      ---      ---
Covers per Week                             650      650      650      650      600
Weeks per Month                    52         4        4        5        4        4
                              ==========  =====================================
Covers per Month               33,750     2,600    2,600    3,250    2,600    2,400
                              ==========  =====================================

Average price per cover    47
Revenue per month               1,586,250  122,200  122,200  152,750  122,200  112,800
Service Charge          @ 12.5%     198,281   15,275   15,275   19,094   15,275   14,100
                              ----------  -------------------------------------
Total Net Revenue               1,784,531  137,475  137,475  171,844  137,475  126,900
                              ==========  =====================================

Total Dress Price          60
                           ==
```

```
VAT Allocation       VAT Rate       %
--------------       --------      ---
Standard Rated          14         100
Zero Rated/Exempt        0           0
Other                    0           0
                                   ---
                                   100
                                   ===
```

```
Sales Allocation
----------------
Month      %    Net      Val    Gross      Debtors  Mar      Apr      May      Jun      Jul
-----     ---   ---      ---    -----      -------   ---      ---      ---      ---      ---
                                                0
Mar        8  137,475  19,247  156,722            156,722
Apr        8  137,475  19,247  156,722                     156,722
May       10  171,844  24,058  195,902                              195,902
Jun        8  137,475  19,247  156,722                                       156,722
Jul        7  126,900  17,766  144,666                                                144,666
Aug        9  158,625  22,208  180,833
Sep        8  137,475  19,247  156,722
Oct       10  171,844  24,058  195,902
Nov        8  137,475  19,247  156,722
Dec        9  158,625  22,208  180,833
Jan       10  171,844  24,058  195,902
Feb        5  137,345  19,247  156,722
         ---  ----------------------                -----------------------------------------------
         100 1,784,531 249,834 2,034,366         0  156,722  156,722  195,902  156,722  144,666
         === ======================               ===============================================
```

Figure 5.7 Accounting report based on Lotus 1-2-3. Reproduced courtesy of Levy-Gee & Co. Ltd.

Aug	Sep	Oct	Nov	Dec	Jan	Feb
---	---	---	---	---	---	---
600	650	650	650	750	650	650
5	4	5	4	4	5	4
=======	=======	=======	=======	=======	=======	=======
3,000	2,600	3,250	2,600	3,000	3,250	2,600
=======	=======	=======	=======	=======	=======	=======
141,000	122,200	152,750	122,200	141,000	152,750	122,200
17,425	15,275	19,094	15,275	17,425	19,094	15,275
-------	-------	-------	-------	-------	-------	-------
158,425	137,475	171,844	137,475	158,425	171,044	137,475
=======	=======	=======	=======	=======	=======	=======

Aug	Sep	Oct	Nov	Dec	Jan	Feb	Debtors
---	---	---	---	---	---	---	-------
							0
							0
							0
							0
180,833							0
	156,722						0
		195,982					0
			156,722				0
				180,833			0
					195,902		0
						156,722	0
-------	-------	-------	-------	-------	-------	-------	---
180,833	156,722	195,982	156,722	180,833	195,902	156,722	0
=======	=======	=======	=======	=======	=======	=======	

data consolidated for a group of companies. If this seems over-elaborate, it must be remembered that even a small organization employing 60 or 70 staff will often have two or three operating companies and a whole series of departments for accounting purposes.

It is easy enough to enter the data for such a model into the worksheet; the problem is remembering the cell reference when you want to retrieve it or define how other rows are to be calculated from it (as in a consolidation). 1-2-3 provides a number of facilities to help in this respect, although processing a complex model can still be frustrating at times.

Fixing titles

The first of these facilities enables you to fix titles, using the command: /WT (/Worksheet Title). This fixes either a group of vertical columns, or a group of horizontal rows, or both. Usually, the purpose is to fix the first row and column which contain the column and row headings respectively. Otherwise, the headings will disappear as you scroll to distant parts of the worksheet, making it difficult to remember what the data refers to.

Windowing

Another useful facility is **windowing**, which enables you to view two or more parts of the model at the same time; a vertical or horizontal line is drawn across the screen, which divides it into two sections. The two sections can be scrolled independently, thus allowing, for example, the top section to fix on rows 1 to 10 while the bottom section scrolls down to row 100 or 120. This could enable you, say, to change the sales volume in row 3 and to see the effect on the company's cash flow in row 120. The sections of the screen are referred to as windows, and some spreadsheet packages allow the screen to be divided into any number of such windows. 1-2-3 only allows two windows, which may be split either horizontally or vertically. This is not a serious practical restriction, because if the screen is divided into more than two windows, then the windows become too small to be of any real value.

Range names

Another way around the problem of handling large models is to attach a name to a single cell or an area of the worksheet, using the command: **/RNC** (/Range Name Create). For example, **SALES-MACHO** might identify cell B2, or **MACHO-ALL** could identify the range of cells A1 ... K6. (A range of cells in Lotus 1-2-3 means a rectangular block of cells: A1 ... K6 means the block with A1 in the top left corner and K6 in the bottom right corner.)

The first range-name (**SALES-MACHO**) could be used in a formula, or in directing 1-2-3 to go to that cell. The second range-name (**MACHO-ALL**) would be useful where a range of cells needs to be referenced, as in a print command.

If the model is not too complicated, creating a few range-names may be all that is needed to make the model easily usable by a human operator. A name such as **PAINT-SALES** or **TAX-RATE** is memorable, whereas a cell reference such as B145 or A75 is not.

Usually, the model can be broken down into a series of tables, each relating to one section of a department's accounts. All that is needed is to name a cell in each page and then command 1-2-3 to go to the relevant cell, normally by using the function key F6. For example, pressing F6 for 'go to' and typing **PAINT-SALES** as the required cell means that 1-2-3 would move to that cell. This would enable the data relating to the Paints operation to be accessed; the user could enter or amend data as he wished, finally moving on to another section of the model in a similar way. At the end, the consolidated results could be printed out by referencing the section of the worksheet containing the group data; attaching a name such as **GROUP-ALL** to that range of cells makes it easier to remember which cells to print.

Macros

The most powerful facility that 1-2-3 offers in setting up a customized system is the use of macros. A macro-program is a stored sequence of keyboard commands, and the advantage of writing macros is that the whole sequence of commands can then be invoked by pressing one key.

Consider, for example, when one wants to print a section of the worksheet relating perhaps to one department. This requires a whole series of commands and responses, and these can be stored as text in cells of a Lotus model. In some cases, a 'return' needs to be typed after a response to a question; Lotus uses the symbol – here to represent the 'return' key. The advantage of using a macro is that typing in all the responses is time-consuming, and it is also easy to leave out a step by mistake; for example, if you forget to define the range, you might find that the whole of a very large table is being printed, rather than just a section.

The first step in setting up the macro is to choose some empty cells in a distant part of the worksheet which is unlikely to be used. For example, the keystrokes might be stored in the range of cells H120 ... H124 as follows:

Cell	Contents	Explanation of command
H120	/PP	Print
H121	RA50...E67˜	Range from cell A50 to E67 (a block)
H122	OP72˜Q	Page length 72
H123	OML5˜Q	Left margin 5
H124	OMR130˜QGQ	Right margin 130
		Go, i.e. do the print

Entering the above is the same as entering any other text, except that when the text is entered into H120, it must be prefaced by ' to show that text is being entered; otherwise 1-2-3 will assume that the command /PP is being invoked immediately.

Note that several commands could be combined in one cell if preferred, and indeed H124 does contain two distinct commands. All the commands could have been entered into one cell, although it would probably make things less clear.

The other step in creating the macro is to give a name to the range of cells H120 ... H124, using the command: /RNC (/Range Name Create). The name must be backslash plus a letter, such as \A or \T. From now on, the macro can be invoked at any time, simply by holding down the ALT-key and typing the appropriate letter. Thus, typing ALT-X will invoke the macro saved as \X (on some machines, the CTRL and SHIFT keys may be used together instead of an ALT key).

In addition to using the letters of the alphabet, you can also name a macro as \0, and this has a special function. This macro will automatically be invoked when you first load the model, and this is especially useful for calling up your own menus in designing a 'tailored' solution to a problem.

There are numerous other facilities available in macros which cannot be discussed here: the macro can allow a user response while the macro is being invoked, as when the print range is to be varied rather than being a fixed part of the worksheet, and loops and tests of various kinds can also be put into the macro. However, probably the most useful feature is to be able to set up your own menus.

Creating menus

It is quite easy to create your own menu in Lotus 1-2-3, similar to the standard 1-2-3 menus, by setting up a macro with /XM in the first cell. This tells 1-2-3 that you wish to call up a menu that is specified below.

Figure 5.8 shows a screen-shot of Lotus 1-2-3 with a user-written menu displayed for the Macho-Biggs model. The menu enables the user to look at any of the companies in the group, or to print or graph the output. Any of the options can be selected just as on standard Lotus 1-2-3 menus, by typing the first letter or by highlighting the option and pressing the return key; the data can be edited simply by choosing the Quit option to return to spreadsheet mode. The user-written menu can be retrieved at any time by typing ALT-A, and can be used after editing to output results or to save the new version of the model.

Figure 5.9 shows the macro for setting up this menu in 1-2-3. Notice that a typical 1-2-3 macro includes a number of coded references to keystrokes, such as:

    ~ return   {GoTo} go to specified cell

    {home} go to start of model, i.e. cell A1

/XMA102 means that the definitions for the menu start in cell A102. The cells in row 102 are used for the menu options (up to 8 options are allowed). Row 103 is used for a longer description of what the option does (to be displayed on line 3 of the screen). Below each option there then follows the macro to be invoked for that option. For example, viewing the consolidated results means going to cell A75, while printing or graphing requires a series of commands.

In this example, only one menu is used, but it would be relatively simple to extend it to several levels of menus. All that is necessary is to include a command such as /XMA120 under one of the options already specified. This could be useful for a fairly complicated model where, having selected a company in the group, one then wanted to select a section of the accounts relating to that company.

A final point of warning about macros in Lotus 1-2-3: they are not for the beginner. It is easy to miss out something in a macro, and it is not easy to see what is wrong. On the other hand, macros can be used by a good programmer to create extremely user-friendly models for particular applications. A number of professional accounting firms have applied Lotus 1-2-3 in this way.

5.5 SPREADSHEET 'ADD-ON' SOFTWARE

A number of companies are now offering 'add-on' packages for Lotus 1-2-3 and Supercalc 4. These are essentially very sophisticated macros

A1:

Macho-Biggs Results

	A	B	C	D	E	F
1						
2			Macho Cycles Ltd			
3			------------------			
4		1989	1990	1991	1992	1993
5						
6	FB Racer - Quantity	100	110	120	130	140
7	- Price	300	310	325	340	350
8	- Revenue	30000	34100	39000	44200	49000

Figure 5.8 Screen-shot of Lotus 1-2-3 showing a user-written menu.

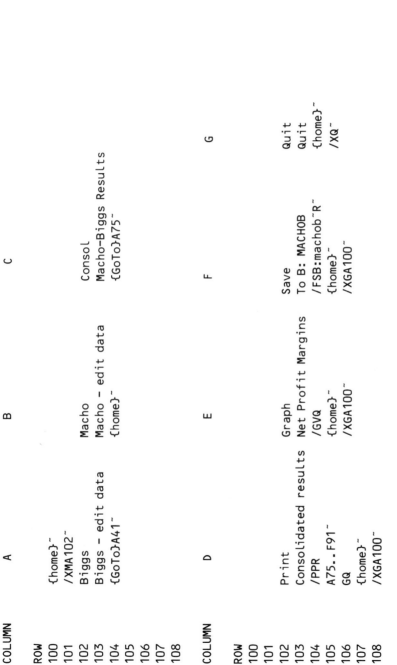

COLUMN	A	B	C
ROW			
100	{home}~		
101	/XMA102~		
102	Biggs	Macho	Consol
103	Biggs - edit data	Macho - edit data	Macho-Biggs Results
104	{GoTo}A41~	{home}~	{GoTo}A75~
105			
106			
107			
108			

COLUMN	D	E	F	G
ROW				
100				
101				
102	Print	Graph	Save	Quit
103	Consolidated results	Net Profit Margins	To B: MACHOB	Quit
104	/PPR	/GVQ	/FSB:machob~R~	{home}~
105	A75..F91~	{home}~	{home}~	/XQ~
106	GQ	/XGA100~	/XGA100~	
107	{home}~			
108	/XGA100~			

Figure 5.9 Macro for the user-written menu for the Macho-Biggs model. It is stored in cells A100 to G108 of the worksheet.

(similar to the Macho-Biggs Model just described) which are written to run in conjunction with the relevant spreadsheet package. They tend to be relatively cheap, certainly save considerable effort, and provide useful models presented in a user-friendly way, which would be beyond the computing skills of most users to achieve.

Probably the best known company specializing in add-on software is 4-5-6 World. They market a wide range of add-ons for Lotus 1-2-3, including various statistical forecasting routines. Another good example of such software is the accounts production package from Levy-Gee, already cited in this chapter. Another example is ICASH from Independent Computer Systems Ltd, a cashflow and profit and loss forecasting system. Use of this software is discussed in Chapter 10 on planning and control.

Finally, another very useful package to run in conjunction with Lotus 1-2-3 is the Spreadsheet Auditor from Computer Associates. This includes a utility for printing large spreadsheets sideways, and a 'pop-up cell noter' for attaching notes to cells. However, the main function of Spreadsheet Auditor is to check spreadsheet models for possible errors of logic; such errors are relatively easy to make on a large model, and not easy to discover without using a package such as Auditor. Indeed, Computer Associates cite one American company who lost $250 000 by underbidding on a contract as a result of a simple error in a spreadsheet model. Spreadsheet Auditor costs £150; whether this is an economic purchase for a practice depends on the extent to which spreadsheets are used and on the degree of complexity of spreadsheet models that are written.

5.6 INTEGRATED SOFTWARE

Integrated software has, until recently, meant software where data can be passed fairly easily from one computer program to another without needing to be re-entered by the human operator. Thus in an integrated accounting system, the nominal ledger can be updated directly from the sales or purchase ledgers. Lotus 1-2-3 integrates with other programs because it has a number of commands which enable it to read in data from other programs, and it can also output tables in a form that can be read by other programs. Lotus 1-2-3 can read in tables written in text form (ASCII) by other programs, as well as binary data files from dBASE3 and the standard .DIF files that are produced by some packages. Lotus 1-2-3 also integrates with word processing packages in that the output from 1-2-3 can be written to an ASCII text file which can then be edited by the word processor; this would be normal in an accounting office where the figures produced need to form part of a larger report.

More recently, the term **integrated package** (or integrated software) has acquired a specific meaning on microcomputers: now generally taken to mean combining spreadsheet, database, graphics and word processing within the one package. Lotus 1-2-3 was the first microcomputer package able to make reasonable claims at such integration; however, it is quite limited in some of its facilities and, in particular, it is totally inadequate for word processing.

There are a number of other packages which take the concept of an integrated package much further, and which do include good word processing facilities. Lotus have developed two such packages: Symphony (for IBM-compatibles) and Jazz (for the Apple Macintosh). Other well-known names include Open Access, and Framework (written by Ashton-Tate, the authors of dBASE3). All these packages have a similar range of facilities, although they differ substantially in how they operate; they cost about £350 or so at 1988 prices.

Integrated packages have not proved popular in accounting practices, probably because they are only advantageous if both typing and computational work are carried out by the same member of staff. In an accounting practice, it is usually desirable to spread work between several members of staff in order to achieve maximum efficiency, and therefore it is sensible to use separate word processing and spreadsheet software.

5.7 COMPARISON OF SOFTWARE

Choice of the correct software for financial modelling (and management accounting analysis) may seem difficult, because of the vast profusion of packages available. The aim of this section is therefore to summarize what is available. The prices quoted are 1988 prices (for spreadsheets and integrated packages). (These are mail-order prices, which are about 30% below recommended retail prices.) In deciding which software to choose, there are essentially four types of package to choose from:

Spreadsheet
The market leaders are Lotus 1-2-3 and Supercalc 4, with Lotus 1-2-3 being by far the best seller. The two packages are very comparable in the facilities offered, and either can be purchased for just under £250. Some large accounting firms have adopted Supercalc 4 in preference to Lotus 1-2-3 — Supercalc 4 has better graphics facilities than Lotus 1-2-3,

and it is also possibly easier to set up macros in Supercalc 4 than in Lotus 1-2-3. Multiplan is another good spreadsheet package, which offers less facilities than Lotus 1-2-3 or Supercalc 4, but costs only about £150. There are also a number of good '1-2-3 clones' which are less well-known, offering much the same facilities as Lotus 1-2-3, but selling for under £100. Twin and VP-Planner are two such packages.

Integrated Packages

Packages such as Open Access, Symphony or Framework offer good word processing and spreadsheet analysis, with reasonable graphics and database facilities, at a cost of about £350. They also include telecommunications facilities, which can be extremely useful for transmitting data from one microcomputer to another via telephone lines. Framework is probably the easiest to use of the three integrated packages listed above. Symphony is rated as a powerful package, but some users find it relatively difficult to use. Open Access is preferred by many users, and is particularly good at handling telecommunications.

Financial Modelling Packages

Packages such as Finar and Micro-FCS provide far more facilities than a spreadsheet, at a higher cost (typically about £1000). Users of such packages tend to be companies already using minis or mainframes with similar software, but there are now a lot of users who only use micros and who have discovered the limitations of spreadsheets. This may imply running out of memory (as is common with Lotus running under MSDOS), but often the main problem is the user not being able to cope with complex models using a spreadsheet package.

Consolidation Packages

Some clients have complex company structures, where the management accounting system requires consolidation of company accounts into group accounts, and possibly consolidation at several levels. Software has now become available on microcomputers specifically designed for this. Two such packages are Planmaster from Planmaster Systems Ltd, and Micro-Multi from Thorn-EMI Computer Software, both of which have been developed from successful mainframe software. However, such software is very expensive (typically upwards of £10000) and is likely therefore not to be of much interest to small- or medium-size practices.

There are arguments for and against spreadsheets, integrated software and financial modelling packages. Cost is a major factor, but probably the most important factor to be considered is the applications for which the package is required. It may well be that for an accounting office a simple spreadsheet package offers all the facilities that are needed. On the other hand, the reason that 1-2-3 has been so popular with business users is that it hits the right level in terms of offering a number of extra facilities without being too complicated.

The general consensus at present is that the integrated packages are not having the same success as 1-2-3, probably because most users do not wish to combine word processing and spreadsheet analysis. As already mentioned, this is undoubtedly the case in an accounting practice; word processing tends to be carried out by secretaries, and accounting calculations by clerks or qualified accountants. Thus, if the tasks are carefully separated, then there is little point in using an integrated package; it is generally simpler and better to use two different packages for the two tasks.

Moreover, the development of more sophisticated operating systems is likely to make highly integrated packages less useful (WIMPs — such as OS/2 Presentation Manager and the Apple Macintosh operating system — were described in Chapter 3). For the moment, a package at the level of Lotus 1-2-3 appears more relevant to many users.

Another consideration is whether to purchase financial modelling software. This is clearly a more expensive option than purchasing a spreadsheet package. Whether such software is worth purchasing depends on the degree of sophistication of the user's requirements: relatively simple models are often best written using a spreadsheet, whereas complex consolidations or monthly reporting systems may be much easier to handle in a package such as Micro-FCS.

A final point of warning if you are concerned about performance: a standard spreadsheet such as Lotus 1-2-3 or Multiplan will perform calculations much faster than a financial modelling package. This may be important for some users, although the time involved in developing a model and setting it up to run usually matter more than the time taken to run it, using the right software will save considerable time.

5.8 CONCLUSIONS

No accounting office should purchase a microcomputer without buying a spreadsheet package (or, alternatively, a financial modelling package), and indeed the combined benefits from word processing and spreadsheet applications are usually substantial enough to justify the cost of a microcomputer. The main problem is to decide which package to standardize on, because standardization is absolutely essential, particularly where an organization is using several micro-computers. The disadvantages of using several different spreadsheet packages far outweigh the marginal advantages that a range of pack-ages may have. The problems arise partly because of the inconveni-ence of transferring data between different packages, but mainly because it makes life more difficult for staff, as each package is slightly different in how it operates.

Nevertheless, it may be worth purchasing both a financial modelling package and a spreadsheet, especially where several microcomputers are in use. It is quite possible to envisage a package such as Micro-FCS being used for a few major applications, while a spreadsheet is used for more minor calculations.

6 Database applications

A database package, sometimes referred to as a **database management system** (DBMS), is a computer program which enables a set of records (referred to as a file) to be set up and to be updated at regular intervals. The features provided in database packages are described in more detail in the next section. It should be emphasized that the packages themselves are designed to keep records in whatever format is specified by the user, and to produce reports on them; they can therefore be used for a wide range of applications. However, this does imply that the user has to define in detail what records are to be kept and what reports are to be produced. If the system is relatively complex, as with an accounts system, this process can be difficult and time-consuming.

Many accounting applications and administrative functions of a practice require files to be set up and maintained. Examples are files of customer details (one record per customer) in a sales accounting system, and files of property leases (one record per property) in a property records system.

For many applications (especially for standard accounting applications), it is preferable to purchase a package written for that specific application, rather than to invest time in adapting a database package for that purpose. Various specific applications packages are described in later chapters of this book. However, there are many simple record-keeping operations for which a database package is ideal; there are also many applications which do not fall into any obvious pigeon-hole, and where the only answer is to use a database package.

6.1 CHOICE OF SOFTWARE

This is an area where there is a vast profusion of choice, with hundreds of packages available, of which probably only about thirty are very serious contenders, No generalizations can be made as to the type of database software most suitable for an accounting practice; the choice depends on the type of work, and the specific applications envisaged. It is also quite conceivable that the practice might purchase several different packages for use with different sets of records. For this reason, illustrations are given in this chapter which use two very different database packages.

Most popular database packages can be broadly classified into one of four categories:

(a) Text data
The most well-known such package is Cardbox Plus, which costs about £300. This package is simple to use, and is designed to provide a 'computerized card index' as a reference to a set of books or journal articles (such as references to auditing guidelines). Cardbox Plus allows variable length records (essential where text summaries are to be kept) and will set up word indexes where specified (for example, to show which summaries contain the word 'goodwill').

Cardbox Plus can also be useful for simple client mailing applications, having the facilities to set up standard letters and to 'personalize' them by extracting names and addresses from the relevant client files. However, Cardbox Plus does not have the facilities necessary rapidly to process large volumes of numeric data, and is therefore unsuitable for many accounting applications.

(b) Simple file management packages: numeric data
There are a number of good packages available, such as PFS (Professional File) and Reflex (the Database Manager) (from Borland), which cost about £70 or so. Simpler database packages tend to be menu-driven, because it is easier for an inexperienced user to remember what to do if presented with a menu. They also tend to have a relatively limited range of facilities. Such a package is often ideal for a user who is setting up his own basic record-keeping system. Section 6.4 shows how client records may be kept for an accounting practice using a package of this type.

(c) Command-driven: numeric data
By far the best known such package is dBASE3 from Ashton-Tate, which is used in the examples in this chapter. Some other well-known

packages are Microsoft Rbase, Dataease, Paradox and Delta 4 from Compsoft Ltd, and there are many others. The full multi-user version of dBASE3 (dBASE3 Plus) costs £550, but older and more limited versions of dBASE3 are available at a lower price. Prices for major competing packages are similar, but there are a number of cheap dBASE3 clones such as Practibase which sell for £100 or less.

(d) Databases with SQL interfaces
SQL (structured query language) has become the standard interface for popular database packages (such as Oracle and Ingres) on minicomputers and mainframes. This ensures that different databases that have been set up using various computers will be compatible, and hence that data can easily be transferred between different systems.

A number of packages with SQL interfaces have been released recently for microcomputers, such as Focus, Ingres PC and PC/Oracle. They are relatively expensive, and are probably most relevant to firms which are also using larger computers and wish to maintain compatibility.

It is likely in the near future that new versions of some of the standard database packages mentioned in (c) will also offer an SQL interface as an option.

One major difference between types (b) and (c) (or (d)) is that the simple file management packages tend to lack the full relational database facilities (see next section). In addition, a command-driven package enables you to customize applications easily and to design your own menus by writing macro-programs (analogous to the macros in Lotus 1-2-3). This is essential where one is designing complex databases with several files cross referencing, but a menu-driven package may be easier for a simple application involving one or two files.

6.2 BASIC DATABASE CONCEPTS

A database consists of a series of data sets, or **files**. Each file contains **records**, each record containing data relating to one member of the set, and the data being kept for that record in a specified format. A simple example is shown in Figure 6.1 for a client file: each record in the file relates to one client of an accounting practice. The records are subdivided naturally into **fields**, such as Name, Address, Area, Size of client, and so on. The records in the file shown in Figure 6.1 are in a fixed format, i.e. each client is allocated a fixed size record, and the fields within that record are also of a fixed size. It is essential to allo-

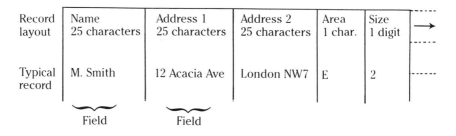

Record layout	Name 25 characters	Address 1 25 characters	Address 2 25 characters	Area 1 char.	Size 1 digit	----→
Typical record	M. Smith	12 Acacia Ave	London NW7	E	2	------

Field   Field

Figure 6.1 Example of file design.

cate sufficient space to each field when designing a record, although to some extent the data may be constrained to fit within this format, abbreviating names and addresses where necessary. A fixed format is usually convenient in most accounting applications, although some database packages are more flexible and do allow variable length fields.

Such files have always been a necessary part of commercial data processing systems written in conventional programming languages such as COBOL. A true relational database language differs in its ability to define easily relationships between different files within the database. For example, one might set up a relationship between a customer file and a sales ledger file in a sales accounting system; the objective here would be to give the user the facility to access immediately the sales ledger records for a particular customer after accessing the customer record.

Another feature which distinguishes a database language from most conventional languages is the flexibility available to set up **multiple indexes** on files. Indexing of files is essential to get fast access to records, this being a requirement of most databases. To understand how indexing is used, consider how books are filed in a library: standard library indexes are usually filed alphabetically in order of *author name*, which in computing terms means that the field *author name* is an index for the file. Alternative indexes would be:

1. *Title*: in alphabetical order of titles
2. *Class No. + Author name*: a combination of the two fields, the classified reference giving books in sequence of author within class number.

Confusion is often generated by the use of the word 'database', which is used to refer both to the set of data files and to the computer package which processes them. Mainframe database packages are often referred to as fourth generation languages (4GL), but unfortunately the definition of a 4GL is very vague and encompasses packages which are not true database packages. (Even the definition of a true database package is open to some academic debate, which will be ignored here.)

The next section discusses what features one might reasonably expect from a good database package running on a microcomputer.

6.3 FEATURES OF A DATABASE PACKAGE

Most computer programs for commercial applications do very few calculations, and most instructions in a conventional programming language (such as BASIC or COBOL) relate to the following operations:

1. input of data from a VDU
2. output of results to a printer
3. updating of files.

Database packages concentrate on making these operations as simple as possible, and the time involved in developing systems can be enormously reduced by using database packages. A simple records system may be developed which would have taken considerable programming effort using a conventional language.

More sophisticated packages such as dBASE3 and Rbase System V may be used to write customized systems for specific user applications where the development cost can be directly compared with conventional programming. Exact productivity gains are difficult to estimate, but it is common to reduce development time by a factor of about seven; thus a set of programs which would take seventy mandays to write and get working in COBOL, may be implemented in under ten days using a database package. An extreme example of the efficiency of mainframe database software was demonstrated in the *Computer News* championships of March 1987, where the winning team from Majorgreen used a package called System Builder to write and fully test an airline reservation system in the space of twenty-four hours, which would have taken conventionally about six man-months.

The features offered by a typical database package are:

1. *To create a file, and define the format of the records*. This includes naming all the fields on each record, the width of each field, and

the field type. The field type may be either numeric (e.g. price) or character (e.g. customer name). Some packages allow other special field types such as date fields.

2. *To create records.* This can usually be done easily by entering data into a standard screen form provided by the package, which prompts the user with the field names defined in creating the file and then automatically creates a new record.

3. *To amend and delete records.* The procedure is usually similar to that for creating records.

4. *To change the file format.* This is a common user requirement: one often finds a need for expanding a field or creating additional fields as use of a database develops. This not only required redefinition of the record format, but also requires expansion of all records that have been created in the old format.

5. *To create indexes.* This facility has been mentioned already in section 6.2, and is essential for rapid access of individual records.

6. *To select records according to specified criteria.* This requires reading through the file and printing a list of relevant records. A typical criterion might be for a property file: [**AREA = East & PRICE < £80 000**].

7. *To sort records into a specified sequence.* For example, customer orders may need to be sorted into product sequence. Often it is more efficient to create additional indexes rather than to sort the data records.

8. *To define report formats (for output to screen or printer).* Standard listings are usually provided by database packages, but it is often desirable to be able to design more professional-looking reports in a clearer format.

9. *To print labels.* This is an important requirement, as database packages are often used to create mailing lists. It should be possible to print names and addresses to any standard size of computer label stationery.

10. *To define screen entry formats.* Most packages allow the user to create their own data entry screens, and to carry out data validation checks before creating or amending the record.

11. *To produce data files in standard formats.* These are required to transfer data to other packages such as Lotus 1-2-3, and to create name and address files for use in word processing applications.

Database packages vary in the precise facilities that they offer, in how easy they are to use, and in how flexible they are. In general, menu-driven packages tend to be easier to use but more inflexible than command-driven packages. In the remainder of this chapter, we discuss typical applications for each type of package.

6.4 SETTING UP A SIMPLE DATABASE

The application considered in this section is to maintain a client list for an accounting practice. This is a typical simple database application, the objective being to maintain an up-to-date circulation list of client names and addresses. The list can be output for several purposes: either as a printed list, or on sticky labels for addressing envelopes, or as a disk file to be used as input to a mailing system which produces personalized letters (see Chapter 14). A database system also allows selected groups of clients to be printed where relevant, rather than having to print the complete list.

The package used in this illustration is Reflex: the Database Manager. This is a package designed for relatively simple applications: typically, involving only one data file which is being regularly accessed and updated. Reflex is a relatively cheap package (about £70) and has sold extremely well to users who wish to set up a simple database. It is a well-presented user-friendly package which does not require any detailed knowledge of database terminology. It is probably the best-selling package of this type, although there are a number of other similar packages equally worthy of consideration.

In some respects, Reflex resembles a manual card index system in the way it presents data; the user enters records into a simple form which they have created. The records are made up of fields, which can be variable in length from record to record. Reflex lacks many of the more powerful database features (such as indexing) and only one file can be open at any time, but it does benefit from simplicity, and provides a powerful and easy-to-use system for many applications.

Reflex offers a series of 'views' on the underlying database; the user does not need to know how the data file is stored on disk. Initially, the user is presented with a 'form view', which consists of a large blank rectangle; you simply define a data entry form on the screen with suitable prompts for each field. Having defined this form, you then enter a series of records into the database; the fields are variable in length, just as with a manual system, up to a maximum of 255 characters. Reflex normally assumes field types by default (if a number is entered in the first record, the field is taken to be numeric); however, you do have the option of defining fields as text, numeric or date.

Figure 6.2 shows a complete form view with a record displayed on the screen; the record is one of a set of client names and addresses, which also includes three fields which can be used for selective printing:

1. **turnover**: for selecting clients by size

Personnel Manager

```
Views  Edit  Print/File  Records  Search  Form
```

```
FORM

Client Name: Brighouse Ltd

Address 1: 22 Browns Rd
Address 2: Walthamstow
Address 3: London E17 8SD
Address 4:

Contact Name: Mrs H Briggs
Job Title: Personnel Manager
Tel No: 01-154 3333
Turnover £000: 700
Type of Client: S
Area: 2
```

Figure 6.2 Reflex: form view. Screen-shot displaying a record for a client.

2. **type of client**: S represents service sector, M represents manufacturing, and R is retail
3. **area**: geographical areas relevant to the firm (coded 1–9).

Reflex offers a limited but powerful set of commands, making it simple and user-friendly. Any command can be rapidly selected from a series of pop-up menus, using either a mouse or a keyboard. Even major changes such as adding new fields or moving them around on the screen are very simple to perform.

Once a set of records have been entered into the database, Reflex then offers a number of different views of the data, which can be selected from the pop-up menu for the views option.

Form view

As already mentioned, this is the view normally used for entering data into the database. One can also scan through existing records very quickly using the function keys, and amend or delete records.

List view
This is shown in Figure 6.3 for client data. It allows a number of records to be viewed at a time, which is often more convenient. Records may be added, amended or deleted as in the form view.

The disadvantage of this view is that usually only a limited number of fields can be viewed at a time, and probably only part of those fields. However, one can scan from left to right across a record, and widen columns which are too narrow. It is also important to remember that one is seeing a view of the database, which may be slightly restricted by the space available on the screen.

Crosstab view
This enables one to set up a two-way cross-tabulation for all records of a given variable classified by two attributes. For example, this could be turnover for clients broken down by Type of customer and by Area code.

Graph view
This enables graphs to be displayed on the screen or to be printed, showing either values for individual records or average values for a group of records.

Report view
Although this may be displayed on the screen, the main purpose is to define the format for printing reports. This is discussed below in more detail.

Sorting and selecting records

Sorting records is very simple in Reflex; the screen used for defining field types initially also allows sort keys to be defined against up to five fields, numbered from 1 to 5 in order of importance. Once these sort keys have been defined, Reflex will immediately display the records in the specified sequence; if the sort keys are changed at any stage, it will then display in the new sequence.

Selecting records is done by setting up search conditions in a table, as shown in the screen shot in Figure 6.4. In this example, the selection is to be: 'All clients in Area 2 or 3 with a turnover of over £200000'. Once search conditions have been defined, Reflex only displays the records which meet the specified conditions. This is described as a 'filter' by Reflex, because the records that do not meet these conditions remain in the database and are not displayed. At any time, the filter may be removed and the whole set of records displayed once again.

J Smith & Co

Views Edit Print/File Records Search List

```
┌──────────┐
│   LIST   │
└──────────┘
```

Client Name	Address 1	Address 2	Address 3	Add
J Smith & Co	33 Acacia Ave	Walthamstow	London E17 9SD	
Texas Toys Ltd	18 Hall Rd	Tottenham	London N17 8GT	
Tamsin June & Co Ltd	Efficiency House	Blackfriars Rd	East Halton	Ess
Morwenna Electronics	12 Folkestone Rd	Leyton	London E11 8JG	
Kerensa (UK) Ltd	15a Hamden Mews	London N12 3WS		
Brighouse Ltd	22 Browns Rd	Walthamstow	London E17 8SD	

Figure 6.3 Reflex: list view. Screen-shot showing sections of several client records.

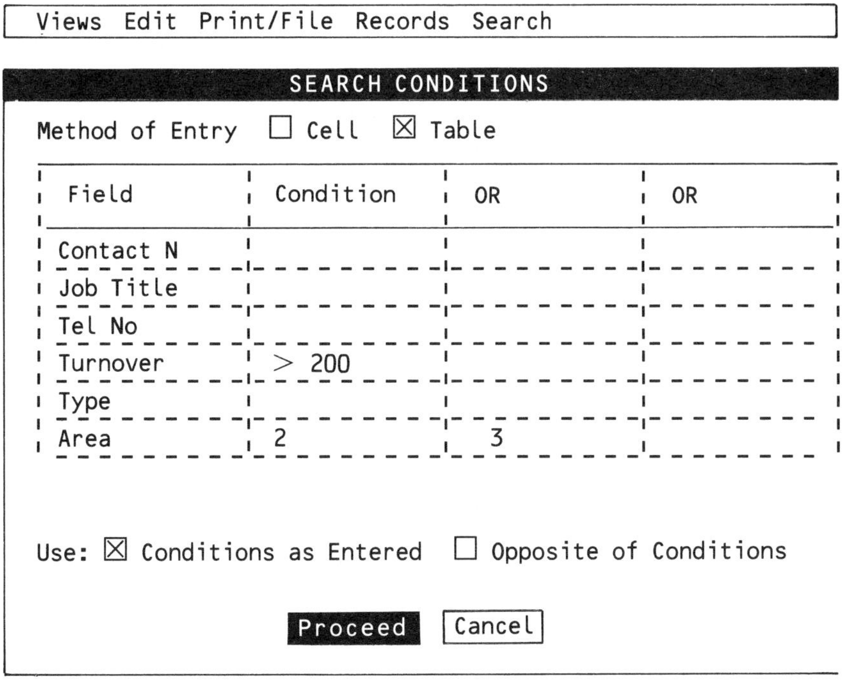

Views Edit Print/File Records Search

SEARCH CONDITIONS

Method of Entry ☐ Cell ☒ Table

Field	Condition	OR	OR
Contact N			
Job Title			
Tel No			
Turnover	> 200		
Type			
Area	2	3	

Use: ☒ Conditions as Entered ☐ Opposite of Conditions

Proceed   Cancel

Figure 6.4 Reflex: setting search conditions. Screen-shot showing the conditions used to select the records for the report printed in Figure 6.5, i.e. those clients areas 2 or 3 with turnover greater than £200000.

Figure 6.5 shows a listing of records which meet these specified conditions; the records have also been sorted into sequence of area codes. The report is printed according to a report view, as discussed in the next section.

Defining a report

This is achieved by using the report view, which initially contains a blank rectangle. It is merely necessary to fill in text or variable names as required, defining on screen the report layout and the widths of variables for printing. Page headers and footers may also be added, using special functions in Reflex to produce subtotals and totals. Producing the report layout for Figure 6.5 represents only a few minutes work.

Producing a 'mail-merge' file (a list of names and addresses to be used for personalized mailing — see Chapter 14) is equally

Arkwright, Faltwhistle and Patel   October 18, 1987
Chartered Accountants

Clients in Areas 2 and 3 over £200,000 Turnover

F Brown   01-999-8753
J Smith & Co   Area: 2   Turnover: 500
33 Acacia Ave   (£'000)
Walthamstow
London E17 9SD

Mrs H Briggs   01-154-3333
Brighouse Ltd   Area: 2   Turnover: 700
22 Browns Rd   (£'000)
Walthamstow
London E17 8SD

Ms J Tamsin   01-100-2323
Texas Toys Ltd   Area: 2   Turnover: 750
18 Hall Rd   (£'000)
Tottenham
London N16 9GT

```
M Frances              01-154-9898
Morwenna Electronics                Area: 2          Turnover:          1200
12 Folkestone Rd                                     (£'000)
Leyton
London E11 8JG

                                    Turnover for Area 2:                3150

Ms I Bell              01-100-7878
Kerensa (UK) Ltd                    Area: 3          Turnover:           120
15a Hamden Mews                                      (£'000)
London N12 3WS

                                    Turnover for Area 3:                 120

                                    Overall Turnover:                   3270
```

Figure 6.5 Reflex: client listing following conditions laid down in Figure 6.4.

straightforward. This simply requires a report design for the appropriate format, plus selection of the option to output to disk rather than to printer.

Finally, printing labels requires yet another report format. Labels are not quite as easy to produce from Reflex as some other packages, but it is by no means difficult.

6.5 A MORE COMPLEX DATABASE EXAMPLE

This section describes an application to keep a record of time worked on client accounts and to bill clients for work done. This example is intended to be illustrative; whilst this is an important application for many practices, they would normally purchase time recording and fees ledger software (as described in Chapter 9 on practice management). Nevertheless, there are occasions when standard software will not cope with the specific requirements of a practice, and it is then worth considering having programs written in a database language.

This example has been considerably simplified to make it clearer, but it would be straightforward to design a system with considerably more information on the records. A realistic system would also require a number of additional files to provide a satisfactory audit trail of changes made to the main data files.

The database package used in this demonstration program is dBASE3 Plus. dBASE3, produced by Ashton-Tate of Los Angeles, has been easily the most successful of database packages on microcomputers, with over 100 000 users in the UK alone. Used as a command-driven system, dBASE3 is more difficult to use than simple menu-driven packages such as Reflex, but it is also far more powerful. However, dBASE3 does have an ASSIST command to guide the inexperienced user. This provides a menu-driven system for creating and manipulating data which is reasonably easy to use.

Whilst perhaps not the first choice for simple applications, dBASE3 is still a very good second choice and might well be the package chosen by a firm that wanted to standardize on one database package for all applications. The intention here is to show the advantages of a command-driven system in certain applications rather than to review dBASE3. This section therefore concentrates on dBASE3 in normal command mode rather than in ASSIST mode.

When you enter dBASE3, it gives a standard prompt of . (a dot) and expects you to type in a command. If you cannot remember the command for a particular operation, there is a very comprehensive HELP system to lead you to the correct command. Some examples of dBASE3 commands are shown in Figure 6.6, together with an explanation of the commands. In most cases, these correspond to the operations performed by Reflex in the previous section. The examples shown here are relatively simple, but even experienced users find it difficult to remember the precise commands when running applications involving several related files. This inevitably requires a reasonably complicated sequence of instructions which can easily be confused. The great advantage of a command-driven system is that a whole sequence of commands can be stored in a file, which can then be activated by one single command. This is usually referred to as **macro-programming**.

Using dBASE3, applications can be set up to run under a customized menu-driven system, with the detailed instructions written in a macro-program. Such a customized system requires reasonably skilled programming to write but, once it has been developed, will be much easier to use than a standard package such as Reflex. We have developed our own menu-driven systems on a number of occasions using dBASE3, and have always found the initial effort to be thoroughly justified.

Figure 6.7. shows the main menu for the system, while the files needed and the record formats are shown in Figure 6.8. The system is one that could be used and maintained easily by clerical staff with little knowledge of computers or database systems. Figure 6.9 shows a section of the macro-program for this system, while typical reports produced by the system for options 6 and 9 in the menu are shown in Figures 6.10 and 6.11.

Such a system could not be set up easily by a simple file-handling package such as Reflex; careful programming is needed to make it sufficiently user-friendly. Both reports shown require simultaneous access to at least two files, and cross-referencing between those files. Thus, the weekly statement takes the name and address of the client, amount paid this week, disbursements and opening balance from the Client file; the hours worked from the Time file; and the chargeout rate from the Employee file.

6.6 DATABASE SYSTEMS: PROBLEMS OF SECURITY AND CONTROL

Many micro-based packages were originally designed for single-user environments where problems of security and control were not seen as major considerations. However, systems used by accountants often tend to be concerned with clients' personal details, where security and

Command	Explanation
CREATE EMPLOYER	Create database file EMPLOYER.DBF (define field length and types)
APPEND	Add new records
BROWSE	Inspect and amend current records
INDEX EMPLOYER ON EMPREF TO EMPIND	Index EMPLOYER.DBF by field EMPREF, creating an index file EMPIND.NDX
DISPLAY TO PRINT FOR AREA = '2'.AND.TURNOVER > 150000	Print all employer records in area 2 with turnover over £150000, printing according to a standard listing format
CREATE REPORT EMPREP	Create a special report format EMPREP.FRM
REPORT FORM EMPREP TO PRINT FOR AREA = '3'.AND.TURNOVER > 150000	Print a similar report, using special report format

Figure 6.6 Typical dBASE3 commands with explanations.

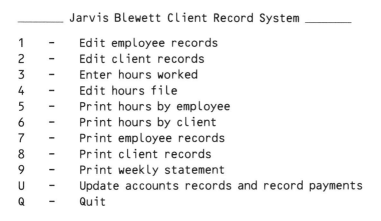

```
_____ Jarvis Blewett Client Record System _____

1  -   Edit employee records
2  -   Edit client records
3  -   Enter hours worked
4  -   Edit hours file
5  -   Print hours by employee
6  -   Print hours by client
7  -   Print employee records
8  -   Print client records
9  -   Print weekly statement
U  -   Update accounts records and record payments
Q  -   Quit
```

Figure 6.7 dBASE3: main menu for client record system.

1) Employee File: EMPLOY.DBF   Index: employee reference

	Type	Length	Format
Employee reference	character	8	
Name	character	25	
Date of birth	date	8	99/99/99
Skill level	character	1	
Chargeout rate.	numeric	8	99999.99

2) Client File: CLIENT.DBF   Index: Client reference

	Type	Length	Format
Client reference	character	8	
Name	character	25	
Address	character	75	
Area	character	1	
Type of company	character	1	
Turnover of company	numeric	5	99999
Amount recd — this week	numeric	9	999999.99
Disbursements — this wk	numeric	7	9999.99
Current balance — w/e	numeric	9	999999.99

3) Time File: TIMER.DBF
           Indexes: employee reference, client reference

	Type	Length	Format
Employee reference	character	8	
Client reference	character	8	
Hours worked this week	numeric	5	99.99

Figure 6.8 dBASE3: record formats for the client record system.

```
*    client.prg  main program for Jarvis Blewett Client
*               Records System
*    Copyright Frank Blewett & Robin Jarvis, 1987
*    Programmer: Frank Blewett     Version 30.7.87
clear
clear all
*         Put main menu on screen, and ask user to select
*
?'    ------Jarvis Blewett Client Record System---------'
?' '
?'     1 - Edit employee records'
?'     2 - Edit client records'
?'     3 - Enter hours worked'
?'     4 - Edit hours file'
?'     5 - Print hours by employee'
?'     6 - Print hours by client'
?'     7 - Print employee records'
?'     8 - Print client records'
?'     9 - Print weekly statement'
?'     U - Update accounts records and record payments'
?'     Q - Quit'
read
wait ' ' to choice
*                 now process option selected
docase choice
case choice = '1'
use employ index empref
browse
......
case choice = '6'
*
*  first, define the two files needed and cross-reference
*
select 1
use employee index empref
select 2
use time index empref
set relation on empref into employee
*
*  next, screen input - to get employee reference
*                       for report
clear
@1,5 say 'Report on Hours by Employee'
@3,5 say 'Employee reference:' get employrf
read
*
*  lastly, find the first record for that employee and
*          print report for all such records
find &employrf
report form chargrep to print while empref = employrf
*
case choice = '7'
..........
```

Figure 6.9 dBASE3: macro-program for client billing system.

Sample report from the dBASE3 demonstration system.

```
JARVIS BLEWETT Ltd                    Client: J Briggs
Chartered Accountants                         137 Folkestone Rd
                                              London E18 5SD

Hours Worked by Employees             Week Ending: 12/02/88

Ref          Name                Date        Hours    Rate      Amount
                                                       £          £
---------    ----------------    ---------   -----    ------    -------
BLEWETTF     Blewett F           08/02/88    3.00     85.00     170.00
JARVISR      Jarvis R            09/02/88    5.50     60.00     330.00
MISSELBR     Misselbrooke P      10/02/88    8.00     10.00     800.00
TEDIOUSA     Tedious A R         11/02/88    8.00      6.50      51.00
TEDIOUSA     Tedious A R         12/02/88    8.00      6.50      51.00
                                             -----              -------
                                 TOTAL       32.50             1402.00
                                             -----              -------
```

Figure 6.10 dBASE3: client record system sample report – hours by client.

Sample report from the dBASE3 demonstration system.

```
JARVIS BLEWETT Ltd                    To:  J Briggs
Chartered Accountants                      137 Folkestone Rd
                                           London E18 5SD

STATEMENT FOR WEEK ENDING: 12/02/88
-----------------------------------

Opening Balance              2130.50

THIS WEEK
---------
Fees for hours worked        1402.00
Disbursements                 143.65

Less
----
Amount received this week    (1230.50)
                             ---------
     CURRENT BALANCE          2445.65
                             ---------
```

Figure 6.11 dBASE3: client record system sample report – weekly statement for client.

control aspects become important. Unfortunately, cheap database packages are sometimes proposed for accounting applications where their use can be dangerous. Particular care is needed in choosing a package for a multi-user environment.

Some relevant points to consider in relation to a database package are the following:

1. Can access to files be restricted, with password protection? Most database packages allow free access for editing files.
2. Can a record of changes be kept automatically? This is needed for any recovery procedure.

The above facilities are essential in order to be able to create an audit trail which cannot be readily bypassed by a user who chooses to use the standard commands, rather than go through the customized menu for the application.

Multi-user systems

1. Can an adequate system of user numbers and passwords be set up, with different levels of user access?
2. Can a log be kept of all transactions entered (including changes to all files), with access to the log restricted only to certain users?
3. Does the package deal correctly with multi-user access to files by locking records for the current user, rather than locking files?

Simple file management packages are not generally designed for multi-user access. Even for a single user, it is unlikely that such a package would adequately meet the criteria listed above. Generally, expensive packages such as Ingres and Oracle which have migrated down from minicomputers tend to be very safe in this respect. Other packages need to be looked at with extreme care to make sure that they provide an adequate level of security for the particular application.

6.7 THE DATABASE APPROACH TO RUNNING AN ACCOUNTING PRACTICE

Many software companies now favour taking a database approach to meet the information problems of professional accounting firms. For example, Star Computer Group PLC is a company which has been very successful in selling to professional accountants in the UK. They have rewritten their software using a UNIX-based database package, precisely because they emphasize the importance of such an approach.

If a computer system is to be truly successful, then it should be possible for the partners in a firm to be able to access immediately any relevant financial data relating to the practice or their clients. Moreover, it should then be possible to manipulate this data: using a spreadsheet to make projections or a graphics package to print graphs, or to integrate the data into a report produced by a word processing package.

Such a totally flexible and 'open-ended' approach is really only practicable if one uses a database package, and this is why companies such as Star are taking this approach. Figure 6.12 shows how the

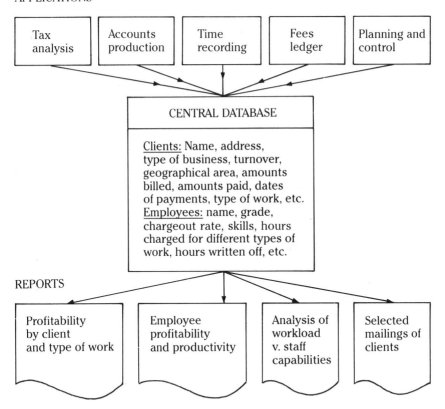

Figure 6.12 Database approach to practice automation. A central database is updated by the various applications. From this any reports required by the practice may be extracted, either as printouts or as disk files to be edited by word processing for use in reports.

various applications used by an accounting practice may be viewed in a database approach. A system like this could be set up on a single-user microcomputer with a hard disk, but it is most valuable in a larger multi-user system so that all the users in the practice are updating and accessing a common database.

For most purposes, this approach does not represent a radical departure. The individual applications will appear much the same to users. The difference lies in the accessibility of information. For this reason, we shall concentrate in the next few chapters on individual accounting applications, but it is important ultimately to think in terms of a total management information system. The benefits of such a system will be seen not in direct cost-saving, but in providing a better service to clients and better financial control of the practice.

6.8 CONCLUSIONS

Most accounting practices will find some applications for which database software will be useful. There are many very good packages on the market, and new packages are frequently launched. There is no one package which is best, and it is a question of choosing the one that is most appropriate in a given situation. The two packages described here are good of their type, but there are strong arguments for making different choices. However, it is important to standardize on one package (or at most two), because if different staff are using different database packages, then that is certainly a recipe for confusion.

Finally, it is worth re-emphasizing the importance of the database concept to accounting firms. Even if multi-user systems currently seem too expensive, prices are continuing to fall. By the early 1990s, accounting practices that want to remain competitive will have to invest in such systems.

7 Preparation of accounts and incomplete records

This chapter will focus on the software available to be used by an accounting practice in preparing clients' accounts. The installation of software and its use will depend upon the completeness of individual client's records, which itself will vary according to the nature of the client's business — for example, a public company will generally require more detailed records than a small firm.

The aim of this chapter is to give the practising accountant an insight into the main features of accounts production software and how it should be used in the work of the practice. Particular emphasis will be given to the possible increases in productivity of the office in dealing with this important source of fee income. Control over the software will also be covered in terms of security and the prevention of loss of records, a subject that creates some anxiety for accountants in the implementation of computer systems.

We shall look at a typical software package in a reasonable amount of detail. This will be set out in one of the later sections of this chapter, where a popular accounts production software package — Auditman — will be considered.

7.1 THE NEEDS OF THE CLIENT AND THE COMPLETENESS OF THE CLIENT'S ACCOUNTING RECORDS

Before accounts production software is used, the particular needs of the client must be considered. These will vary, mainly depending on:

1. whether the client is a company
2. whether the client is an unincorporated organization, i.e. sole trader, partnership or some other legal entity such as a charity.

These factors will determine the format of the accounts, the timeliness of their production, the sophistication of any further analysis required for management purposes and the state of the records that are kept by the client. All are fundamental in meeting the client's requirements for the production of accounts.

In the case of a company, the law stipulates that proper accounting records must be kept on a day-to-day basis (the software used for this application is considered in Chapter 8). Normally, the accounts will be complete, i.e. the nominal accounts and a trial balance can be extracted from the records. Accounts preparation would therefore be restricted to the production of final accounts, with formatting under the *Companies Act* 1985.

Unincorporated organizations are not subject to the same rules as companies, and their requirements are therefore very different. For example, the main need of accounting information for the sole trader is for preparing statements for the Inland Revenue, and therefore day-to-day records of the business are not usually maintained in the same detail as those of companies. Nevertheless, many unincorporated organizations maintain detailed records for their own management control and planning requirements or for VAT returns. The completeness of accounting records therefore tends to vary among unincorporated organizations and this will affect the starting point in the preparation of the client's accounts.

A typical small to medium size practice will usually have a range of clients whose needs vary for the reasons described above. Any software installed, together with the systems and procedures of the practice for the processing of these accounts, must be flexible enough to cater for these variations. Variations in the completeness of client's records is therefore a major problem. In one of the case studies of accounting practices using account production software, studied by Bhasker and Williams (1986), one practice classified work into three types:

1. very incomplete records

2. partially incomplete records.
3. complete records.

The practice's systems for account preparation were designed around this classification: input procedures and the job descriptions of employees varied according to the particular work classification.

7.2 THE STAGES IN A COMPUTERIZED ACCOUNTS PREPARATION SYSTEM

Figure 7.1 illustrates the stages, in a summarized form, of accounts preparation using a computerized system. This illustration assumes

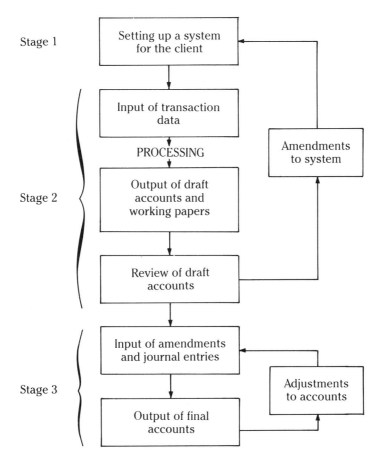

Figure 7.1 Stages in computerized accounts preparation.

the records kept by the client are in the partially incomplete category, i.e. a limited amount of records of transactions are kept, such as a listing of the sales, but the majority of the documentation is in the form of source documents, for example bank statements and stubs from cheque books. The design of programs for this type of software very much tends to mirror the model of accounts preparation under a manual system, and therefore they should be understandable to accountants. This is an important factor in the acceptability of computer software because it has been frequently acknowledged that if a computer process closely mirrors manual procedures, the accountant will have a feeling of confidence in the system.

Stage 1: Setting up a system for the client

The first stage in this process involving the work of the practice, after receipt of the documentation from the client, will be the setting up of a system and the organizing of input for the client. This will depend on the status of the client, that is whether or not the client is new or established.

If the client is new, client files will have to be set up. These files will normally include the client's name, the registered office, and the accounting period covered (e.g. a year). Nominal accounting headings, in terms of codes and descriptions, will need to be set up taking account of the client's requirements. Some of the headings will be standard within the system (for example, 'cash at bank'), whilst others will have to be created by the user. There must be flexibility within the system to cater for all clients. The codes and descriptions will be used to classify revenue, expenditure, assets and liabilities. The extent of the detailed breakdown of each of these items will depend upon the amount of analysis required for the final accounts and for management information purposes. VAT requirements will also be set up at this stage. Most software available, if required, will automatically calculate the input and output VAT for each relevant transaction. Options should also be available for differing rates of VAT. For new clients the balances to be brought forward, for example the opening cash balances, will have to be set up for relevant accounts defined in the nominal coding procedure.

The structure and the numer of nominal account headings are clearly a critical element in a successful process of producing accounts. It is important that these headings are carefully considered at this stage. Any future amendments could be costly in respect of computer and staff time. The setting up of the client's records and the relevant nominal headings requires a reasonable amount of technical expertise, and the staff responsible for this task should therefore have the appropriate accounting skills and experience.

The organization of input for established clients — and for new clients once their files have been set up — involves the process of coding the source documents and any other records. The codes will either be written on to the source documents or onto a form that has been specifically designed. Using a special form is often favoured, as it speeds up the operator input to the computer. Coding requires a reasonable amount of technical expertise to identify the expense and match it with the appropriate nominal account.

Stage 2: The preparation and review of draft accounts

The ease of inputting data is to a large extent dependent upon the efficiency and efficacy of the previous stage. At this stage, during the input of data, the software should also allow any narrative that is required to be added to the data relating to transactions. This will give the user the option to write a more detailed reference against a transaction. A number of packages offer a facility to help reconcile data input on the screen and such calculations can form part of the working papers (such as bank reconciliations) that are important to the audit trail. Another useful facility is the capability of automatic balancing as this generally gives a better audit trail since a balancing entry is made for every posting.

The keying in of data may either be carried out by a skilled operator, who would normally have very little expertise in accounting, or a member of staff with a reasonable technical knowledge such as an audit clerk. A trained key operator will be much faster at inputting data, but the audit clerk is likely to be more efficient in many situations because of his ability to resolve errors.

Security is important in the inputting of data to prevent access by unauthorized staff to clients' records. This will normally take the form of using passwords for entry into the system, which are normally an option on such software. The practice must give considerable thought to this aspect to protect clients' confidentiality.

The output, at this stage, will be in the form of draft accounts and working papers, such as a trial balance. The accounts can then be reviewed. It is important that the software gives the user the opportunity to interrogate specific accounts for errors and to make adjustments such as for depreciation. During the review, particular attention should be given to the appropriateness of the nominal codes defined in Stage 1 of the process; any amendments should be made at this stage. Final journal entries relating to corrections, amendments and end-of-year adjustments can then be prepared for input.

Stage 3: The preparation of final accounts

After the input of adjustments the final accounts are prepared and printed. It is important that the software chosen for this type of work has a word processing facility; this will enable notes to the accounts to be made as well as provide a facility for report writing. This is particularly important where the requirements of the 1985 *Companies Act* and Accounting Standards are relevant to the client because a considerable amount of supplementary information is then required to support the accounts.

Another important facility in the preparation of the final accounts for clients who are companies is that the formats available should conform to those prescribed by the 1985 *Companies Act.* The majority of the more popular accounts production software on the market does have this facility.

To ensure that files are not corrupted or lost, it is important that back-up copies are made on to diskettes or tape cassettes. Back-up procedures should be installed at varying stages of the process for preventive purposes, and the design of the procedures, because of their importance, requires careful thought.

This particular illustration, as stressed earlier, focused on a system for accounts production for a client whose records were incomplete. For clients whose records are in a more complete state, the procedures and stages would be similar to those illustrated in Figure 7.1, except that the point of entry into the system and a number of the routines would differ. For example, with a client who prepared his own records and produced his own trial balance with the appropriate working papers the point of entry, after auditing these records and preparing the necessary adjustments, would be at the later input stage.

7.3 DECIDING WHAT TO PUT ON THE COMPUTER AND THE DIVISIONS OF WORK

The implication from the last two sections is that the completeness of client's records will determine the point of entry into the computerized system for accounts preparation. In practice, this is not strictly true; from our own survey of professional accountants, there seem to be differences in opinion as whether it is economical to employ the computer for incomplete work. However, there does seem to be a great deal of agreement that from extracted trial balances onwards, computers are extremely efficient and economical in producing final accounts.

A potential constraint on the use of a computer in the early stages of the accounts preparation is the chargeout rate used for computer time that some practices employ. For example, we know of one medium-size practice which charges out £50 per hour for computer time compared to approximately £13 per hour for articled clerks. Using such an unrealistically high rate for their computer, this practice has concluded that an articled clerk's time for preparing accounts up to the trial balance is cheaper than using a computer.

The worrying point here is the method upon which the £50 per hour for computer time was established. Although we have no information regarding the basis of the calculation in this particular case, it is generally accepted that such decisions should only take account of marginal costs as any fixed cost — such as the purchase cost of the computer and software — is irrelevant to the decision. It is also difficult to assess the full cost and benefits of a computerized system for a practice before it has been installed. Probably the best method is to consider particular accounting routines and compare them with the manual version. Another reasonable basis for this assessment is advice from an experienced user.

It should, however, be stressed that for a computer system to be used efficiently and economically for the preparation of accounts, the following factors should be taken into account:

1. The balance in the division of work between technical staff and other staff, for example key operators and articled clerks. The practice should carefully consider the particular roles of staff so as to obtain the optimum benefits from using this resource.
2. The planning and detailed procedures for particular types of work. There is strong evidence to suggest that if a practice implements formal detailed procedures that are comprehensive and understandable to staff, the work programmes will be completed more efficiently. It may be appropriate to implement procedures for categories of accounts production divided into incomplete, partially complete and complete, as suggested earlier in the case study by Bhasker and Williams (1986).
3. The need for internal controls and internal checks. Although a number of controls are built into the software, a considerable part of the process of accounts preparation is outside the computer and it is therefore appropriate that this process is subject to strong internal controls and checks so that control can be maintained.

It is our opinion that the prejudices against the use of computers in the early stages of accounts preparation are mainly due to past difficulties with software experienced by accountants, and due to these dissatisfied users communicating their experience to others. However, the nature of the software market is dynamic and competitive. Software is constantly being updated by the better software companies to take account of amendments arising out of user comments and dissatisfaction. There is strong evidence to support the view that more and more users who originally were dissatisfied with the software are now using it for all the stages in accounts production.

7.4 CHOICE OF SOFTWARE

There seems little doubt that the most appropriate accounts production software for small- to medium-sized accounting practices are ready-written programs produced by software companies. This software is relatively cheap, there are very few, if any, development costs involved, and it is extremely user-friendly.

The alternative to this ready-written software is customized programs written specifically for a practice. Although presumably all the peculiarities of the particular practice can be accounted for, the development time is considerable. We have knowledge of one medium-sized practice which wrote its own program and the development time was estimated to be six months, involving one partner's time and a number of senior staff — and the program after this still had a number of bugs. This practice has now installed a ready-written software package! Therefore, writing your own programs is costly and it is unlikely that the benefits will exceed the costs.

There are undoubtedly dozens of accounts production software packages on the market. It is also true that a number that have been introduced over the last five years have now disappeared. It is therefore important to choose a company that has installed its software at a large number of sites. The software produced will then have been well tested and there will probably be strong back-up support in terms of maintenance and training.

Computer Services Midlands (CSM) Ltd have the characteristics described and have produced an accounts production package, Auditman, that has been one of the market leaders for a relatively long time. Auditman has gone through a number of development stages and the current version is known as Auditman II; there have been well over 2000 installations of this software. The system runs on either hard disk or twin floppy disk microcomputers. Another company that has similar qualities is Star Computers PLC which markets a package that runs on the Star Auditor 1000 computer, a UNIX-based multi-user microcomputer. This system is also popular with small firms of accountants.

7.5 MAIN FEATURES AND FACILITIES OF ACCOUNTS PRODUCTION SOFTWARE

This section will consider the main features and facilities of accounts production software packages, using Auditman as an example. Auditman was originally designed for relatively large practices but it is apparent from CSM's customer range that the software is also appropriate to small and medium practices. Auditman caters for all types of legal entities and all states of records, from incomplete to complete.

Auditman is relatively simple to operate and very user-friendly. One of the important features that is of considerable help to the user is pop-up menus. The arrangement of these menus guides the user through possible tasks. Each menu identifies facilities to assist the input of information and has the ability to recall the input for amendments and corrections. The main features to aid data input are:

1. up to 1000 codes are available for nominal accounts
2. double-entry controls on input — postings cannot be made without the relevant double entry, thus if only one entry is input an error message is shown on the screen
3. prepayments and accruals/self-reversing facility — postings this period will be reversed automatically in the next period (e.g. rates paid in advance)
4. the automatic calculation of VAT, gross and net amounts
5. the ability to add narrative to input transactions
6. bank and cash reconciliations with a balancing facility on screen to aid this process
7. batch total checks and checks for account balances
8. new nominal ledger accounts can be added whilst posting — a user is not required to go back into the 'set up file' routine.

The input procedures and these user facilities are designed in a way that does not require a great deal of technical expertise. Thus a key operator with a relatively small amount of technical experience, backed up by the practice's own procedures for data input, should be able to cope with this task. This is not to say that senior staff should not be capable of inputting data. In fact, it is very important that such staff understand the process, so that they can be a party to designing the required procedures, both for backing up the computerized system and for reviewing the working papers generated by it.

At the review stage, after entering the input and before printing draft accounts, the user can call up on the screen or print a number of working papers to check the data input. These working papers include a trial balance, audit trail and nominal ledger accounts. All the working papers will show the operator's initials, the date and the last posting number entered into the system. Figure 7.2 shows the audit trail menu.

The facility for formatting the final accounts is based on what CSM describe as interactive formatting. This is a simple 'question and answer' technique on screen used to design the formatting requirements of clients. Although this system is based on standard formats, it does have a considerable amount of flexibility relative to some other software on the market. The system also provides a facility for automatic notes to the accounts, enabling the user to specify relevant standard notes for clients from a simple table. The notes are then automatically called up into the final accounts report. The word processing facility, which can be linked to the system, gives the user the additional flexibility to add to the notes and other reports related

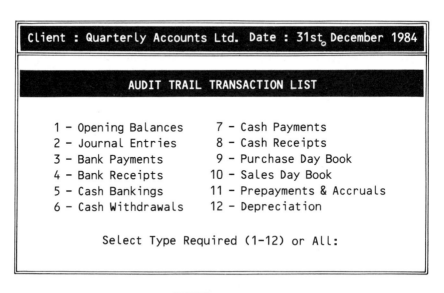

Figure 7.2 Auditman II: screen-display of audit trail menu. Reproduced courtesy of CSM Ltd.

M. D. WARREN

BALANCE SHEET AT 31ST DECEMBER 1985

	1985		1984	
	£	£	£	£
FIXED ASSETS		2,551		2,250
CURRENT ASSETS				
Trade Debtors	4,138		2,700	
Sundry Debtors				
and Prepayments	305		300	
Bank Account	1,065		–	
	5,508		3,000	
CURRENT LIABILITIES				
Bank Account	–		750	
Sundry Creditors				
and Accruals	193		180	
Value Added Tax	435		190	
	628		1,120	
NET CURRENT ASSETS		4,880		1,880
		7,431		4,130
REPRESENTED BY:				
CAPITAL ACCOUNT				
Opening Capital		4,130		3,970
Capital Introduced		1,450		–
Net Profit for the year		2,376		2,755
		7,956		6,725
Drawings	100		2,595	
Private Payments	425		–	
		525		2,595
		7,431		4,130

Approved

Figure 7.3 Auditman II: a sample accounts production job. Reproduced courtesy of CSM Ltd.

M. D. WARREN

TRADING AND PROFIT AND LOSS ACCOUNT
FOR THE YEAR ENDED 31ST DECEMBER 1985

	1985		1984	
	£	£	£	£
SALES		9,500		9,375
COST OF SALES		4,550		4,420
GROSS PROFIT		4,950		4,955
LESS OVERHEADS				
Salaries and Wages	300		–	
Motor Running Expenses	987		875	
Telephone Charges	84		50	
Sundry Expenses	25		75	
Heating and Lighting	19		15	
Insurance	30		25	
Rent & Rates	250		250	
Bank Interest and Charges	13		10	
Accountancy Charges	165		150	
Depreciation – Vehicles	751		600	
Depreciation – Plant & Equip.	150		150	
(Profit) Loss on Sale of Assets	(200)		–	
		2,574		2,200
NET PROFIT FOR THE YEAR		2,376		2,755

Figure 7.3 (continued)

M. D. WARREN

SCHEDULE OF MOVEMENTS OF FIXED ASSETS
FOR THE YEAR ENDED 31ST DECEMBER 1985

	Motor Vehicles	Plant & Equipment	Total
COST:	£	£	£
At 1st January 1985	3,200	750	3,950
Additions in Year	1,652	–	1,652
Disposals in Year	(800)	–	(800)
	4,052	750	4,802
DEPRECIATION			
At 1st January 1985	1,400	300	1,700
Write Off on Disposals	(350)	–	(350)
Charge for Year	751	150	901
	1,801	450	2,251
NET BOOK VALUE			
As at 31st December 1985	2,251	300	2,551
As at 31st December 1984	1,800	450	2,250

Figure 7.3 (continued)

to the accounts. Figure 7.3 illustrates the reports generated for the final accounts preparation for a small business using Auditman. At this stage the final working papers with a full audit trail can also be printed.

A particularly interesting facility of Auditman is the ability to generate management accounting information. This facility is a potential additional fee earner to the practice, as extremely useful management information can be supplied to the client. The management accounting facility includes the ability to set up period budgets for items of expenditure and revenue, and compares the budget with the actual performace. The reports generated are of good quality for presentation to clients. Further management information in respect to forecasting and financial modelling can be produced by linking Auditman up with a spreadsheet package, such as Lotus 1-2-3. The information in the form of balances, nominal ledger accounts and budgets from any period may be transferred from Auditman to the spreadsheet and used for analysis.

In general, the main savings in using a software package such as Auditman compared with manual accounts production is the elimination of a substantial amount of manual analysis, cross checking and typing. The software also gives the accounting practice the possibility of additional fee income through facilities such as the production of management accounts.

7.6 CONCLUSIONS

The process of producing accounts clearly lends itself to computerization. This is reflected through the popularity of this type of software. However, there is evidence to support the view that there still remain a large number of small- to medium-sized practices that are not yet using such software, even though there are clear cost savings to be made.

A number of the accounts preparation packages on the market now also have linked management accounting facilities. For example, the accounts production program is often linked to a budgetary control system. The cost of running both systems together is relatively cheap; this means that the practice is then able to offer, even to relatively small customers, an additional fee earning service at an economical price. Chapter 10 on planning and control considers these link facilities in more detail.

8 Ledger accounts and integrated accounts

The focus of this chapter will be on the possible applications of computers to the main routine accounting functions of the client, where records are kept on a day-to-day basis. In the case of a company, under the 1985 *Companies Act* such records are required to be kept; the Act specifically refers to the records for sales and purchases (i.e records of goods sold and purchased, other than in ordinary retail trade transactions, with details of the goods, buyers and sales sufficient to enable them to be identified). It is also the case that some businesses, which are not incorporated, may wish to keep day-to-day records for management control purposes. These accounts will either be kept by:

1. the client maintaining his own accounts
2. an accounting practice maintaining the client's accounts on a bureau basis
3. a computer bureau, other than the practice, maintaining accounts for the client of an accounting practice

In all the situations above, where computer software is the means by which these records are maintained, accountants need to have a good working knowledge of the software and its limitations in their key role as auditors or preparers of accounting information. Accountants will also need this knowledge to be able to advise clients on whether it is appropriate to computerize their accounting system, and whether particular software seems adequate.

The aim of this chapter, therefore, is to give the practising account-ant an insight into what is perceived as the more important aspects of the software available for maintaining a client's accounting records. Whilst a comprehensive analysis of the range of software available for these applications will not be undertaken, it is appropriate, within the aims of this chapter, to consider in detail a specific package to obtain the required insight into this type of software. This will be achieved by considering one of the best-selling sales ledger packages in one of the later sections.

8.1 CHOICE OF SOFTWARE

For clients of small- to medium-sized firms of accountants the most common, and probably the most appropriate software used for routine accounting applications are ready-written programs produced by software companies. The software is written to perform a specific accounting application, for example particular ledger accounts, such as the sales ledger. Each separate program written for a particular application can be interlinked to form an integrated suite of account-ing software.

Although accounting software allows the different accounting ledgers to be integrated, the extent of any integration for a particular client will depend upon that client's needs and experience. For example, a client installing such software for the first time may decide to use only the sales ledger software. Although greater savings could be made if the sales ledger were to be integrated with sales invoicing and stock control, it is important to gain experience with a relatively simple system. As experience is gained and the client gains confi-dence, he will probably begin to integrate the separate programs.

An alternative to these ready-written programs is to write one's own customized programs for specific applications. Developing programs in a conventional language, such as BASIC, is extremely expensive. Some users have written accounting software using dBASE3 (the database package previously mentioned) or spreadsheets. Although the cost is not as great for this compared with software written in conventional languages, it is still considerably more than that for ready-written programs. In general, these customized programs are unjustified, but in some cases it may be worthwhile for particular specialist appli-cations.

8.2 ADVANTAGES AND DISADVANTAGES OF ACCOUNTING APPLICATION SOFTWARE

Such software is standard in that it is designed for universal use. Thus individual firms do not need to write their own programs, which as suggested earlier, can be a very time-consuming exercise and therefore expensive.

Clearly, the reliability of the software to handle a firm's accounting requirements is very important to a user; the loss of control of one of the main accounting functions could be very costly because it could result in the loss of information required to make decisions and control the business. The fact that this type of software is widely used and hence has been well tested suggests that it is usually extremely reliable. Customized programming requires thorough testing and even then there are often problems of reliability, even if only minor changes have been made to the standard software. Although software firms periodically announce new updated versions with added facilities, the main features of accounting software have not dramatically changed since its introduction to the microcomputer software market in about 1980. Thus the inherent reliability of accounting software, being well tried and tested, is an important advantage to a potential user. It is also important to purchase well-known software that is known to have a large number of users; less well-known software may not provide the same degree of reliability. The demand for this type of software and a highly competitive market have resulted in the price being in a range that should not be prohibitive for a small practice. Typically prices in 1988 were about £200 per module, or £1000 for a complete integrated accounts package. The most popular software for this type of application currently being used are Pegasus, Multisoft and Sagesoft. Very much cheaper software is available but is probably best avoided, because of doubts about the quality and reliability of the software.

Good quality accounting packages will be well documented, the user manuals (instructions) being relatively clear and free from jargon and written specifically for one specialist user group, i.e. preparers of accounts. Because such software has been popular and in constant use, the software companies have developed a considerable amount of expertise over the years. As a result, the software has been developed to a point where it is user-friendly and relatively easy to use, while coping with most difficult accounting problems.

The nature of such software is that an accounting database is maintained, which can be accessed for various purposes. This means that management control information, for example aged debtors analysis, can be generated very quickly from the same information that produces routine accounting information. Such control information can be produced immediately and at a much lower cost than from a typical manual accounting system. It will also be totally accurate if the database is correct, whereas manually produced information cannot be totally reliable.

Another major advantage is that a reputable supplier of this software will normally supply a good after-sales service, giving advice from their experience of the installation of the software with other clients and maintaining and improving the software. A good micro-computer dealer will usually be able to draw up a programme for training staff and implementing software.

Some of the advantages argued for these packages above, however, are outweighed by the disadvantages for particular users. Being a 'standard' package normally means that it is not flexible to cater for individual needs. The potential user, therefore, must be particularly careful to ensure that any software proposed for purchase meets their particular design and procedure requirements. A number of practices have become very proficient in giving advice to clients and potential clients. This 'new' role of the accounting firm has also been a signifi-cant contributory factor in the increase of fee income for these practices. There are a number of books published to assist firms of accountants in giving advice to clients with regard to the installation of computers and relevant software. (A particularly relevant publi-cation is the Chartac *Workpack* (1987).)

It should also be recognized that the user of such a package is also dependant to an extent on the supplier, which can be a disadvantage if the after-sales service is poor. Many dealers can offer low prices but have no understanding of accounts, operating a 'pile them high, sell them quick' policy.

8.3 INTEGRATED ACCOUNTING SOFTWARE

Integrated accounting software is a suite of accounting packages. Each separate program (normally referred to as a module) is linked with others within the suite, so that data input only needs entry into one of the modules for its effect to be recorded automatically in other relevant modules throughout the suite.

The suite of packages will clearly be chosen to reflect the needs of particular users. For example, a small retailer would probably have a need for a purchase ledger, as in transaction terms the recording of purchases and the associated needs of VAT accounting will probably be a relatively large proportion of the accounting requirements of this type of business. Also there may be a need for some form of stock control program for such a business, which would link with the purchase ledger, and the sales ledger if one is kept. The sales will be mainly for cash rather than for credit, and it is therefore unlikely that there is a need for a conventional sales ledger that details customer records. A nominal ledger program may also be included in the suite; other expenses such as wages and rates as well as cash received from sales would be directly entered into this ledger via the journal.

Figure 8.1 details a simple example of such a suite of modules that

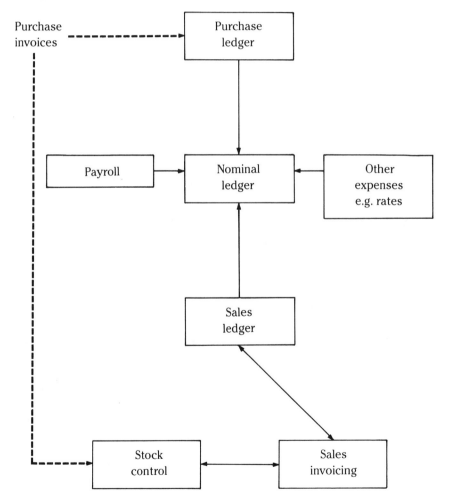

Figure 8.1 An integrated accounting system.

could be relevant for a small client. Six modules are shown in the boxes and the continuous lines illustrate the links between each module. For example, the sales ledger, which will primarily have details of customer accounts, is linked with the nominal ledger and sales invoicing packages. The functions that are not in boxes and that have broken lines to modules within boxes, e.g. purchase invoices, are relevant inputs to the modules — in the case of purchase invoices, the purchase ledger.

The majority of the integrated packages on the market offer a fairly comprehensive standard range of modules; for example, the Pegasus Senior Integrated accounting suite has the following modules:

1. Sales ledger
2. Invoicing
3. Nominal ledger
4. Stock control
5. Bill of materials
6. Purchase ledger
7. Job costing
8. Payroll
9. Information manager.

(Information manager is one module which does not carry a specific application; its function is that of data management, allowing special reports to be produced from data that has been recorded in other modules.)

Each module can be purchased as a stand-alone package or with one or two other related modules; it is often the case for small businesses that only one or two modules are required. This is particularly relevant when a business first installs an application package and there is the natural anxiety of losing control of the business. Often a new user will initially use the software in parallel with the manual system, thereby ensuring that if the computerized system is corrupted, there is always a fall-back available.

Pegasus is probably the best selling of the packages, used by clients to maintain their own accounting records and by bureau services. From recently published figures there are over 50 000 users of Pegasus in the UK. There are basically two versions available: a single-user version, and a multi-user version. The latter is designed for use in a local area network.

The following section will consider some of the main characteristics and features of the sales ledger and its relationship with other relevant ledgers with particular reference to Pegasus software.

8.4 SALES LEDGER

The design of the sales ledger software, not surprisingly, is based on manual accounting systems and is thus built on logical accounting models which should be familiar to accountants. Figure 8.2 illustrates a typical sales ledger model detailing relevant inputs and outputs generated by the processing function of the computer. This illustration will be used as a basis to consider some of the main characteristics and features of a sales ledger package.

The inputs can be divided into two categories:

1. *customer records* the inputting of new records and amendments to those records
2. *transactions* that are current in relation to the day-to-day trading activities, e.g. invoices.

Installing customer records is the first stage in the process. These inputs once processed create a master file, which is identified in Figure 8.2 as output. The data on these files are often referred to as 'standing data'; as this phrase implies the data tends to stay the same and is only changed from time to time when a new customer is enlisted or there is a file amendment, e.g. change of credit rating. Figure 8.3 gives an example of a Pegasus customer record. Two particular facilities which are extremely useful to the user are identified in this record: the 'code' box which permits the user to define particular options for sales analysis (the type of reports generated under this analysis will be considered later) and the 'short name' box which enables the user to search and quickly obtain records for reference.

Once the customer's records have been set up, transactions can then be posted to the sales ledger, thereby updating the balance on the customer account; Figure 8.2 shows a list of typical current transaction inputs.

Before proceeding to some of the details relating to the posting of these current transactions, it is worth considering the two methods used in computerized sales ledgers for processing balances on customer's accounts. Sales ledgers are either 'open item' or 'balance forward' accounting systems.

The **balance forward** method will only show individual current transactions on the customer's account for a defined accounting period, e.g. a month. At the end of the accounting period there will normally be a period-end procedure, which basically tidies up accounts. The effect of this procedure, when using the balance forward method, is that the current transactions in the period are

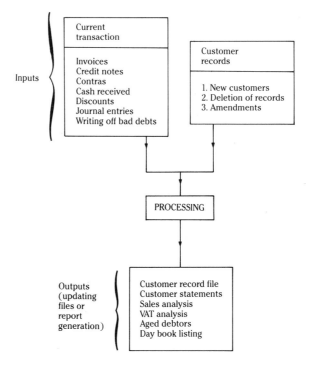

Figure 8.2 Sales ledger model.

accumulated with the balance brought forward from the previous month; thus individual transactions relating to previous months will not be visible.

The **open item** method results in any transaction posted to the account being shown separately until the particular transaction is cleared, e.g. the receipt of cash in respect of a particular invoice, irrespective of time. Only this system of accounting will enable the user to match a particular invoice to a receipt at any time. Clearly this method takes up more disk space to store the extra invoice details, but the benefit is more detailed information. Since disk space is now very cheap, an open system is usually the best choice.

The Pegasus system gives the user the option of using either method; however, some cheaper packages adopt a balance forward approach as it is easier to program and therefore cheaper to install. The user should therefore be careful to make sure to choose a package that suits the particular needs of the business.

It is essential that the software chosen allows sufficient flexibility in

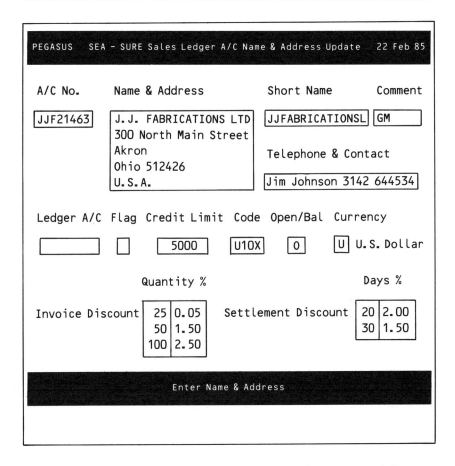

Figure 8.3 Pegasus: customer record. Reproduced courtesy of Pegasus Software Ltd.

defining computations; for example, a company may wish to allow discounts which vary according to customer, type of product and quantity sold. Flexibility in defining printed outputs is also essential; users will want to define their own invoice layout, and to produce various special reports of their own. Pegasus uses a set of 'parameters' which gives users a reasonable range of options for changing their requirements within the system, including discounts and VAT rates. Users can also design their own output forms, such as the customer invoices and statements. This facility, which gives a reasonable amount of flexibility, is clearly important to users and therefore the process of determining the parameters and designing output statements should be carefully considered prior to installation. Changing parameters once the system has been set up can be disruptive and should be avoided where possible.

Recently, the government has become concerned with the large amount of credit taken over and above the stated terms by customers of small firms. They have indicated that there may be legislation, in the future, formally giving small firms the right to charge interest on overdue accounts. Thus, for the user of a computerized sales ledger system the ability to include interest charges into the system would be important. The implication is that any potential purchaser of such software should ensure that the software is flexible enough to cater for such changes in legislation. The Pegasus software does, in fact, already have this facility within the parameters of the sales ledger. However, not every future tax change can be catered for; this does emphasize the importance of buying well-known software in the knowledge that it will be updated if need be.

Most current transaction inputs will be sales orders, used to create invoices. The input procedure will depend upon whether or not a sales invoicing package is integrated with the sales ledger. The process of creating an invoice manually is a very time-consuming activity. This process is particularly suited to computerization provided most customer records are on the computer, and the stock system is integrated with invoicing. To generate an invoice, it is then only necessary to enter the customer code (which will call up relevant information from the customer record in the sales ledger), and the product code and order quantity for the stock items (thus retrieving relevant information from the stock system); the rest of the relevant data will be generated in the processing and printed on the invoice.

The process for input of invoices, when the sales invoicing software is not being used, is controlled through a batching system that generates internal checks; a similar procedure applies for all other current transaction inputs. A useful facility is the ability to list these current transactions, which is an important element of the audit trail, and these lists are also useful for investigating queries.

The input of current transactions, as shown in Figure 8.2, will result in the updating of files within the system and the creation of reports. Users will clearly want to be able to generate customer statements on a regular basis, for example once a month, as well as having the option to print a particular customer's statement due to a customer query. Users can design their own statements when using Pegasus and the Pegasus Manual gives a helpful insight into this facility.

A very helpful facility, common to the majority of sales ledger software, is the ability to create debtor's letters. The Pegasus software has a choice of three standard letters and a facility for users to design their own. The information relating to this letter is derived from the sales ledger. This facility is clearly a great time saver compared to manual systems requiring typists to produce individual letters etc.

For effective credit control, sales ledger packages normally offer an aged debtors analysis. This analysis is particularly useful for small companies because of their inherent problems with cash flow. Figure 8.4 shows a Pegasus aged debtors listing; this report has separate columns showing the current, the previous two months' totals and a single total for amounts owing over a three month period. The customer contact and telephone number are also shown which is useful in the chasing of debtors. The time saved in producing this listing compared with the production of the report manually is very considerable.

Another task that tends to be time consuming manually is the analysis of sales, for example by product. The links within the sales ledger software makes the task of generating such analysis much easier than corresponding manual systems. The types of analysis that can be produced using Pegasus are:

1. by type of customer, e.g. customers in a defined geographical location
2. by product type
3. by a combination of type of customer and product.

This range of analysis clearly gives firms the ability to generate management control information as well as providing a good foundation for planning.

Also generated from the sales analysis in the Pegasus system is the associated VAT output on sales. The information derived from the analysis will give the user the required information to complete the Customs and Excise Return for VAT output. The facility to use varying

SEA - SURE PRODUCTS (M-U) LTD.

23.02.88	Aged Debtors List		Page 1						
Account	3 Months	2 Months	1 Month	Current	Unallocated	Total	Cr Lim	Orders	Account Name
COX00325	0.00	139.38	148.40	-0.42	238.28	525.64	5000	0	PAUL R COX LTD.
JJF21463	0.00	915.57	0.00	1076.23	155.53	2147.33	5000	0	J.J.FABRICATIONS LTD.
PAL14134	12.50	-12.50	152.01	391.28	-215.00	328.29	250**	0	** PALMERS STEEL LTD
	12.50	1042.45	300.41	1467.09	178.81	3001.26			

Figure 8.4 Pegasus: aged debtors listing. Reproduced courtesy of Pegasus Software Ltd.

rates of VAT within the sales ledger is an important feature. This should also be borne in mind when purchasing software which includes purchase ledger packages.

The output reports identified in Figure 8.2 such as customer statements, and referred to in the text tend to be standard in the Pegasus system with some flexibility in design through given parameters. Full control over reporting can, however, be obtained through a separate program called the Report Generator. The type of flexibility described is important for particular users, and this should be a major consideration in the purchasing of such software.

The main security features of this type of software tend to be based on the use of passwords, with an audit trail that can only be accessed by those with the highest level passwords — there are three levels defined in the Pegasus system. Only specified personnel, defined by the user, are allowed access to particular levels.

8.5 INTEGRATION OF THE SALES LEDGER WITH THE NOMINAL LEDGER

The relationship and the links between the sales ledger and the nominal ledger are shown in Figure 8.1. As can be seen from this diagram, the nominal ledger is the central point of an integrated accounting suite.

The integration of the sales ledger with the nominal ledger in a computerized system is extremely time saving compared with a manual system. The process of physically transferring balances from the sales ledger to the nominal ledger in the case of a manual system is redundant when using integrated software. When an integrated accounting package is being used the balances are automatically transferred by an updating routine, without the need to rekey the entries. This updating routine can be completed when the user wishes. Integration of these two ledgers also has the advantage that totals will not be misposted.

In the case of Pegasus, the information from the sales analysis is the source of balances to be transferred to the nominal ledger. The program is once again centred on codes, similar to the sales analysis coding. It is clearly important that the user spends a reasonable amount of time in determining what codes and the combination of codes to use. Any confusion at this point could seriously damage the ability to maintain an adequate reporting base.

8.6 SECURITY AND CONTROLS

The maintaining of accounting records using computer software poses a number of problems relating to security and control. These are of particular concern to the practising accountant; the main issues involved can be classified as follows:

1. security — the prevention of fraud
2. the loss of control — losing information that is required to maintain control of the business and is used for decision-making purposes
3. the audit — adequate internal control and audit trail.

Evidence from the Audit Commission's Computer Fraud Survey (1985 and 1981) identifies that approximately half the types of computer fraud committed relate to the processing of sales and purchases data. Thus a great deal of emphasis should be placed on security when purchasing and installing sales and purchase software.

Internal controls were also identified in the same survey as the main method of discovery of fraud. It is therefore reasonable to assume that strong internal controls are a significant factor in the prevention of computer fraud. In computerized systems an important element of internal control will be internal checks which are embodied within the program of the software. This is particularly critical at the input stage of the process. In general, a good package should subject all the input to validity checks and have facilities for reconciliation of input data. For the majority of the more popular integrated packages these types of internal checks are present; for example, balances of accounts are automatically transferred between ledgers and accounts within ledgers. Another internal check that is considered wise to adopt for input is the manual maintenance of batch totals, which can then be checked periodically with the balances generated by the package.

In section 8.4, reference was made to the significance of adequate passwords for security purposes within the internal control system. Passwords are particularly important for multi-user systems and integrated packages. Each module of the integrated package should ideally have different passwords. Clearly, if a system of passwords is to be effective it is important that there should be precise divisions of responsibility between staff and separate passwords allocated. The password, of course, should be confidential to the particular user. There is also a strong case for passwords being changed periodically. There are many examples where a password has become common knowledge to a number of unauthorized personnel within a department thus making the security vulnerable.

Loss of control due to losing information is a common anxiety experienced by computer users; this is particularly the case with new users. The loss of control information can be very costly. For example, following the loss of a listing of outstanding debtors and customer accounts, it would take a considerable amount of time to recreate such records, as well as an inevitably costly delay in receiving payment from debtors. Sections 8.2 and 8.3 of this chapter made reference to such situations, which because of their importance are worth re-emphasizing briefly here:

1. If the software chosen is widely used it implies that it has been well tested, which also suggests that it tends to be more reliable and therefore there is less chance of losing control.
2. Certainly in the early days of using a package it is wise not to be too ambitious, and to run the package parallel with a manual system.

In the context of maintaining control, the provision of hard copies and the periodic creation of back-up files should also be a significant feature of the internal control system.

The ICAEW Auditing Guideline 407, *Auditing in a Computer Environment*, details the main principles that should be followed when auditing a computerized system. For the practising accountant, reference should be made to this Guideline when auditing such a system. The strength of the internal control system, which has been emphasized earlier, is also an important ingredient in an effective audit.

Of particular importance when using application software is the existence of a good audit trail. All changes to standing records via the input of transactions or file maintenance (for example, setting up new customers' records) should be recorded and logged. Normally the system will provide a computer printout detailing such changes.

The main aspects regarding the subject of security and control relating to this particular application software have been summarized above. For more detail regarding this important subject, reference can be made to the following texts:

1. Bhaskar and Williams (1986)
2. Jenkins *et al.* (1986)
3. Chartac *Workpack* (1987)
4. Auditing Guideline 407 (1984).

9 Practice management

This chapter is principally concerned with time recording and the fees ledger. The two aspects are closely linked and are both important in the efficient management of the accounting practice. Professional accountants usually emphasize strongly to their clients the value of tight credit control, but are not always strict in applying this to their own practices. Indeed, our research has shown many instances where partners have allowed their clients excessively long periods to pay, often allowing them an average of six or even nine months to pay invoices.

The main aim of this chapter is to give the practising accountant an insight into the key features of time recording and fees ledger software, and the implications for the efficient management of the practice. Apart from providing valuable information on credit control for the practice, this application can also help to determine whether the practice is achieving its professional marketing objectives, and whether it has the appropriate level of staff skills.

The development in the use of software for the planning and control of clients' businesses has led to similar developments in the practice. In recent years, some small- to medium-sized practices, for their own management purposes, have introduced forecasting and budgetary control models. This development will also be considered in this chapter.

Another issue of concern which is discussed in this chapter is the professional marketing of the practice. The information on work undertaken for clients which is available from a computer-based time recording and fees ledger system also provides a useful database for the accounting practice to market its services more effectively to its clients.

9.1 THE NEED FOR TIME RECORDING AND FEES LEDGER

For any practice, it is essential to keep a precise record of the work undertaken for each client; this may well include auditing, financial planning and taxation advice, with different specialist sections of the practice working for the client. Any particular task for the client will involve staff at various levels (clerical staff, articled clerks, accounts seniors and partners), who will have to be charged out at a series of different rates. The client will also possibly be charged for any disbursements such as travelling expenses or for use of the practice's facilities, such as telephone calls or the use of a computer for accounts production on behalf of the client.

Keeping track of these various charges is a significant administrative task, and it is sensible to consider using a computer for this; it is this task which is performed by time recording software. From the time recording system, it is a relatively simple matter to calculate the amount owing by the client; for this reason, time recording software is usually combined with a fees ledger.

The fees ledger for the practice is similar in principle to the sales ledger for a client described in the last chapter, since it simply records amounts owing and payments. However, most practices do not use their computer systems for generating invoices, preferring to send a less detailed bill to their clients. Nevertheless, it is occasionally useful to be able to produce an itemized invoice, where a client wishes to query the amount of their bill.

Figure 9.1 shows the structure of a typical time recording and fees ledger system. The time recording provides useful information on the type of work undertaken by the practice, as well as enabling work-in-progress and completed work to be compared with budgets. The fees ledger provides useful credit control information, such as aged debtors analysis.

9.2 CHOICE OF SOFTWARE

There are a number of well-proven time recording and fees ledger packages on the market, such as the Minuteman II time recording and fees ledger package from CSM Ltd and the time, fees and practice management system marketed by Star Computer Group PLC. The package used to illustrate this chapter is the PACS time and fees ledger system, which has been used by many accounting practices, including some leading firms. For convenience, time recording and fees ledger is considered in the next section as a stand-alone appli-

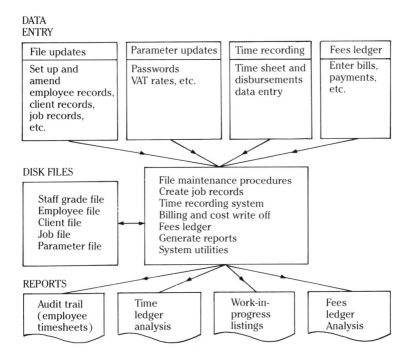

DATA
ENTRY

File updates	Parameter updates	Time recording	Fees ledger
Set up and amend employee records, client records, job records, etc.	Passwords VAT rates, etc.	Time sheet and disbursements data entry	Enter bills, payments, etc.

DISK FILES

Staff grade file
Employee file
Client file
Job file
Parameter file

File maintenance procedures
Create job records
Time recording system
Billing and cost write off
Fees ledger
Generate reports
System utilities

REPORTS

Audit trail (employee timesheets)	Time ledger analysis	Work-in-progress listings	Fees ledger Analysis

Figure 9.1 Overview of time recording and fees ledger system.

cation, since this is the simplest approach. However, as indicated in Chapter 6, there are strong arguments for taking a more integrated 'database' approach, encompassing other aspects of practice management. This is advocated by companies such as Star Computer Group PLC, and this approach will be discussed later in the chapter.

9.3 PROCESSING OF TIME RECORDING AND FEES LEDGER

The stages in processing can be deduced from Figure 9.1. The first stage is to set up the standing data files, namely the staff grade file, the employee file and the client file. The major effort in setting up this system will be creating these files, although some file maintenance will be needed from time to time as changes occur. The staff grade file contains chargeout rates for each grade; the employee is allocated a grade on their employee record, but can be allocated a different chargeout rate from the standard for their grade if this is appropriate.

The second stage is to create job records for each client, which are used as a basis for time recording. Theoretically, all work for a client could be put on to the same job record; in practice, where different tasks are ongoing, it is essential to create separate job records for each task. This makes it easier to analyse the type of work undertaken by the practice, and it enables budgets and target dates to be set for each job against which performance can be measured. This also ensures an early warning where a job is likely to run well over budget.

The third stage is to enter the time sheet data into the system; this can be done by junior staff, using diaries from the previous day, and takes only a few minutes each day. Only the time worked is entered at this stage, since the chargeout rates for any employee can be retrieved from the various employee files. Finally, details of any disbursements also have to be entered against the relevant jobs.

A series of reports based on the time ledger are available on an ongoing basis, including the following:

1. *Audit trail (time sheet)*: a listing for each employee of times worked in a specified time period on various jobs.
2. *Time ledger account*: shown in Figure 9.2, this is the account for each client enabling a clear comparison of actual costs and booked costs to be made in order to assess client profitability.
3. *Analysis by work type (or by employee)*: a listing for each client, either for the whole account or between selected dates.

Similar analysis of disbursements is also available. Although PACS does provide a standard set of reports, there is considerable flexibility to modify the report formats to suit the user's particular requirements.

A very wide range of work-in-progress listings are available, since the listings may be defined by the user to include whatever parameters are relevant. For example, each client may be allocated a manager and a partner, thus enabling reporting by management groups; the work-in-progress listings can then be for any of the following selections:

1. all clients/jobs
2. by partner
3. by manager
4. by partner by manager
5. groups of clients.

For example, Figure 9.3 shows a listing of work-in-progress by partner, including details of fees billed to clients.

PACS also includes exception reporting facilities, which enables jobs to be identified which have gone over budget or exceeded last year's billing. Alternatively, one may choose to list all jobs which are outside

```
P.A.C.S. Ltd.              TIME LEDGER LISTING              Run Date 02.03.88
-------------              -------------------

Client No. 2031            PHILLIPA HOLDINGS LTD.
                           ----------------------

   Date        Description         Emp   Actual  Units --- Ledger Values -----
                                   No.    Costs                D/R       C/R
-----------  --------------------  ---   ------- ----- -------------------------
WE 03/02/88  Meeting - Client       1     50.00    10    100.00
DD 04/02/88  Writing up Cash Book   6     15.00     6     30.00
WE 05/02/88  P.A.Y.E.               7     25.00    10     50.00
WE 12/02/88  Directors Loan Acc.    7     25.00    10     50.00
D  15/02/88  Travelling Expenses                          25.69
D  15/02/88  Subsistence                                  10.00
D  16/02/88  Final Accounts         1     50.00    10    100.00
WE 19/02/88  Final Adjustments      4     20.00     5     40.00
D  29/02/88  Invoice No. 2500                                        -200.00
WE 29/02/88  Review Accounts        5     20.00     5     40.00
             --------------------         ------- ----- -------------------------
             TOTAL                        205.00    56    445.69    -200.00
             --------------------         ------- ----- -------------------------

             ACCOUNT BALANCE  -          245.69
             =================================
```

Figure 9.2 PACS: time ledger account for a client. Reproduced courtesy of PACS Ltd.

specified tolerance levels (e.g. not within 20% of target costs).

The remainder of the system is concerned with the processing of the fees ledger. At the end of a job, a final bill is sent to the client and the job record is closed. At that stage, it may be necessary to write off some of the costs incurred for various reasons. For longer jobs, it may also be necessary to send interim invoices to the client; if so, the invoice amount will be debited against the time ledger account for the job.

A fees ledger system is very similar to the usual sales ledger run by a client; for example, there is an aged debtors report which is very similar to Figure 8.4. The fees ledger system includes a full audit trail on posting, invoices and cash; regular statements of account may be produced for clients, as well as the VAT reports that are necessary for completing VAT returns. Finally, the system allows selected names and addresses of clients to be printed out, either as listings or as address labels.

Finally, it should be emphasized that the distinctive feature of this type of software lies in its ability to draw together information from the time ledger and the fees ledger. For example, Figure 9.4 shows an employee profitability analysis, which is useful for highlighting em-

```
P.A.C.S. LTD.                    BY PARTNER - THIS PERIOD            Run Date 02.03.88
-------------                    -------------------------
```

PARTNER 1 --- M. Thatcher

Client Name	No.	Last Invoice	Memo Column	Opening Balance	Costs	Disb.	Billing	W/O	Total Balance
Lindsay Jarvis Plc	2	16/02/88	Dec 31	444.00	114.00	0.00	-20.00	-24.00	514.00
Channel Seven Ltd	10	23/02/88	Jan 31	368.00	160.00	0.00	0.00	-160.00	368.00
Phillipa Holdings Ltd	2031	29/02/88	May 31	264.38	156.00	25.58	-200.00	0.00	245.96
				1076.38	430.00	25.58	-220.00	-184.00	1127.96

PARTNER 2 --- N. Kinnock

Client Name	No.	Last Invoice	Memo Column	Opening Balance	Costs	Disb.	Billing	W/O	Total Balance
Morwenna Micros Ltd	23	23/02/88	Sep 30	103.00	87.00	0.00	0.00	-25.00	165.00
Kerensa Travel Plc	2031	29/02/88	May 31	215.65	156.00	20.50	-200.00	0.00	192.15
				318.65	243.00	20.50	-200.00	-25.00	357.15

NO PARTNER ALLOCATED

Client Name	No.	Last Invoice	Memo Column	Opening Balance	Costs	Disb.	Billing	W/O	Total Balance
Tamsin Records Ltd	206		Mar 05	200.00	320.00	15.25	0.00	-200.00	335.25
ZZZ NON CHARGE HOLS	34			300.00	300.00	0.00	0.00	0.00	600.00
ZZZ NON CHARGE WORK	36			210.00	0.00	0.00	0.00	0.00	210.00
				710.00	620.00	15.25	0.00	-200.00	1145.25
CLIENT LEDGER CONTROL ACCOUNT				2105.03	1293.00	61.33	-420.00	-409.00	2630.36

Figure 9.3 PACS: work-in-progress listing by partner. Reproduced courtesy of PACS Ltd.

ployees who book excessive amounts of non-productive time, or who cause excessive write-offs of booked time.

9.4 CONTROL OF THE PRACTICE

As already indicated, time recording and fees ledger software can be extremely useful in maintaining control over the work of the practice. Entering and checking manual records can be time-consuming, but the

P.A.C.S. LTD.   BY PARTNER - THIS PERIOD   Run Date 03.05.88

No. Employee Name	Last Time Sheet	Opening Balance	Time Costs		Total Time	-- Allocated --		Unallocated Time
			C(hg)	(N)Chg		Billing	W/O	
1 M Thatcher	29/04/88	1500.00	1300.00	600.00	1900.00	-238.67	-61.33	3100.00
1 UNITS --	29/04/88	150	130	60	190		-30	310
2 N Kinnock	29/04/88	1500.00	1200.00	300.00	1500.00	0.00	0.00	3000.00
2 UNITS --	29/04/88	150	120	30	150		0	300
7 J Lindsay	29/04/88	750.00	150.00	0.00	150.00	-140.00	-80.00	680.00
1 UNITS --	29/04/88	150	30	0	30		-44	136
		3750.00	2650.00	900.00	3550.00	-378.67	-141.33	6780.00
		450	280	90	370		-74	746
DISBURSEMENTS		101.51	87.65	0.00	87.65	-65.25	-20.40	103.51
		3851.51	2737.65	900.00	3637.65	-443.92	-161.73	6883.51

Figure 9.4 PACS: employee profitability analysis. Reproduced courtesy of PACS Ltd.

major effort with a manual system lies in extracting information from the records; as so often with computer systems, the major benefit lies in the quality of information immediately available.

Another benefit of a computerized system is that, assuming the software has adequate password control, it allows different tasks to be allocated to various employees, while maintaining clear control of the system. For example, it may be desirable for junior members of staff to enter details of hours worked from diaries each day; however, they would not usually be allowed to see progress reports on jobs, charge-out rates or details of the client fees ledger.

In a well-organized system, staff at the appropriate level of seniority can be allocated to each task, by giving them an account number and password with the relevant level of access to the system; access to files and reports can be similarly defined. Thus, a computer system can be used to ensure that management information is immediately available where needed, but is not available to other employees.

In the same way, a time recording and fees ledger package such as PACS will include full audit trail facilities such as one would expect from any good accounting package. Access to this should be limited to only a few users.

9.5 HARDWARE FOR PRACTICE MANAGEMENT

It should be emphasized that such a system can only be operated effectively if the hardware is flexible enough. A single-user micro-computer can probably not offer sufficient access to make such a system viable, except for a very small practice. A system which has to provide access to several users for data entry and for retrieving information almost certainly requires multi-user hardware: a network of microcomputers, or shared access to a minicomputer or supermicro. Such a system requires substantial investment, but even then the benefits for the practice can justify such an expenditure. A practice may prefer to gain experience initially on a smaller system, but the benefits in practice management will be reduced.

A more difficult decision with a medium-sized or larger practice may be to decide whether to buy one system or several. The performance of a network is likely to be degraded if a large number of micro-computers are sharing the same files; on the other hand, the cost per user of a multi-user computer tends to increase rapidly as the number of users increases beyond a certain point. For a slightly larger practice, it may well be worth considering buying several 'subsystems' with the ability to pass data between them. Generally, it is a question of selecting the system that fits the organization best; if partners operate in a very independent fashion, there may be little need for them to access data about the whole practice, and it may be best for different sections of the practice to operate separate computer systems.

9.6 DATABASE APPROACH

So far we have discussed time recording and fees ledger software which operates as a stand-alone package; we will now briefly consider an alternative approach as advocated by a number of companies, including Star Computer Group PLC. The basic principle is to set up a complete database of client information to meet all possible computer requirements for practice management.

Under the Star system, data relating to clients is drawn together from a series of subsystems such as fees ledger and accounts production, allowing considerable flexibility in reporting. This also links in with the Star word processing software, allowing personalized letters to be sent to selected clients regarding tax changes or other matters of interest. Because the latest version of the Star software has been rewritten in a database language (a fourth generation language), it offers excellent facilities for designing input screens and reports to meet the precise needs of particular users. Indeed, this potentially offers practices a totally open-ended approach to information management.

9.7 PLANNING AND CONTROL

The introduction of planning and control information systems into a practice can enhance its efficiency and profitability. The major benefits of planning and control to the practice are:

1. The planning process forces the practice to look ahead and thereby anticipate undesirable situations; it may be that preventive action can be taken once the problem is recognized. For example, if it were identified that an overdraft facility in the future would exceed the agreed level, then this might lead the practice to push debtors harder for payment.
2. The identification of the relative profitability of the services offered to clients will be of considerable help in any planning decisions relating to the future expansion or contraction of these services.
3. Performance of the practice at varying levels can be judged against budgets and comparisons can be made, for example, between the performance of different offices owned by the practice. The measurement of performance will also extend to work where no fee income is generated.

In an earlier section of this chapter relating to the processing of time recording and the fees ledger the capability of constructing budgets was referred to as a facility often offered with such software. Whilst this budgetary control information can be very useful, the structure of the control system will mirror the program for the time recording and the generation of fees. In such cases, therefore, these systems tend to be inflexible and may not reflect the total needs of the practice.

An alternative to the budgetary control facilities available with time recording and fees ledger software is to use a spreadsheet. Spreadsheets have the advantage of flexibility and therefore the models can be designed to meet the practice's own particular requirements. The use of spreadsheets is becoming increasingly popular for this type of application in accounting practices. This popularity seems to be derived from their wide use in general business applications, as well as from articled clerks who have developed computing skills at educational establishments prior to their employment.

From our own survey of small- and medium-sized practices, the most popular spreadsheet application has been cash forecasting. This is not surprising, as for all small businesses cash is relatively more critical to the survival of this size of firm. Another popular application is the estimation of budgets for fee income, identifying the targets for varying functions (such as payroll) and varying levels of responsibility (such as senior managers). These budgets can be extended to work-in-progress and debtor levels.

In our discussions with practitioners in the small- to medium-sized firm category, it is very clear that they see a productive future in developing planning and control systems for the management of their practices. More emphasis, it seems, is being placed on the function of the management of the practice. It is clear, from our experience, that the sole practitioner can also benefit from these types of planning and control systems, although perhaps to a lesser extent.

9.8 MARKETING OF THE PRACTICE

There is strong evidence to support the view that if a practice is to grow, then there is a need for the practice to market itself. The information relating to clients held on a computerized time recording and fees ledger can be used as a very good database for extracting information relating to the client for this purpose. For example, the practice may wish to advertise a new service to clients and their bankers via a 'mail shot'. The service already offered to clients and other related characteristics (e.g. type of business) can be scanned to select relevant clients. The relevant information, e.g. names and addresses, can then be quickly extracted and printed.

Another useful aspect of the use of computer software related to marketing is the ability of the practice to produce its own advertising material. The quality of this material through word-processing software, and especially from desk-top publishing facilities, is excellent. These facilities are covered in more detail in Chapter 13 on word processing and the electronic office.

The cost of marketing the practice has dramatically decreased through the use of computer software. From our survey, it seems that even for relatively small practices, this is a viable business approach to expanding the profitable services that can be offered to clients.

10 Planning and control

This chapter will focus on the services that the professional practice can offer relating to the client's requirements for planning and control information. This could include, for example, the supply of periodic cash forecasts or the provision of a budgetary control system.

A number of texts have traditionally referred to these services as 'decision support services'. We feel that this description is too restrictive and that 'planning and control' describes the function more precisely.

The chapter begins by considering the important issue of the demand for this type of information service in relation to small- and medium-sized practices. This will be followed by an examination of the type of software available which can be used to produce planning and control information. Finally, we will examine the specific types of planning and control information that can be produced using microcomputers.

10.1 THE DEMAND FOR PLANNING AND CONTROL INFORMATION

In recent years the demand for planning and control information required by businesses has increased significantly. This is particularly so in the case of businesses which are the clients of small- and medium-sized firms of accountants.

One of the major reasons for this increase in demand is due to the change in bank lending policy. Banks are the main providers of finance to small businesses, and it is businesses of this size that are normally the clients of the small- and medium-sized accounting practices. Banks have recently been pursuing a policy of requiring forecasts from potential borrowers to aid them in their lending decisions. There is also a tendency for banks to monitor these forecasts after the loan is granted and to require explanations for any deviations from the forecast. Often the information required will be on a quarterly basis. Previously, the banks' policy was to use only historic annual accounts for lending decisions. Whilst this change in bank policy may not have filtered through to all branches it does seem that eventually these policies will be universal. As a result of this increase in demand, practices are increasingly producing this information for the client in support of their loan applications and for bank monitoring purposes.

There is also evidence that clients who originally required cash forecasts to support loan applications have recognized the value of these forecasts for their own management purposes. A number of practices in our survey highlighted the provision of cash forecasts for management control purposes as a growing market.

Another major reason for the expansion of this market is the dramatic decrease in the cost of producing this information, which is directly due to the introduction of computers into the practice. The work involved in producing planning and control information invariably contains a considerable amount of analysis which is more efficiently managed through computer systems rather than manual systems. In fact, often these services were not marketable using manual systems because the cost was prohibitively high, and clients would not be willing to pay such high fees. However, there is still a need for the practice to market these services; this will be referred to later in the chapter.

The provision of these services for clients is potentially a major source of fee income for accounting practices and a strong base for the expansion of their fee earning capacity. Indeed, from our own survey of small- to medium-sized firms this has certainly been a reality for a number of these practices, where fees from this source are now making a significant contribution to the overall profitability of the practice.

10.2 TYPES OF SOFTWARE

The types of software available for producing planning and control information can be classified into:

1. software used primarily for maintaining and producing the client's accounting records, which will also generate management control information

2. software that is designed for specific aspects of planning and control, e.g. cash forecasts

3. spreadsheets and financial modelling packages where the users are free to design their own models and applications.

The majority of the software on the market designed primarily for the maintenance of ledger accounts also provides management control information. For example, in Chapter 8 the Pegasus sales ledger software was considered, and reference was made to its credit control capability through the aged debtors and sales analyses. This type of control information is clearly very important to the efficient running of the business. As this type of management control information has already been considered in detail no further reference will be made to it in this chapter.

Software that has been primarily designed for maintaining and producing accounts will often be linked with a budgetary control system. A good example of this type of software is Auditman, the accounts production software considered in Chapter 7. The budgetary control system within Auditman will be considered in more detail later in this chapter.

The advantage with spreadsheets and financial modelling software, such as Micro-FCS, in generating planning and control information is that the user is not restricted to any defined parameters of a program. The flexibility of both these types of software means that they can be used for virtually the whole range of planning and control applications, e.g. budgetary control, cash forecasting and investment appraisal. Indeed, if the practice has developed sufficient skills with one of these types of software it is likely that the software will be used for all planning and control services offered to clients. Chapters 4 and 5 detail the methods by which models can be constructed using these two types of software and give some examples of applications. Later in this chapter, we illustrate some more specific applications of this software.

As previously mentioned, this area of the practice's work is expanding and software companies have responded by developing specific software for this market. For example, the Chartered Accountants, Levy-Gee & Co. have developed with CSM Ltd a number of planning models which are being used by small- to medium-sized practices as additional services to clients.

With the exception of the management control information generated by the ledger accounts — such as aged debtor analysis — the other software described above will be considered in the context of applications for planning and control in the following sections of this chapter. This is not to say that the software considered is the most appropriate for a particular application. This will depend on many factors related to an individual practice.

10.3 BUDGETARY CONTROL

The main advantages of installing a system of budgetary control are that:

1. It compels management to look ahead — without forward planning a business may drift along meeting undesirable situations that should have been anticipated and avoided.
2. It gives the business a means by which it may judge actual performance and thereby highlight strengths and weaknesses within the business.

A system of budgetary control is clearly a desirable management information service for businesses to be run efficiently. However, for smaller businesses, high costs compared with insufficient benefits have often made such businesses think twice about installing a budgetary control system.

The introduction of computers has dramatically reduced the cost element for smaller companies. This is particularly true where the company is using a computer for accounts recording, and where software is used that links this with the production of management accounts. This obviates the need to enter the relevant data into the microcomputer, and the software will also include predefined structure of budgetary control reports using the nominal codes defined for accounts recording. Thus there will often exist a link with a budgetary control program where a nominal ledger is produced for both types of software described in Chapters 7 and 8.

Where this link exists, the user will normally input the budget data at the beginning of the year into the budgetary control system. This will be divided into defined periods for each nominal code heading. The actual balances on the nominal ledger accounts at the end of each period will automatically be transferred to the budgetary control system. These transferred balances will be compared with budgets and a variance report will be generated. This automatic transferring process saves a considerable amount of time. There is a strong argument to support the view that even for small companies a system of budgetary control is cost effective when using such software.

The software Auditman, referred to in Chapter 7, is a good example of such software which links accounts production with the production of management accounts. The following are the main reports generated from this software relating to management accounting information:

1. A list of nominal accounts, comparing actual and budget, with an analysis of variances. This is illustrated in Figure 10.1, which shows a typical such report from Auditman comparing the actual with budget for nominal ledger codes.
2. A management report comparing any periods in the current year with any in the previous year, giving actual, budget and variance details.
3. A set of accounts comparing the 'rolling year', that is any comparative range of periods equal to a full accounting year, e.g. the first 7 months this year plus 5 months from last year, etc.

Figure 10.2 shows an example of the last type of report generated by Auditman. This illustration shows an analysis of the profit and loss account, comparing actual with budget for two specified periods.

The particularly attractive aspects of Auditman's management accounting program are the rolling year facility and the ability of the user to specify the number of periods that are required to be analysed. The user can choose up to 16 periods for this purpose.

Spreadsheets are also a popular means for developing budgetary control systems. The modelling process underlying the philosophy of spreadsheets very much lends itself to the construction of budgets. The main advantages of spreadsheets, compared to systems such as that of the management accounting facility of Auditman and other

Actual vs. Budget Comparison.   Period Range 01/01/88 – 31/03/88

Code	Account	Actual	Budget	Variance	%Variance
1	Sales	-104171.30	-100969	3202	3.17
10	Opening Stock	37103.00	39047	-1944	-4.98
11	Purchases	60457.43	49063	11394	23.22
17	Closing Stock	-49692.00	-43220	6472	14.97
30	Salaries and Wages	19182.00	20044	-862	-4.30
35	Motor Running Expenses	8871.00	5209	3662	70.30
39	Telephone Charges	773.46	629	144	22.89
40	Entertaining	1464.45	1395	69	4.95
41	Printing and Stationery	429.39	445	-16	-3.60
42	Advertising	1920.00	3162	-1242	-39.28
45	Heating and Lighting	447.25	439	8	1.82
48	Insurances	705.50	497	209	42.05
49	Rent and Rates	2620.00	2690	-70	-2.60
55	Bank Charges	579.90	666	-86	-12.91
59	Legal and Professional Fees	400.00	377	23	6.10

Figure 10.1 Auditman: nominal accounts listing. Reproduced courtesy of CSM Ltd.

PERIODIC PROFIT AND LOSS ACCOUNT

For the Period 01/01/87 - 30/09/87

	Period 01/01/87 - 30/09/87			Period 01/10/86 - 30/06/87		
	Actual	Budget	Variance	Actual	Budget	Variance
SALES						
Sales	338560.00	311842	26718	328136.00	296625	31511
	338560.00	311842	26718	328136.00	296625	31511
COST OF SALES						
Opening Stock	37103.00	121752	-84649	75423.00	0	75423
Purchases	174304.00	149625	24679	160470.00	135000	25470
Closing Stock	-46621.00	-124029	-77408	-80391.00	0	-80391
	164786.00	147348	17438	155502.00	135000	20502
GROSS PROFIT	173774.00	164494	9280	172634.00	161625	11009

Figure 10.2 Auditman: profit and loss account. Reproduced courtesy of CSM Ltd.

accounts production software, is that the user designs the model and the structure of the report. Thus there is greater flexibility to extract precisely the data the user wants, and to perform calculations and produce tailored reports. In the setting of budgets there are facilities such as sensitivity analysis which is particularly useful in testing scenarios in the planning process.

If spreadsheets are being used in isolation from accounts preparation software, the data relating to the actual performance would have to be input separately from accounts generated by accounts preparation software. This process of copying data is time consuming and expensive. To overcome this limitation a number of accounts production software systems have facilities to link with spreadsheets. Data can be automatically transferred from the accounts production software to the spreadsheet program for further analysis. This is clearly a very useful facility which should be considered when purchasing software of this nature.

Financial modelling software, such as Micro-FCS, also has characteristics that lend themselves to the construction of budgeting models. As previously mentioned in Chapter 4, the modelling process is different from spreadsheets and is more suitable for handling complex models. This software is very powerful and has very good 'what if' facilities. However, it is much more expensive than spreadsheets, and for a small practice it may not be an economic proposition.

10.4 CASH FORECASTS

From small businesses, which will normally be the customers of small-to medium-sized practices, there is a growing demand for cash forecasts. The provision of these forecasts represents the most productive way in which a practice can expand its fee earning capacity.

Similar to budgetary control applications, the modelling process of spreadsheets and financial modelling software is particularly applicable to the construction of cash forecasts. Both types of software are very user-friendly in respect of the construction of such forecasts. For the practice to construct its own models using such software does take time and therefore money; however, there are many positive aspects to constructing your own models. In particular, those who use either spreadsheets or financial modelling packages for such applications will gain greater versatility in their use; they will then be able to apply these skills to other productive applications. Another key advantage is the user will have much greater flexibility in meeting the specific requirements of the practice.

An alternative to users designing their own models using spreadsheets and financial modelling software is a package specifically programmed for cash forecasts. These programs are invariably written for use with spreadsheets. A well-proven package is one developed by the chartered accountants Levy-Gee and CSM Ltd, and is marketed by both firms. In general the advantage with such packages is that, not only are they well proven but the practice does not have to spend time to develop its own models.

The model developed by Levy-Gee and CSM is part of a number of planning models they market — the sales analysis model was illustrated in Figure 5.7 of Chapter 5. The cash flow model is a twelve month projection and is generally flexible enough to cater for different types of clients, e.g. restaurants, pubs and farmers. There is also a facility to build in varying assumptions, i.e. a 'what if' facility. This facility, it should be said, is essential for such applications and it would be very surprising if it were not included. Figure 10.3 shows a sample printout from this package.

Another popular software cash forecasting package used by a number of accounting practices is ICASH from Independent Computer Solutions (Software) Ltd. This software runs under Lotus 1-2-3 or Symphony. The market for this type of package is rapidly expanding, and it is strongly recommended that any potential purchaser should choose a package that has been proven.

```
                                          EASY PROJECTIONS LTD - CASH FLOW FORECAST
                                          ============================================
                                          1ST JANUARY 1989 TO 31ST DECEMBER 1989
                                          ========================================
                         T.B. @ 01/01/89                Cash Movements
                         ----------------               --------------
                     DR      CR     Jan    Feb     Mar     Apr     May     Jun     Jul     Aug     Sep
                     ---------------------------------------------------------------------------------------
Receipts
--------
Sales            45,000         26,012 31,651 41,871 54,141 60,375 59,685 55,545 55,545 52,785
Discnt on Sales                      0      0      0      0      0      0      0      0      0
                                ------------------------------------------------------------------------
Total receipts                  26,012 31,651 41,871 54,141 60,375 59,685 55,545 55,545 52,785
--------------
Payments
--------
Purchases               40,000 23,834 32,683 43,712 36,843 33,471 34,466 44,246 44,298 62,462
Salaries/Wages           1,150  1,150  1,150  1,150  1,150  1,150  1,150  1,150  1,150  1,150
Telephones                                     6,000
Printing etc         500   500    500    500    500    500    500    500    500    500    500
Motor & Travel
Genrl Expenses
Commission
Rent & Rates
Light & Heat
Insurance
Repairs/Renewal
Audit & Acctcy
Bank Charges
Stock & WIP      65,000
Fixed Assets
VAT on Expenses          (500)                 (550)                 (600)
VAT               3,971  3,971      0      0  4,170      0      0  6,840      0      0
Resrves/Capital          41,029
                                ------------------------------------------------------------------------
Total Payments                  28,955 34,333 51,362 42,113 35,121 36,116 52,136 45,948 64,112
--------------
```

Opening Bank Bal.	0	25,000	(25,000) (27,943)(30,625)(41,407)(29,378) (4,124) 18,707 22,115 31,712
Net Month. Movement			(2,943) (2,682) (9,491) 12,028 25,254 23,570 3,409 9,597 (11,327)
Bank Int @ 17.0%			0 0 (1,291) 0 0 (739) 0 0 0

```
                                ------------------------------------------------------------------------
CLOSING BANK BALANCE            (27,943)(30,625)(41,407)(29,378) (4,124) 18,707 22,115 31,712 20,385
====================            ========================================================================
NET PROFIT
==========          ------------------
            £ 110,000 110,000
              ==============≠====
```

Figure 10.3 Cash flow forecast. Reproduced courtesy of Levy-Gee & Co.

Oct	Nov	Dec	Total		Adjustments		P&L Account		Balance Sheet	
			DR	CR	DR	CR	DR	CR	DR	CR
50,025	56,235	65,205		609,075	90,000			609,000	125,925	
0	0	0		0				0		0
50,025	56,235	65,205		609,075						
60,056	46,323	30,047	492,440				66,964	446,425		60,949
1,150	1,150	1,150	13,800					14,800		1,000
			6,000					6,000		
500	500	500	6,000					6,000		
			0					0		
			0					0		
			0					0		
			0					0		
			0					0		
			0					0		
			0					0		
			0					0		
			0				65,000	61,425	61,425	
			0					0	0	0
(600)			(2,250)			(2,250)		0	0	0
2,948	0	0	12,034		64,714	90,000	(2,250)		0	14,974
			0					0	0	41,029
58,158	47,973	31,697	528,024	609,075	154,714	154,714				
20,385	12,252	20,514	25,000	0						
(8,133)	8,262	33,508								
0	0	0	2,030				2,030			
12,252	20,514	54,022	54,022	0			54,022			
							23,420	0	0	123,420
			£ 609,075	609,075			£ 661,425	661,425	241,372	241,372

10.5 INVESTMENT APPRAISAL

The types of decision information service that can be offered to clients under this heading include:

1. project appraisal
2. the assessment of whether to expand a particular line of business
3. cost reduction programmes

The methodology used in such appraisals is discounted cash flow, that is the determination of the net present value or the internal rate of return. The time period involved in such decisions is relatively long and therefore the uncertainty is greater. Any software used must have a good range of 'what if' techniques so that this uncertainty element can be assessed in rational terms.

A system that does have the qualities required for such applications is the financial modelling software Micro-FCS. In particular, the range of 'what if' facilities are useful. There are two major commands:

1. sensitivity
2. target.

These commands were described in detail in Chapter 4 on financial modelling.

Another important feature of financial modelling packages is their flexibility. It is the user that models the application, and this does therefore give a great deal of freedom to the user *vis-à-vis* application packages. Figure 10.4 shows an illustration of a report generated by Micro-FCS.

There are also a number of packages on the market that are specifically written for investment appraisal. Cash Value from Hoskyns Group Ltd is typical, and is being used by a large number of customers. This package has sensitivity analysis and a standard report generation facility. One of the major differences from a modelling packages is that built in to the program is a facility for the assessment of taxation related to investment decisions. This is extremely useful as the process of building tax into such models can be quite complex.

10.6 USE OF GRAPHICS

'A picture is worth a thousand words.' Often key points can be put across extremely effectively by using graphs, particularly where comparisons are being made, such as between the performance of different companies or the relative advantages of competing invest-

B-J Holdings Ltd - Forecast Results over Next 7 Years

YEAR

	1	2	3	4	5	6	7
Sales Volume		100,000	108,000	116,640	125,971	136,049	
Revenue		60,000	65,448	71,391	77,873	84,944	
Raw Materials		13,000	15,120	16,913	18,996	21,337	
Labour		10,000	11,880	13,857	16,163	18,852	
Fixed Overheads		20,000	21,800	23,762	25,901	28,232	
Advertising		5,000	4,000	3,000	2,000	1,000	
Sub Total		12,000	12,648	13,859	14,813	15,523	
Capital Expenditure	15,000						
Change in Working Cap	12,000	1,090	1,189	1,296	1,414	(16,989)	
Pre Tax Cash Flow	(27,000)	10,910	11,459	12,563	13,399	32,512	
Tax Paid		(7,800)	6,240	6,956	7,622	8,147	8,538
Net Cash Flow	(27,000)	18,710	5,219	5,606	5,777	24,365	(8,538)
Cost of Capital	12%	12%	12%	12%	12%	12%	12%
DCF	(27,000)	16,706	4,161	3,990	3,671	13,825	(4,326)
NPV	11,028						
IRR(Yield)	29.64%						
Payback(Years)	3.55						

Figure 10.4 Investment appraisal of a seven-year project using Micro-FCS.

ments. In many cases, graphs form an essential part of a professional report; no practice that wishes to market itself successfully can afford now to ignore this tool.

Whereas, in the past, producing graphs was prohibitively expensive, the position in this respect has been transformed in recent years by the cheap availability of the hardware and software to print good quality graphs. Micro-FCS has excellent graphics, and even Lotus 1-2-3 and most other spreadsheets have reasonable facilities. Alternatively, a specialist graphics package such as Microsoft Chart may be preferred. Lotus 1-2-3 will produce line graphs, pie charts and bar charts; 1-2-3 graphics are not very flexible, but they are adequate for many users.

Good quality black-and-white graphs can be printed out on most standard dot matrix printers; the only other hardware requirement is that the microcomputer used has a graphics board installed, but these are usually supplied as standard on current business microcomputers.

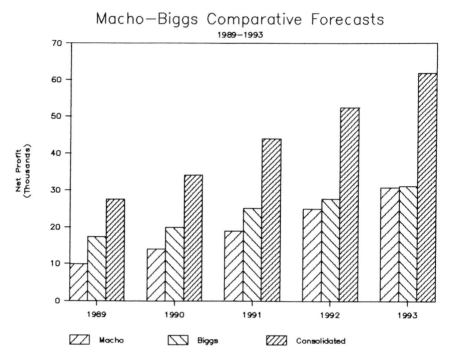

Figure 10.5 Use of graphics.

(Graphics boards were mentioned in Chapter 2 on hardware; they allow the screen to be addressed, when in graphics mode, as a set of dots — or pixels — rather than as rows of characters.) For example, Figure 10.5 shows a bar chart produced by Lotus 1-2-3 and printed on a Taxan Kaga KP-810 printer; the graph compares forecast net profits for companies in the Macho-Biggs Group, whose results were given in Figure 5.4. Graphs such as this are relatively easy to produce, although slow to print out because the graph has to be printed out dot-by-dot rather than printing whole characters as in text. The graph in Figure 10.5 highlights the forecast performance of different companies in the group far more readily that a simple presentation of a set of accounts.

More sophisticated graphics facilities are available which enable good quality colour graphs and charts to be produced, either as drawings or as colour slides. These can be produced by 1-2-3, but it may be preferable to use a specialist graphics package. The additional hardware requirements are either a graph plotter, a colour printer or a photographic device such as the Polaroid Palette, which produces colour photographs or slides direct from a disk file. It may be difficult to get such equipment to communicate with a microcomputer and it is probably not recommended to the occasional user — attempts at using colour graphics can be very time consuming, and frustrating.

Thus most accounting practices are unlikely to use colour graphics, and their needs are likely to be met by printing graphs from a dot matrix printer; however, this may not be true of their clients. For applications such as sales and promotion, colour graphics can help to improve the quality of presentations, and make substantial savings. It is also the case that good presentation of management information can be extremely important to the management accountant, and accountants in large companies often use sophisticated colour graphics equipment. However, effective use of colour graphics is rather beyond the scope of this book, and not yet a matter of great concern to accountants in small- to medium-sized practices.

10.7 LEASING

A major restriction on the growth of small businesses is the sources of finance available to purchase new modern equipment. The purchase of capital equipment can place a massive strain on cash flow for this size of business through the one-off payment. One way around this problem is leasing.

When a business leases an asset the asset can be used immediately and the payments will normally range over the effective life of the asset, thus easing the problems of cash flow. The amount and timing of the payments will be known with certainty through the leasing agreement. So the certainty of such fixed-term commitments makes cash management easy and is therefore very attractive to small companies.

The problem for small businesses in the decision to lease equipment is, however, the question of the relative cost of leasing compared to the outright purchase of a piece of equipment — more commonly known as the 'lease-or-buy' decision. The skills of the practising accountant can clearly help in such decisions.

The calculations required in a lease-or-buy decision, including the calculation of the implicit rate and the present value of the lease payments, are complex and lend themselves to computers. A software package, produced by Deloitte Haskins & Sells, called Lease Plus can be a useful acquisition for small- to medium-sized practices as an aid to advising clients on lease-or-buy decisions. This software was primarily designed to help accountants prepare the information to comply with the lease accounting requirements of SSAP 21; however, a number of small- to medium-sized practices are primarily using it to help them to advise clients. The main features of this software are to:

1. calculate the implicit rate of a lease
2. calculate the present value of the lease using the implicit rate
3. produce schedules of amortization and depreciation over the life of the lease
4. produce reports of leases complying with SSAP 21.

The use of leasing as an alternative source of finance for small businesses is certainly growing. Small business agencies are actively advising firms of this alternative. There is clearly a role for the practising accountant to advise clients which could contribute significantly to the fee income of the practice.

10.8 OTHER RELEVANT APPLICATIONS

Spreadsheets have been cited as relevant to the majority of the planning and control applications covered in this chapter. There has been a tendency in recent years for software firms to develop add-on facilities to spreadsheets.

An interesting package of this nature, marketed by Sagesoft, is Options. Options focuses on risk analysis in a far more sophisticated way than the normal type of 'what if' scenarios developed on spreadsheets. Options may, if preferred, be purchased with its own spreadsheet, and there is also a facility for graphical analysis. Figure 10.6 illustrates a report generated from Options showing in percentages the probablity of success or failure of a project.

```
                                                              £
99% chance of ------ NETT PROFIT/LOSS exceeding     - 15209.46
90% chance of ------ NETT PROFIT/LOSS exceeding     -  6945.08
80% chance of ------ NETT PROFIT/LOSS exceeding     -  3100.86
70% chance of ------ NETT PROFIT/LOSS exceeding     -   227.09
60% chance of ------ NETT PROFIT/LOSS exceeding        2191.39
50% chance of ------ NETT PROFIT/LOSS exceeding        4500.00
40% chance of ------ NETT PROFIT/LOSS exceeding        6808.61
30% chance of ------ NETT PROFIT/LOSS exceeding        9227.09
20% chance of ------ NETT PROFIT/LOSS exceeding       12100.86
10% chance of ------ NETT PROFIT/LOSS exceeding       15945.08
1%  chance of ------ NETT PROFIT/LOSS exceeding       24209.46
```

Figure 10.6 Options: risk analysis showing profitability in percentage of chances of success or failure.

10.9 CONCLUSIONS

The applications referred to in this chapter are seen as a principal way of increasing an accounting practice's fee income. However, it is important to stress that the information relating to the planning and control of a client's firm is not governed by legislation, thus the business does not have to produce this information to satisfy any statutory requirements. Also, it may not be apparent to clients that such a service will give them much help to run their businesses efficiently at a reasonable cost. Thus there is a need for the practice to market these services and thereby communicate to clients the advantages of using them.

The cost of marketing these services can now by quite reasonable. In particular, the desk-top publishing facilities referred to in Chapter 13 on word processing make it a feasible task for the practice to produce its own publicity at an economical cost. The practice could use mail-shots to existing and potential clients, and to organizations such as banks that may be willing to recommend them because of the quality of their services.

11 Stock control

This chapter is concerned with stock control, a topic which is extremely relevant to many professional accountants who frequently have to prepare and audit accounts for clients whose major asset is stock; even quite small businesses may have many thousands of pounds tied up in stock. In our research interviews, managers of small businesses often have expressed disquiet at having large amounts of stock, sometimes well over £100 000 in value, without knowing exactly what there is except at occasional stock-checks. Because the control of stock levels is important, and often critical to their clients, professional accountants must be in a position to advise them. The introduction of computer software is an important development in this area, and it is essential that the practice should have the knowledge and understanding to advise on this; there are also auditing implications, that the practice needs to be aware of.

It is clearly a matter of concern when so much money is tied up in stock, particularly as cash constraints are often critical with a small business; reducing average stock levels by even 10% can be of considerable benefit. There is also strong empirical evidence that inadequate funding is the major reason for insolvency in small businesses, and that such cash flow problems are often caused by holding excessive stocks. Moreover, a well-organized stock control system which shows clearly the precise asset value of current stocks can often be useful in persuading a bank manager to extend credit; apart from finding the information useful, it is likely to give him confidence that the business is well managed. A manual stock control system cannot usually readily produce such information, whereas a computer-based system will.

A second major concern is usually the **shrinkage cost**: shrinkage being the loss of stock due to deterioration or, more usually, pilfering. A computer-based system can also be beneficial in this respect because of the better quality of information available, but perhaps more especially because of the greater discipline that it imposes on the organization. Auditing a computer-based system is usually easier than auditing a manual system because it is merely a matter of ensuring that the procedures for preparing and checking the various computer inputs are being correctly operated. With a computer system, a list of current stock quantities can be readily obtained at any time; this makes it much easier to carry out periodic stock-checks on selected items, and increases the chances of necessary stock checks actually being carried out. Another useful feature of a computer system is that it becomes much easier to recognize slow-moving stock items; this is useful in identifying the stock items that are obsolete and should be written off.

11.1 OPERATIONAL RESEARCH APPROACH

Other important objectives for stock control are presented by operational researchers. They see the problem of stock control as essentially being to mimimize total costs, these costs being to some extent economic or opportunity costs rather than true accounting costs. In a simple operational research model, one assumes that prices are fixed, and that demand for the stock item is constant from year to year. The following additional costs then need to be considered in order to determine an optimal stock-holding policy:

1. **Order costs** where a fixed cost for ordering a batch is assumed; this cost represents the delivery and clerical costs associated with an order.
2. **Holding costs** representing the cost per unit held of a particular item of stock, including both warehouse costs and cost of capital.
3. **Stockout costs** representing the economic cost to the business of being out of stock of the particular item because of loss of customer goodwill.

An operational research model would typically seek to find the optimum order quantity so as to be able to find a trade-off between, on the one hand, holding too much stock and incurring high stock holding costs and, on the other hand, holding too little stock and then incurring high order costs because of the excessive number of orders made. A second trade-off is likely to occur between stockout costs and holding costs; stockouts may be reduced by holding additional 'buffer' stock during the reorder period, but at the price of incurring additional holding costs. Again, the optimum balance needs to be struck.

Thus the two parameters required for each item in a stock control system are the order quantity (how much is to be ordered each time) and the reorder level (the stock level at which a new order must be issued). Some specialist stock control packages will track demand using exponential forecasting methods, and will then recalculate the optimum values for these parameters. Most microcomputer stock control packages do not include any such optimization procedures; nevertheless, they do usually allow the user to specify order quantities and reorder levels for each product. Some packages also allow a warning level to be defined for each product, to indicate when stock is getting extremely low.

Another major factor to be considered is the effect of variable pricing, as the models discussed so far consider only fixed prices. Even where there are no seasonal fluctuations, discounts are often available for large orders, and this can change the optimum ordering decision. Moreover, if price increases are expected, it may be prudent to build up stocks prior to such an increase. It is possible to construct more complex models which cover factors such as discounting, but this is unlikely to be worth doing for most small businesses. The sensible conclusion is that the basic operational research models can provide a useful guide in many situations, although the assumptions made will sometimes prove unsatisfactory. It is also important to emphasize that these are not just theoretical ideas of interest to academics; the **economic order quantity** approach has been used by businesses for many years, and has proved to be of considerable practical value.

Finally, 'ABC' analysis of stock can often be useful in determining whether major efforts should be made. This implies classifying stock by value into one of three categories:

A: high-value items, few in quantity, but representing up to 80% of stock by value
B: medium-value items
C: low-value items which may represent 80–90% of stock by quantity, but less than 5% by value.

A simple 'two-bin' ordering system (reordering when the stock level falls below a certain level in a bin) is usually adequate for 'C-type' items. On the other hand, 'A-type' items tend to be so expensive that they are ordered in ones or twos when needed, and customers are not usually surprised if such items are not available *ex* stock. The major effort in planning stock levels always has to be made in designing the ordering procedures for the 'B-type' items. Over a period of time, a computer-based system can be extremely useful in this respect, both by monitoring the usage of different stock items, and by highlighting key items.

11.2 STOCK CONTROL SOFTWARE

Having outlined some of the possible benefits from computer-based stock control, it is now appropriate to look in more detail at relevant software. Almost invariably, the stock control software encountered on microcomputers by professional accountants will be designed as one module of an integrated accounting system. It may, however, be used as a 'stand-alone' package, rather than be linked to sales invoicing. Occasionally, stock control may form part of a production scheduling system, but such software is more likely to be encountered on larger computers than on microcomputers.

A stand-alone stock control package is a relatively simple piece of software, since it merely has to keep a stock list together with relevant stock quantities, and to print reports periodically. This is an obvious application for a database package, and a small client may set up a perfectly adequate stock control system in this way; this saves the cost of stock control software, which may, in any case, be too complex for the particular application. However, a system set up by a client using a database package will probably not satisfy any reasonable auditing requirements; controls will be lacking, and there will probably be no audit trail. Since the major justification for using a computer is likely to be increased control, it is usually worthwhile purchasing stock control software, rather than using a database package.

The software we will consider here is the Pegasus stock control package, which integrates with the Pegasus Senior accounting software considered already in Chapter 8; most integrated accounting software includes stock control packages with facilities similar to those described in this section. Pegasus is probably not suitable for a large multi-site stock records system. The costing methods available are restricted to **last in, first out** (LIFO) and **average cost**. Pegasus will not cope with a FIFO (first in, first out) system, as is sometimes necessary, because of the very detailed records that FIFO requires. (Although it is recognized that the LIFO method of costing does have the advantage that stock items are charged out at the latest price, it should of course be remembered that for stock valuation purposes the method is outlawed under SSAP 9).

Figure 11.1 shows a typical stock record listed by the Pegasus stock record print routine, together with details of recent stock movements for that item. As indicated previously, the reorder level and reorder quantity are defined by the user so as to minimize total costs, while the minimum stock level is used to provide an emergency reminder if the stock should ever fall below that level. The cost price is used for

```
P11MERC190    /01    AUTO PAINT - MERC. BLUE
```

Cost Code		Supplier Code	TUR04327
Stock Category	BS	Suppl Part No	190-SL1414-028
Factor		Supplier Code	
Assembly Indicator	N	Suppl Part No	
Unit Weight	0.00	Supplier Code	
Unit Volume	1.00	Suppl Part No	
Discount Code A	40.00%	Alternate Ref	P1123/01
Discount Code B	20.00%	Analysis Code	111S3
Discount Code C	15.00%	Bin Location	P1
Qty Issued 1 Mth	283	VAT Code	1
Qty Issued 2 Mths	246	Cost Price	1.85/LITRE
Qty Issued 3+ Mths	873	Sell Price 1	3.95/LITRE
Last issued	25.02.88	Sell Price 2	3.80/LITRE
On order	450	Re-order level	150
Allocated	85	Re-order Qty	420
In stock	120	Minimum Stock	50
On Order	450	Re-order level	150
Allocated (Orders)	65	Re-order Qty	420
Allocated (B.O.M.)	0	Minimum Stock	50
Allocated (Manual)	15	Free Stock	35
In Stock	120		

Type	Date	Ref/order	Qty	
P/Order	11.02.88	PAD7532	10	Bal 400 Due 13.02.87 From TUR04327
Receipt	12.02.88	PAD7534	50	
S/Order	17.02.88	SED1321	150	Completed
Issue	24.02.88	000001	45	

Figure 11.1 Pegasus: stock record print. Reproduced courtesy of Pegasus Software Ltd.

stock valuation, the two selling prices being intended for different groups of customers. In addition, the stock record contains the following stock quantities:

1. quantity in stock
2. quantity allocated
3. quantity on order.

For reasons of control, these stock quantities cannot be amended directly when the main part of the stock record is created or amended. Instead, they are amended via the accounts system or by using the routines for entering stock movements or updating orders. Alternatively, the quantity in stock may be changed by making a stock adjustment as a result of a stock check. In accounting terms, it is clearly important to separate stock adjustments from the regular stock issues.

The most useful feature of a stock control system is the 'on-line' access, to be able to determine immediately, in response to a customer request, whether a particular item is in stock. Pegasus also offers a number of reports, as well as facilities for defining customized reports where necessary. The standard reports available are:

1. *Stock movements report.* Details of all deliveries, issues and returns for each stock item in current period.
2. *Outstanding purchase orders report.*
3. *Stock valuation report.* This is shown in Figure 11.2, and is clearly important for accounting purposes.
4. *Reorder report.* This lists all items below reorder level and not currently on order, and is shown in Figure 11.3. Warnings are also

```
        B & J PRODUCTS LTD

28.02.88         Stock Valuation Report        Page 1

Stock Ref/Location              Quantity   Cost  Selling  Cost    Selling  Potential No
                                           Price Price    Value   Value    Profit    Days

A001      /01   TRACTION ASSEMBLY     87   38.28  54.96   3330.36 4781.52  1451.16
A001      /02   TRACTION ASSEMBLY     30   38.28  54.96   1148.40 1648.80   500.40
P1123     /01   AUTO PAINT - D BLUE  128    1.65   4.27    211.20  546.56   335.36   26
P1123     /02   AUTO PAINT - D BLUE   18    1.65   4.27     29.70   76.86    47.16   27
R13       /02   SHEET METAL 10/10     30   25.14  38.84    754.20 1165.20   411.00

                Actual Stock Value                        5473.86 8218.94 2745.08
                Value including Minus Qty Items           5473.86 8218.94 2745.06
```

Figure 11.2 Pegasus: stock valuation report. Reproduced courtesy of Pegasus Software Ltd.

```
        B & J PRODUCTS LTD

27.02.88        Re-order Report          Page 1

 Stock             In    Qty      On   Re-order              Supplier  Supplier
Reference Location Stock Allocated Order Qty                 Reference Name

A002      /01      10    24        0    5+  MINUS STOCK  WIL04225 Williams Ltd
TRACTION SUSPENSION ASSEMBLY
M101      /02      20     0        0   50                 FUR01224 Furndale Ltd
COOLING RADIATOR
T12       /01      25     0       20   50   BELOW MIN     TUR04327 Turner Supplies Gmbh
TIMBER - 16/4/2
```

Figure 11.3 Pegasus: reorder report. Reproduced courtesy of Pegasus Software Ltd.

added where the item is below the minimum level or out of stock. This report should normally be printed at least once a week and used as a basis for purchase ordering.

5. *Price list.* This includes both specified and discounted prices.
6. *Stocktake list.* This lists all stock items together with bin locations, either with or without stock quantities.
7. *Issues report.* This lists all stock issues for the current period for a specified range of stock items.
8. *Issues history report.* This is shown in Figure 11.4; it is particularly useful for highlighting 'slow movers', enabling obsolete stock to be eliminated.

11.3 SECURITY AND CONTROL

Tight control is essential in a stock control system if losses are to be kept to a minimum; where the system is perceived to be lax, pilfering and other losses will be much more common. Thus there need to be clear definitions of who is authorized to carry out various tasks in relation to the computer system, with a password control written into the software. As with other Pegasus modules, the stock control module has three levels of password authorization:

1. Level 1 — access to all routines, including parameter updates.
2. Level 2 — reorganization routines and daily processing.
3. Level 3 — daily processing only.

Many clients will have only one employee using the stock control system; for larger systems, the Level 1 user will be able to use the

B & J PRODUCTS LTD

27.02.88	Issues History Report			Page 1
	This Period	Last Period	Period 2	Period 3
A001 /01	23	45	32	65
TRACTION ASSEMBLY				
M101 /02	45	72	53	137
COOLING RADIATOR				
P1123 /01	191	212	178	456
AUTO PAINT - D BLUE				

Figure 11.4 Pegasus: issues history report. Reproduced courtesy of Pegasus Software Ltd.

audit trail prints to investigate where problems arise.

Finally, it is important to remember that a well-run computer system is not a substitute for a well-managed warehouse; it can only run in parallel with the physical system, and adequate control of the actual goods is also necessary. However, a computer system can be valuable in indicating problems, and in facilitating more regular stock-checks.

11.4 USERS OF COMPUTER-BASED STOCK CONTROL

Although there may be some saving in clerical costs by using a micro-computer, that is not usually the major consideration in a stand-alone stock control system. Instead, the benefits are likely to be tighter control, and better and more immediate information. However, where stock control is linked into a sales invoicing or manufacturing system, there may also be a worthwhile reduction in such costs.

The cost of setting up and running a stock control system can be fairly high because of the time required for data entry. Setting up a stock list initially can be very time consuming, as it may well include several thousand stock items; when the system is running there may be a large number of low-value transactions to be processed. These costs are probably acceptable if the new system is replacing an existing clerical one, but for many clients, such as small retailers, this will not be the case. Those clients will usually have kept only very limited records of stock because of the disproportionate amount of paperwork entailed in keeping accurate records. In such a situation no saving in clerical costs can be made, although a computer system would offer greater management control.

Clearly, a system which leads to a substantial increase in administrative costs is unlikely to justify itself. Whether it is likely to be worthwhile depends on the type of business that the client is running, and the way in which the stock control system is to operate. As a rough guide, it is convenient to classify users of stock control systems as either manufacturers, wholesalers or retailers, each of which may require a different approach.

Of these, the wholesaler's system is likely to be the most amenable to computerization. Typically, wholesalers buy in large batches from manufacturers or importers and sell the same goods in smaller quantities to retailers. The turnover of individual items is high, and therefore the cost of operating a computer system represents only a small fraction of their total operating costs. Most wholesalers use a computer for accounting, and hence stock control forms an essential part of their integrated accounting system. Moreover, the administrative cost of running the stock control system tends to be fairly low because stock issues and returns usually occur as a result of sales invoicing transactions.

It is much more difficult to generalize about manufacturers — no two manufacturing systems will ever be the same. Large manufacturers will normally use systems based on minicomputers or mainframes rather than microcomputers. However, smaller accounting practices will have many clients involved in assembly work or small-scale manufacturing, for whom stock control is a major problem. These manufacturers will need to stock raw materials prior to production as well as some finished goods. Although the stock control system for finished goods may be similar to that for a wholesaler, the situation can be more complex — small manufacturers often only stock very popular items and make other items to order. For raw materials, the stock control system may need to be linked in with the production scheduling system in order to ensure that the materials needed for production are available. However, a small manufacturer can often make effective use of a computer as a decision aid without having to computerize all their operations; for them, a simple stock control system, possibly linked to purchase or sales invoicing, could be useful.

Smaller accounting practices will usually find that among their clients it is principally retailers who need to concern themselves with problems of stock control. However, although many retailers use microcomputers for their purchase ledger and word processing, they have been less ready to use computers for stock control. This may seem surprising, but there are a number of reasons:

1. Retailers often have no sales invoicing system, because all sales are by direct payment, reducing any potential saving in clerical costs.
2. Recording 'stock issues' (i.e. sales) may impose a substantial administrative burden. Retailers often prefer to count stock on shelves periodically, rather than attempting to keep ongoing stock records.
3. The effort in setting up a stock system may be prohibitive because of the very long stock list maintained.

Large stores have been using computers for many years for stock control, using Kimball tag readers or electronic tills to provide the computer input. In the past, such equipment was far too expensive for the small retailer, but current technology has developed to such an extent that it is now feasible for them to use a microcomputer for stock control. A number of off-licence chains are using microcomputers, as are some car spares retailers; it is likely that many other small retailers will follow suit.

One particularly useful development has been that of electronic tills designed for the small retailer which can automatically update stock records. Such a till can either be used as a stand-alone stock control system or connected to the microcomputer that processes the accounts. Another advantage is that the shop assistant merely has to type in the stock code, leaving the till to retrieve prices and calculate totals. Electronic tills have also proved extremely popular for use in bars in drinking clubs; clubs hold stocks of considerable value, where shrinkage is a very major problem.

Another major development is likely to be in setting up stock lists. For some retailers, this is not a serious problem; for example, club bars have only a very limited number of stock items and some shops may only have a few hundred stock items. However, builders' merchants or retailers of car spares may need to hold many thousands of stock items; for them, the answer is likely to be to get their stock lists and future updates on disk from external sources, either from their trade association or from commercial specialists. Where retailers with a large number of stock items do use computers, the previously slow service to customers does improve noticeably; this also represents a cost saving to the retailer, because time saved for the customer is time saved for the retail assistant. Such systems also yield considerable benefits for management in terms of maintaining financial control, and financing operations is often the major consideration when a high proportion of company assets consist of stocks.

11.5 STOCK CONTROL: THE AUDIT IMPLICATIONS

In the introduction to this chapter, the importance of stock control for small businesses was emphasized. For many small businesses this asset, in terms of value, will probably be the largest item in the balance sheet. The audit, in such cases, will therefore tend to focus on stock.

Earlier in this chapter we referred to the problems of businesses which do not employ a continuous stock record system. Reference was made to the inevitable lack of control and the requirement for a physical stock-check at least once a year. From the auditor's point of view, it is likely that these weaknesses in the internal control system will be questioned; this will probably result in some form of qualification in the audit report. It is also the case that the audit work related to the physical stock-check will be time consuming and burdensome. In contrast, where an effective continuous recording system is maintained, as for example by using a computerized system, then the auditor will normally be able to place a greater reliance on the internal control system. The auditor's involvement in testing the relevant aspects of the physical stock-checking will also be reduced.

When a client is using a computerized system of stock control, the emphasis in the approach to the audit does tend to differ from that for a manual system. One of the major tasks in the audit will be substantive tests on stock movements and on the stock values shown in the accounts. The information required for these tests will often be available from reports generated by the software. This will result in the auditor spending significantly less time in extracting and analysing the information from stock records. For example, the Pegasus software generates a routine report that analyses the history of stock movements (see Figure 11.4); this information will be required by the auditor to identify potential obsolete stock. It is unlikely that this analysis would be readily available from a manual system.

Where relevant audit information is not produced in the form of reports on a routine basis, access and extraction is relatively quicker and simpler using stock control software. For example, it is much easier to scan through items of stock on a screen or from a printout rather than ploughing through a manual set of records. The capability to select and extract information quickly is also useful to the auditor when testing the effectiveness of the recording system with actual stock items.

The time taken in carrying out substantive tests (to ensure that the value of items in the accounts are correct), which often tends to be time consuming and tedious work, will therefore be decreased substantially. However, due to the more complex nature of software systems, it is important that the client maintains strong internal controls, and thus there is a greater need for the auditor to carry out compliance tests on these controls (these are tests to ensure that internal controls are complied with).

The use of such systems for stock control does mean there must be an effective audit trail; in the development of the software for accounting applications, systems analysts have been very aware of the need for an adequate audit trail. However, there is still a need for the user to ensure that references and comments against recorded transactions are sufficient to follow the transaction through the accounting system. The auditor has a responsibility to advise the client that such references and comments are adequate to ensure that an effective audit can be carried out.

11.6 CONCLUSIONS

Many clients are likely to derive considerable benefits from using computer-based stock control; some of these, especially retailers, could not have considered using such a system until very recently. The benefits for the client are principally improved information and better financial control, which may also make auditing more straight-forward and thus reduce audit fees. Other possible benefits for the client are reduced administrative costs, and the goodwill generated by providing a better service to the customer.

For the accounting practice, it is important to encourage clients to take the most efficient approach possible. Moreover, a professionally organized client will make the task of the auditor much smoother, enabling the practice to operate according to planned schedules. A computer-based stock control system will enable the accountant to plan carefully the client's financial requirements, and to take steps well in advance when it is necessary to raise extra capital.

12 Payroll

Payroll has always been seen as an obvious application for computers, and the earliest commercial computer in the UK was developed by Leo in 1954 specifically for payroll calculation. Although simple in principle, payroll calculation tends to be awkward and detailed, and in addition to the actual payslips, it is also essential to produce regular reports in different forms for various parties (internal reporting on departments, and external reports for the Inland Revenue, DHSS, etc.).

Thus, at first sight, payroll seems an ideal application for a computer and that is probably the case for companies with more than about fifty employees, especially if a significant proportion of staff are weekly paid. For small businesses, a manually processed payroll is probably yet another weekly chore for an already harassed manager; however, the benefits realized by computerization may be outweighed by the costs. Computerized payroll requires a significant initial investment in terms of purchasing software and training staff; payroll is also subject to annual government budget changes, and frequent amendments to government legislation. The net result is that with only a few staff on the payroll, it is probably not worth the effort for a small client to run his own payroll on a computer, particularly as it would be necessary for him to register as a user of personal data under the 1984 *Data Protection Act.*

The professional accountant therefore has two services that he can offer his clients in relation to computerized payroll. For larger businesses which process their own payroll, the professional accountant's role may simply be to offer advice and to audit their system periodically to ensure that adequate checks are applied. However, smaller businesses will often find it more efficient to have their payroll processed on a 'bureau' basis, and many accounting practices now run such services for their clients. Apart from the question of efficiency, a major concern with payroll is preserving confidentiality; indeed, payroll files inevitably contain personal data which is covered by the 1984 *Data Protection Act*. It is much easier for a small business to maintain confidentiality if the payroll is processed externally, such as by their accountant, rather than at their own office.

12.1 CHOICE OF SOFTWARE

Whether the payroll is processed by the client or by the practice on a bureau basis — or indeed by the practice for their own employees — the software used is likely to be similar. The package used to illustrate this chapter is the payroll module from the Pegasus Senior accounting software. All integrated accounting packages include a payroll module, and most payroll programs operate in a fairly similar way to Pegasus, although they may differ in the degree of security offered. For most smaller businesses, Pegasus is a good, basic payroll package with adequate security and all necessary reports. However, some packages do offer greater sophistication in their range of analysis and reporting. A client with a multi-company organization and a need for a wide range of reports across departments and companies, together with a need to apportion costs, might find a more expensive payroll package such as Omicron more appropriate.

Although there is a wide range of payroll packages available, it is extremely important to choose a package which is well proven, and backed by a company that has the resources to update the software as necessary, whenever new government legislation is introduced. To cite just one example, in April 1988, new government pension rules were introduced which vastly increased the number of possible deductions that could be made. This required considerable updating of software; one very large computer bureau, CMG Services, had to rewrite their payroll and pension package at a cost of £1m. Admittedly, the CMG software is designed for very large companies, but even updating microcomputer software can be a costly matter.

12.2 PROCESSING PAYROLL BY COMPUTER

Every business tends to have individual variations in how employees are paid, and a totally standardized system will be of little use to most companies. Payroll packages tend to be highly parameterized; they allow a wide range of flexibility in the type of special payments and deductions that may be made.

Figure 12.1 shows the various stages involved in processing a

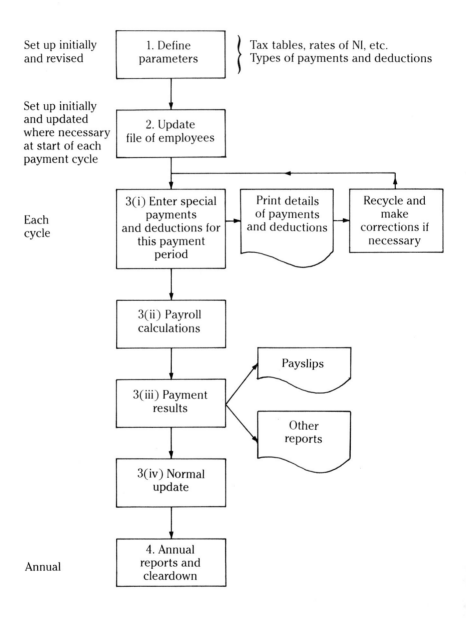

Figure 12.1 Stages in payroll processing.

payroll by computer. The process is likely to be very similar, whatever software is used, but there will be major variations according to the type of business. For example, a professional office may have only monthly paid staff with no overtime and few special payments, whereas a small building firm may have both weekly and monthly paid staff with a wide range of special payments. Where a business has both weekly and monthly staff, it is usual to process the two groups completely separately.

Thus, the first stage in setting up a computerized payroll will be to set up the various parameters required. Standard parameters will include tax tables and national insurance rates, but special payments and deductions will also have to be set up for the particular company (or group of staff within the company).

In the main, these parameters will be left unchanged once they have been set up, subject only to government tax changes and other periodic revisions. However, changes in government legislation will sometimes require more fundamental changes in programming logic; in such situations, well-known and reputable software companies will rapidly produce updates for their clients. This highlights the importance of choosing software which has a large customer base.

The second stage in the payroll process is to create a file of employees, which will include relevant personal details as well as data required for payroll calculations (tax code, earnings year-to-date, tax paid year-to-date, and so on). Entering this data is the major task when the system is first set up; this file will also need to be regularly updated as personnel details change.

Finally, at the end of each payment period, details need to be entered of all special payments to be made for items such as overtime and expense claims. These details need to be scrutinized very carefully and corrected where necessary before the individual payslips are printed out.

12.3 FEATURES OF PEGASUS PAYROLL SYSTEM

Pegasus allows either weekly, fortnightly, four-weekly or monthly payments to a group of staff, the only restriction being that a separate file must be used for each different payment period. Staff may be paid either in cash, directly to a bank or giro account, or by a cheque printed by the computer on special stationery.

In addition to fulfilling the standard requirements for PAYE tax, national insurance and statutory sick pay, Pegasus allows up to 30 different types of payments or deductions to be defined by the user.

Typical payments may include standard pay, overtime, shift allowances, commission and expenses; deductions may include health schemes, union dues, car loan repayments and private pension schemes. In printing the payslip, Pegasus prints only those payments or deductions relevant to the particular individual.

Apart from the various statutory reports and a coinage analysis showing what coins and notes are required from the bank for wage packets, Pegasus also produces various reports for management control purposes, such as the employee print shown in Figure 12.2. Another useful report is the departmental analysis of the payroll — a section of this is shown in Figure 12.3. The assumption underlying this analysis is that the first two characters of the employee code act as a departmental code.

Lastly, the payroll system also produces an update file for the nominal ledger. This can be used simply to update standard accounts such as PAYE, NI employer's contributions and wages control; more usefully, reference codes within the employee record may be used to modify the nominal codes and hence to post the employee costs against various cost centres. Hence, the Pegasus payroll does integrate with the nominal ledger to offer an effective management accounting system.

J-B PRODUCTS LIMITED

07.03.88   **Employee Records**   Page 5

P1AD012 Mr A Davenport

Code	0033	SSP Days	1	Gross T.P.	259.45	Gross T.D.	7692.95
Tax Code	359H	Days/Week	5	Tax T.P.	125.00	Tax T.D.	1311.00
N.I. No.	PP123565N	Sex	M	Net T.P.	9.63	Pens'n T.D.	123.12
Paid by	Giro					S.S.P. T.D.	9.35
C/Centre	PD02			Average Pay	150.37		
Birth Date	22.10.47	Hol Ent	20	S.S.P. Rate	9.3500		
Start Date	12.01.75	Director	N				

<------------National Insurance------------>
                                                    ´ERS   ´EES   C/OUT
Bank A/C   24566523 Co-operative Bank
            20-45-80 Wellingborough   T.P. A   15.46   13.32

          Note: T.P.= this period, T.D. = year to date

Figure 12.2 Pegasus: employee print. Reproduced courtesy of Pegasus Software Ltd.

J-B PRODUCTS LIMITED

07.03.88	Departmental Payroll Analysis - Period 48		Page 1

Department P1

<——— Pay Elements ———>			<——— Voluntary Deductions ———>			
Payments	Type	Amount	Units	Deduction	Type	Amount	Balance

Payments	Type	Amount	Units	Deduction	Type	Amount	Balance
Basic Pay	T	346.50	77.00	Pension	X	0.00	26.45
Overtime 1	T	10.00	2.00	Insurances		2.00	14.00
				Loan	R	5.00	
				Cleaning	N	0.50	15.15
				Union Subl	A	1.15	9.60

This Period Totals

Taxable Pay	356.50	Cash Equiv	0.00	Pensions	0.00
Non-Taxable	0.00			Voluntary	8.65
S.S.P.	0.00	Tot Taxable	356.00	P.A.Y.E.	76.79
CI Hol Pay	0.00	NI 'ERS	37.20	NI 'EES	32.03
				True Net	239.03
Total Pay	356.50				356.50

Figure 12.3 Pegasus: departmental analysis of payroll. Reproduced courtesy of Pegasus Software Ltd.

12.4 SECURITY AND CONTROL

Clearly, the need for adequate security and control in respect of payroll is a major consideration for the following reasons:

1. *requirements of confidentiality*: personal details, and possibly salaries, must be kept private
2. *need for accuracy*: employees tend to get very upset if mistakes are made in their payslips
3. *danger of fraud*: payroll offers relatively simple opportunities for fraud if control is poor, and criminal cases do occur frequently.

Thus there is a need for strict control at all stages in the preparation and processing of payroll. The precise controls would depend on the size of the business, and on whether the system was to be run by the client himself or by the professional accountant. Some typical controls might be as follows:

Separation of responsibilities
Ideally, one member of staff should be responsible for preparation of data input and another for computer input and processing. This

enables independent checks to be made on results, ensuring a high degree of accuracy. The chances of fraud happening are also reduced, since collusion becomes necessary.

Password control

Passwords and at least two levels of authorization are essential, and a senior member of staff should set up the various parameters. These may not be changed by other users with a lower level of authorization, their role being the regular input and processing of payroll data. In fact, Pegasus allows three levels of password:

Level 1 — Parameter updates, nominal analysis, payroll update, special update/reports
Level 2 — Payroll calculation
Level 3 — All other processing.

The senior member of staff, as a Level 1 user, will also have sole access to the audit trail, thus enabling him to monitor the work of junior staff where necessary.

Where an accounting practice is processing payrolls for several clients, each payroll will have separate files, with a different set of passwords for each client.

Input controls

Large companies make considerable use of standard controls such as existence and range checks, and batch control totals. Pegasus includes checks for existence of employee codes, but does not include more sophisticated checks, which are probably not appropriate to a small business with only a few employees.

Output controls

These are likely to provide the best means of control in any organization, but will be especially effective in a small business. Errors often become immediately obvious when reports are examined by the employee responsible for preparing data input, or by the manager concerned.

If these points seem slightly daunting to a small business, this is deliberate; payroll does require extreme care. In some respects, a computerized payroll requires less care than a manual payroll, since only the data input requires checking rather than the actual calculations. Indeed, it is doubtful whether it is worthwhile for a small business with only a few employees to process their own payroll at all, given the complications involved and the availability of bureau services.

12.5 CONCLUSIONS

For all but the smallest practices, it will be worthwhile running the practice payroll on a computer. Apart from the saving in clerical costs, the practice will also gain experience which will be useful if it is to advise clients effectively.

On the other hand, processing a computerized payroll (or indeed any payroll) may seem somewhat daunting to many clients; for them, it may well be sensible to have it run on a bureau basis, even if they have their own microcomputer for accounting applications. Thus, computerized payroll offers a number of useful opportunities to an accounting practice that is seeking to offer a complete service to its clients, and is an essential tool for a practice that wishes to market itself professionally.

13 Word processing and the electronic office

Any professional accounting office spends a considerable amount of time sending out relatively standardized letters to clients. They will also need to send out standard letters to other businesses as part of their audit function, for example requesting confirmation of balances from the client's bank or confirmation of accounts from debtors. Use of a computer for word processing can considerably reduce the amount of typing involved, as well as improving the quality of presentation.

Similarly, most practices need to produce reports for the client or for the client's bank, which go through a process of drafting by accounts seniors and redrafting by partners. Often, the report needs to be retyped, resulting in further cost to the practice. In particular, the 1985 *Companies Act* lays down strict legal requirements for the production of annual accounts for any company. These must contain a directors' report, together with various notes to the accounts and a statement on accounting policies; it may also contain a chairman's statement. Although this can usually all be typed out using an accounts production package, there is likely to be a large amount of typing involved and it is probably not efficient to have accounts staff doing this work. It is usually better to produce the figures using an accounts production package, and to output these results to a disk file; this can then be edited by word processing, allowing the main typing work to be done by secretarial staff.

The implication therefore is that any accounting practice, however small, will realize considerable benefits from using a computer for word processing even if they do not use a computer for any other applications. However, maximum benefit will be achieved if a computer is also used for the various accounting applications within the practice, and if these applications are fully integrated with word processing. Clearly, this involves organizational problems as well as technical ones. These will be discussed, together with the concept of the electronic office system, based on an integrated system and a centralized database for the practice. Many professional accountants now feel that the only efficient way to run a practice is to implement practice automation based on such a system.

Another application of increasing importance to professional accountants is **desk-top publishing** (DTP), enabling accountants to market their services positively in a competitive market. Desk-top publishing allows users to do their own electronic typesetting for very little outlay, and can be used to produce good quality publicity material at very low prices. Whilst not appropriate to normal accounting work, this is ideal for producing the type of periodic newsletter or information sheet that many accounting firms circulate to their clients.

13.1 WORD PROCESSING

The essential characteristic of a word processing system is that documents are not printed directly; instead, the document is displayed on a screen and recorded on to a disk file. This means that corrections can easily be made, and the document only printed when complete and correct. Reports can also be redrafted without complete retyping, and standard letters can be set up which are then modified appropriately for individual recipients.

As with all computer applications, word processing requires appropriate hardware together with suitable software to drive it. The typical hardware would be a single-user microcomputer, possibly attached to a local area network, connected to a suitable printer. The microcomputer should either have a monochrome or a high quality colour screen, together with a letter quality printer. A number of possible choices for the printer were described in Chapter 2; either a daisy-wheel printer or a laser printer would be suitable, or even possibly a good quality dot matrix printer.

There are a number of popular word processing packages on the market, selling for between £200 and £400; some well-known packages are Lotus Manuscript, Wordstar, Wordcraft, Word Perfect, Displaywrite, Multimate Advantage and Microsoft Word, but there are many others. Many thousands of copies have been sold of each of these packages — indeed well over a million copies of Wordstar alone. Each package tends to have slightly different features which appeal to different users, but for the basic work of an accounting office, it probably does not matter greatly which of these packages is selected. However, it is essential for the firm to standardize on one word processing package to avoid compatibility problems; for example, a file produced by Wordcraft could not be directly read by Wordstar because each package inserts its own different control characters into the text. It may also be necessary to consider compatibility with other software, such as desk-top publishing software.

Finally, there are a number of cheaper word processing packages on the market, costing from £50 to £100 and designed for cheap microcomputers such as the Amstrad. These tend to be restricted in their facilities, and are often 'cut down' versions of more expensive software. In general, such software is not a sensible choice for a professional office, although it might be useful for a single practitioner wishing to purchase a cheap word processing system.

Most word processing packages operate in two modes: a file mode (which is usually the opening mode) and an editing mode. The file mode allows files to be printed, as well as allowing essential tasks to be performed such as copying, renaming or deleting files. There should also be the option of selecting a different subdirectory, which is essential if different types of documents are to be kept on separate subdirectories; the use of subdirectories was explained in Chapter 3, and efficient organization of files is essential in a busy accounting office. Typically, the files relating to different partners would be on different subdirectories; alternatively, files relating to particular types of work might be on the same subdirectory, as might the files relating to one large client. Within a subdirectory, the file extension (see Chapter 3) also provides a useful means of classifying files into groups.

A typical word processing session would involve choosing the edit option from the file menu, editing and saving a document as a file, and then returning to file mode to print the completed document. Figure 13.1 shows the opening file menu for Wordstar, while Figure 13.2 shows a document being edited on the screen.

There are usually two forms of editing: **document** and **non-document**. Accounting offices will use document mode for most of their work; a document file is assumed to consist of paragraphs, so that where text is inserted, the paragraph can automatically be reformed within the correct margins. A non-document file consists of separate lines with no specified margins; non-document mode is used mainly for creating computer programs or macro-programs in data-base languages, but may be needed for creating lists of names and

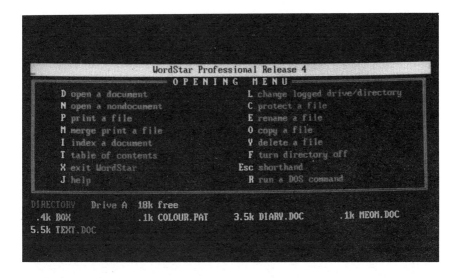

Figure 13.1 Wordstar: opening file menu. Reproduced courtesy of MicroPro International Ltd.

addresses for a mailing system.

The main difference in word processing as opposed to conventional typing is that a 'carriage return' is typed only at the end of the paragraph, and not at the end of each line. In the case of word-processing, there is a facility known as **word-wrap**: when the right-hand margin is reached, the word that is currently being typed automatically drops down to the next line. The operator simply carries on typing until the end of the paragraph; because the paragraph is treated as one entity, text can be inserted and the paragraph immediately reformed to the correct margins.

Most word processing software is of the **wysiwyg** type: 'wysiwyg' stands for 'what you see is what you get'. It is never possible to emulate precisely printed output on a screen, but in a wysiwyg system, the print layout will be reproduced together with underlining and possibly different typefaces if the computer has a graphics board. The alternative to a wysiwyg system is one where the document is typed in a standard format and only formatted correctly at the printing stage; some professional journalists prefer this approach, but for an accounting office the wysiwyg approach is simpler and much more appropriate.

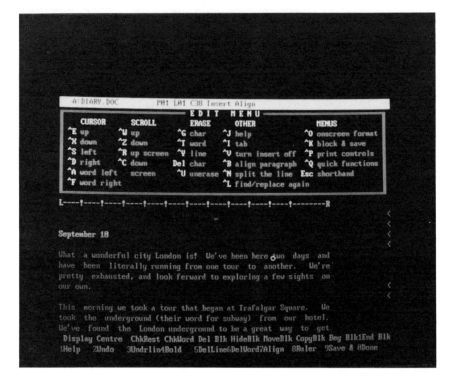

The figure shows a Wordstar document editing screen. The status line reads:

```
A:DIARY.DOC        PH1 LB1 C38 Insert Align
                    === E D I T   M E N U ===
    CURSOR        SCROLL        ERASE      OTHER                MENUS
^E up         ^U up         ^G char    ^J help           ^O onscreen format
^X down       ^Z down       ^T word    ^I tab            ^K block & save
^S left       ^R up screen  ^V line    ^V turn insert off ^P print controls
^D right      ^C down       Del char   ^B align paragraph ^Q quick functions
^A word left     screen     ^U unerase ^N split the line  Esc shorthand
^F word right                          ^L find/replace again

L----!----!----!----!----!----!----!----!----!----!-------R

September 18

What a wonderful city London is! We've been here two days and
have been literally running from one tour to another. We're
pretty exhausted, and look forward to exploring a few sights on
our own.

This morning we took a tour that began at Trafalgar Square. We
took the underground (their word for subway) from our hotel.
We've found the London underground to be a great way to get
Display Centre  ChkRest ChkWord Del Blk HideBlk MoveBlk CopyBlk Beg BlkiEnd Blk
1Help  2Undo  3Undrlin4Bold  5DelLine6DelWord7Align  8Ruler  9Save & 0Done
```

Figure 13.2 Wordstar: document editing. Reproduced courtesy of MicroPro International Ltd.

The other main features offered by a word processing package are as follows:

1. *To delete or insert text.*
2. *To over-type existing text.*
3. *To re-set margins.* Necessary for wide documents, or where paragraphs are to be indented.
4. *To reform paragraphs.* Necessary where text is inserted or deleted in the middle of a paragraph, or where margins have been changed.
5. *To move or copy blocks of text.* Often in a long report it is useful to move a section in order to add emphasis.
6. *To find a specified text string.* For example, it is useful to check all occurrences of the word 'table' in order to check that all the tables in a report are numbered in the correct sequence.
7. *To replace a text string.* For example, one might wish to replace

the string 'ICA' with 'Institute of Chartered Accountants' each time that it occurs.

8. *To insert another document (by reading another file).* This is essential where a number of standard paragraphs are to be merged into a letter.

9. *To check spelling.* Inbuilt spelling checkers now usually have over fifty thousand words, and should have English rather than American spellings. There should also be facilities to add words to the dictionary (such as proper names) and to suggest alternatives where a word is misspelt.

10. *To count words.* Essential for journalists writing articles of a specified wordage, and also for authors of books such as this.

11. *To customize standard letters, by a mail-merging facility.* This is extremely important for an accounting practice, which will often need to send out similar letters to groups of clients. Figure 13.3 shows a typical standard letter prepared on Wordstar; this can be 'merged' with a file of names and addresses to produce a series of personalized letters, one of which is also reproduced.

The package used for writing this book was Wordstar (from Micro-Pro), which for many years has been probably the best-selling word processing package, although more recently it has had a number of strong competitors. Wordstar is a good, basic package but it does lack the sophisticated facilities of some competing software (including Wordstar 2000, a more recent product from MicroPro).

A major competitor of this type has been Microsoft Word, and Figure 13.4 shows a screen shot of this package in operation. This offers a wide range of different character sets, which are displayed on the screen as they will be printed; the document can be printed when ready on a laser or a dot matrix printer. Microsoft Word also allows two windows to be opened, with a different document being edited in each window; blocks of text can then be copied across from one document and inserted into the other one. While many accounting offices may feel that this degree of sophistication is more than they require, nevertheless there are many situations where such facilities are extremely useful; for example, one may wish to produce sheets of financial advice for clients which draw on the text of previous similar notes. This sort of 'cutting and pasting' between documents is vastly simpler to do where a windowing facility is available, as with Microsoft Word; on the other hand, occasional users of word processing tend to find Word more difficult to use, perhaps partly because of the wide range of facilities offered.

Thus, it is important that the practice considers very carefully its

```
                              B & J Accts Ltd
                              957 Folke Road
   &Name&                     London N17 9SD
   &line1&
   &line2&
   &line3&                        &date&


   Dear &name2&,
                   We   have   to   inform
   you   that   your account   is   now
   seriously in arrears. Unless  we
   receive   the   sum   of   £&amount&
   within   seven   days,   we   regret
   that   your   account   will   be
   stopped.
                 Yours faithfully


               for B & J Accts Ltd




                              B & J Accts Ltd
                              957 Folke Road
   J Biggs Ltd                London N17 9SD
   274 Browns Rd
   New Cheam
   London E18                 4 April 1988


   Dear Mr Biggs,
                   We   have   to   inform
   you   that   your account   is   now
   seriously in arrears. Unless  we
   receive   the   sum   of   £355.80
   within   seven   days,   we   regret
   that   your   account   will   be
   stopped.
                 Yours faithfully


               for B & J Accts Ltd
```

Figure 13.3 Wordstar: mail-merging showing a standard letter and the resulting personalized document.

word processing requirements and selects a package which meets its needs, ensuring both that the package is powerful enough and also that it does not demand an unreasonable level of skill from the staff who will use it. It is important to consider not just the obvious immediate uses, but also any future applications that are likely to develop, as practices discover ways of providing a more professional service to their clients. Because of the high initial training investment,

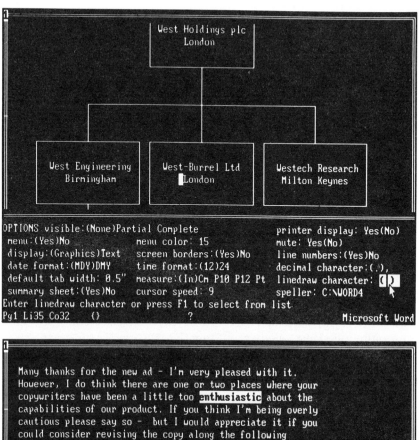

OPTIONS visible:(None)Partial Complete
menu:(Yes)No   menu color: 15
display:(Graphics)Text   screen borders:(Yes)No
date format:(MDY)DMY   time format:(12)24
default tab width: 0.5"   measure:(In)Cm P10 P12 Pt
summary sheet:(Yes)No   cursor speed: 9
Enter linedraw character or press F1 to select from list.
Pg1 Li35 Co32   {}   ?

printer display: Yes(No)
mute: Yes(No)
line numbers:(Yes)No
decimal character:(.),
linedraw character: ⟨|⟩
speller: C:\WORD4

Microsoft Word

Many thanks for the new ad - I'm very pleased with it.
However, I do think there are one or two places where your
copywriters have been a little too **enthusiastic** about the
capabilities of our product. If you think I'm being overly
cautious please say so - but I would appreciate it if you
could consider revising the copy along the following
lines...

                    Introducing VOICE.
                 The Hi-Fi you can't hear.

══════════════╣ **Word Finder   Thesaurus** ╠══════════════
enthusiastic:
adj • anxious, ardent, avid, breathless, desirous, eager, excited, fain,
        impatient, impetuous, keen, passionate, raring, zealous;
      • ardent, excitable, fervent, fiery, flaming, hot-blooded, impassioned,
        intense, passionate, stirring, sweaty, torrid, **zealous**;
      • alert, animated, bouncy, bright, brisk, buoyant, chipper, dashing,
        dynamic, ebullient, energetic, exuberant, frisky, frolicsome, gay,
        jumpy, kinetic, lively, peppy, pert, playful, rousing, scintillating,
        spirited, sprightly, spry, vivacious;
      • buoyant, cheerful, ecstatic, elated, exuberant, positive.
  ↑↓↔:point   ENTER:replace   ESC:exit   CTRL-F6:look up

Figure 13.4 Microsoft Word: screen-shot. Reproduced courtesy of Microsoft Ltd.

and the cost of converting to a different package, it is likely that the word processing package selected now will still be in use in ten years' time, so it is essential to make the right choice.

Finally, some practices have bought dedicated word processors from specialist companies such as Wordplex and Philips; in essence, these are simply microcomputers equipped with suitable software. They tend to be more expensive and less flexible than standard micro-computers, but do usually include very high quality software and equipment, often having A4-sized screens. Apart from possible com-patibility problems with other microcomputers used, they are probably not a good choice for a small- to medium-sized practice, where it is crucial to have flexibility; a standard microcomputer bought for word processing has the advantage that it can be used as a 'stand-by' for general accounting work when another microcomputer breaks down, or where a peak workload occurs.

13.2 THE ELECTRONIC OFFICE

The term electronic office system (an often misused concept) refers to an integrated management information system for an organization. In large companies, such a system will normally be run on local micro-computers in offices which are connected to a large minicomputer or mainframe. It also requires a centralized database, together with the facility to transfer data freely between different computers and differ-ent applications. Finally, there will be facilities to send electronic messages to other users or groups of users. Obviously, word process-ing is an integral part of an electronic office system, being needed in order to create documents before they are sent as messages.

Where large companies do not have electronic office systems, it is not unknown for tables of printed computer output produced by the accounts system to be carefully typed into a spreadsheet or retyped as part of a report by a secretary using a word processor. Often, the accounts system is on a mainframe computer which is not linked to the microcomputer used for word processing and spreadsheet analy-sis. Such a process must be avoided in an accounting practice for two reasons: it wastes time and hence money, and it provides an oppor-tunity for errors to be introduced in transcribing data.

Electronic office systems have proved valuable in certain situations for large organizations (the Stock Exchange computer system being a notable example), but most accounting practices could not afford the level of computing power required. Nevertheless, the concept is worth considering as a model of what might be achieved, and many aspects are worth implementing, even in a relatively small firm. One obvious point is the integration of different applications.

Integration of word processing with other applications is essential if an accounting firm is to operate efficiently, and to maintain a high quality of presentation for their clients. Most reports are likely to include a number of tables or other numerical output produced by the firm's accounts production software or spreadsheet package.

Technically, there is no difficulty in designing a system where tables of output can be readily transferred between different applications, and in particular to word processing for re-editing. It is merely necessary that suitable facilities are available, namely:

1. *Hardware*: A multi-user system or a local area network is desirable so that files can be readily accessed by the various staff who are responsible for different stages in the process of analysis. A less satisfactory alternative is for data to be transferred on diskette between different microcomputers, or for the same single-user microcomputer to be shared between several different users.

2. *Software*: Compatibility between different packages is essential if data is to be transferred. As a minimum, any reports produced by the applications package should be available as a disk file (an ASCII text file) instead of printed output; such a file can then be edited by word processing. This is a standard facility with most spreadsheets and database packages, but it is not always available in accounting software.

It is also highly desirable to be able to 'import' data from other packages into a database or spreadsheet; although data can be imported from an ASCII text file, it is not generally very convenient. It is preferable if tables can be output in one of the standard binary data formats, for example the .WK1 format used by Lotus 1-2-3 Version 2. CSM accounting software (see Chapter 8) allows certain data to be output in this format, so that it can then immediately be read into a 1-2-3 model.

13.3 ORGANIZATIONAL IMPLICATIONS

Large companies have invested heavily in microcomputers in recent years, and it is now common to find senior executives who have microcomputers on their desks. Unfortunately, surveys do not demonstrate automatic benefits, and in many cases executive productivity has actually reduced becase of acquiring a microcomputer. The reduction happens because the executives often spend their time typing into the computer at very slow speeds, without considering the efficient use of their very expensive time.

This is a disturbing finding in relation to professional accounting practices; whereas such executive inefficiencies may be hidden in a large company, no accounting firm can afford to be profligate in the use of staff time. Qualified accountants are considerably better paid than secretaries, and are usually considerably slower at typing.

It is also important to remember that there is a high initial cost in using computers in terms of the cost of training staff. Apart from the obvious costs of training courses, staff need to spend time familiarizing themselves with software and gaining experience before becoming competent. Training costs will increase substantially if staff have to be trained in all applications, rather than just certain aspects of the work.

It is therefore essential in using computer systems to define clear responsibilities for different tasks. Where financial plans are evaluated on a computer, it may be sensible for the plan to be sketched out by an accountant and then entered into a spreadsheet model by a clerk. Where a large amount of text needs to be added in producing final accounts, it is sensible for this text to be added by a typist at the word processing stage, rather than it being typed by accounts staff.

Hence, maximum efficiency will only be achieved if the organizational implications are carefully considered. Not only is a review of procedures necessary, it is also likely that there will be a shift in the type of work required from staff, with less emphasis on basic routine accounting. With care, it should be possible to use computers to provide a better service to clients and to increase the income of the practice.

13.4 DESK-TOP PUBLISHING

Desk-top publishing (or DTP) is essentially a greatly enhanced version of word processing, allowing the facilities of full electronic typesetting. Figure 13.5 shows the sort of output that can be produced, in this case using Ventura (one of the better-known DTP packages) and a Ricoh laser printer. This system can be run on most standard business microcomputers (such as an AT-compatible or an IBM PS/2 Model 50), a laser printer being also essential. Ideally, a high-quality enlarged monochrome screen will be used, but this is not essential; a mouse is also highly desirable because of the interactive way in which much of the page layout work will be done. Many accounting practices will have a suitable microcomputer in use already with a laser printer for word processing, and then the only additional cost of a desk-top

Ventura Scoop

SPECIAL EDITION   APPROPRIATE TECHNOLOGY LTD   JULY 1988

Aptec Shows Off Ventura Publisher at Café Royal

SAN FRANCISCO (VP) — Xerox Corporation has introduced its first electronic publishing software product that runs on industry standard personal computers. Xerox chose the Seybold Conference to announce the price and availability of the software package. Conference attendees were impressed by the speed of the product and its depth of functionality.

Product will be widely available.
The Xerox Desktop Publishing Software Series: Ventura Publisher Edition will be made available through Xerox authorized dealers (including ComputerLand), and the Xerox Business Software Center via an 800 number, and the Xerox general line sales force. Commented one observer, "This breadth of distribution represents Xerox's committment to the mainstream of the PC-based market."
Ventura Publisher Edition allows personal computer users to merge text and graphics to create publishing-quality documents, such as newsletters, technical manuals, books, bids and proposals, that might otherwise be sent to a print shop or typesetter. The package runs on the Xerox 6065, IBM PC/XT, IBM PC/AT, and all PC compatibles. It supports most popular laser printers, including the Xerox 4045, the Apple Laser-Writer and the Hewlett Packard Laser Jet.

Pioneers in the field
"As one of the pioneers in the field of electronic publishing, Xerox fully understands users' requirements for a desktop publishing software product," said James N. Brown, vice president, office systems marketing, Xerox Business Systems Group.
Pricing for Ventura Publisher Edition is $895, with volume discounts available. For further information or to place an order, call 800-822-8221.

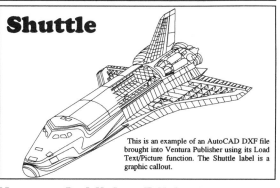

This is an example of an AutoCAD DXF file brought into Ventura Publisher using its Load Text/Picture function. The Shuttle label is a graphic callout.

Ventura Publisher Edition Redefines Desktop Publishing

MORGAN HILL (VP) — Xerox Ventura Publisher Edition has added new meaning to the term "Desktop Publishing." Before the introduction of Ventura Publisher Edition, Desktop Publishing refered primarily to advanced drawing packages that were extended to handle different text fonts.
These types of packages were characterized by a hand-intensive approach that attempted to mimic what graphic artists and typesetters were used to doing using the personal computer screen as an electronic paste-up board. While this approach was easy for artists to pick up, it did not result in much time-saving because the user was still faced with the drudgery of hand-adjusting each piece of text on the page.
Fortunately, the software developers at Ventura Software Inc. recognized this and adopted a Style Sheet approach. In the same way that a spreadsheet defines the rules for

Illustration of nozzle produced in AutoCAD. Line-Art can also be brought in from Mentor Graphics EE CAD, DXF compatible CAD packages, Lotus 123, GEM Draw/Graph. Images can be brought in from PC Paintbrush, GEM Paint, MicroTek, Dest, and other scanners.

a complex set of repetitive calculations, a Style Sheet defines the rules for complex layout. Once these rules are defined, non-typesetters can quickly achieve typesetter-quality results simply by applying or tagging each paragraph as a Headline, Sub-Head, etc.

> *Ventura Scoop was created with Xerox Ventura Publisher Edition. This is a complex page with many fonts being used in combination with a large amount of graphics. Many printers will not successfully print a page this complex.*

APPROPRIATE TECHNOLOGY LTD, APTEC HOUSE, SOUTH BANK BUSINESS CENTRE, PONTON ROAD, LONDON SW8 5AT. TEL- 01-627 1000. TELEX- 261797 APTEC G. FAX- 01-498 0496

Figure 13.5 Output from Ventura desk-top publishing. Reproduced courtesy of Aptec Ltd.

publishing system would be the cost of the software, typically about £750.

Some of the facilities available in a typical DTP system are:

1. different font sizes and different character thicknesses for emphasis (as on headings)
2. use of different character sets, or italics, as required
3. division of page into columns, or horizontal subsections
4. importing text files produced by any common word processing package
5. importing charts produced by graphics packages, to scale those charts up or down as necessary, and to move them around on the page as required
6. fitting text around such charts, thus avoiding blank spaces
7. enlarging or moving headings on the screen.

The above list is only a brief indicative summary of the features in what are very powerful software packages. Indeed, for many practices the problem will be finding a package that is simple enough to use on an occasional basis rather than looking for esoteric features. The major point is to ensure that the package does interface with the word processing and graphics software and the laser printer that are to be used. This will not usually be a problem, especially as most accounting practices will tend to use standard packages such as Lotus 1-2-3 or Supercalc. In any case, most DTP packages also interface with specialist graphics design packages, such as Autocad (the picture in Figure 13.5 was produced by Autocad).

DTP packages do have some text editing facilities, which are needed where text needs to be abbreviated to fit into an available space. However, the usual procedure would be to type text initially by word processing and then to import it into the DTP system. The major point to be considered is the level of skill required in order to perform effectively. Although most DTP software is reasonably user-friendly, nevertheless the wide range of facilities implies that a longer learning process is necessary. In addition, there are non-computer skills of graphic design which need to be acquired if truly professional work is to result. Thus, one would expect only one or two secretarial staff in an accounting office to be trained to use desk-top publishing, whereas many staff might be able to use word processing.

The advantages of using desk-top publishing for an ambitious accounting practice are considerable; it enables even quite small practices to produce extremely professional newsletters to send out to all their clients. Alternatively, they may send information sheets to selected clients on particular financial topics of interest to them. All this can be done at very low marginal cost with a modest initial invest-ment, but it will considerably enhance the professional image of the practice in the eyes of current and potential clients. Thus, desk-top publishing is a valuable tool in selling the services of the accounting practice; our experience is that selling is a key aspect of managing the practice, which is often sadly neglected by many small- or medium-sized practices.

13.5 CONCLUSIONS

There is no doubt that any practice will benefit from word processing, but they will gain most if word processing is seen as a computing application which must be totally integrated with other applications, rather than just being seen as a secretarial aid. Word processing can not only save money, but will also help the practice to enhance its professional image to clients, and thus to market itself more success-fully. This particularly applies to practices that are able to make efficient use of desk-top publishing in producing promotional material.

Points mentioned elsewhere about security are especially true of word processing; confidential documents produced on the word processor must not be immediately accessible to any unauthorized members of staff. Even practices which are careful about the security of their accounting systems often forget the dangers inherent in a word processing system. It is essential that adequate procedures for security are established, which should include at least a password protection for system access, and preferably facilities for encrypting files and establishing passwords for any important files. Such pro-cedures are especially important where networks or other multi-user systems are in operation.

14 Taxation

The development and use of software for taxation applications by accounting practices has been much more problematic and slower than other accounting applications. In the past, software houses have lost considerable sums of money in attempting to produce a marketable taxation package. However, there are strong arguments to support the view that computerization in this area is feasible and will yield cost savings. A number of tax packages are now being used, although many accountants still claim that it is quicker to perform tax computations manually.

In this chapter, we will be examining the important issue of the suitability of taxation packages, particularly in relation to small- to medium-sized practices. The taxation packages on the market tend to be designed for specific tax functions, for example the computation of personal tax liability; for the majority of small- to medium-sized practices, income tax will form the major proportion of their tax work. The features of this type of software will be considered in detail.

14.1 THE CASE FOR TAX SOFTWARE

In general, the processing of a client's tax liability involves:

1. providing information to meet the requirements of a number of standard formats for submission to the Inland Revenue.
2. updating information in respect of client details and changes in legislation relating to taxation, for example accounting for the changes in tax rates set by the *Finance Acts*.
3. the computations necessary in calculating the tax liability of clients
4. keeping a diary for the management of the tax work in the practice.

The majority of this work therefore involves keeping records and retrieving information from them; it therefore lends itself to computerization.

Recently, the Inland Revenue has been investigating the feasibility of fully computer-generated returns. It is likely, if such a system were to be implemented, that a practice which already uses tax software to prepare substitute returns for clients would be in an advantageous position.

Software houses have for a long time recognized that the nature of taxation lends itself to computerization. They have also recognized that the market is large enough to justify a heavy investment in developing and marketing such software. The major problems in the development of tax software have been twofold: initially, the problem of producing software that could cope with the intricacies of taxation legislation; secondly, convincing accountants who specialize in tax that the introduction of software in this field can be justified on economic grounds. Advances have now clearly come about with the design of a number of tax packages that have successfully met the necessary requirements and are being used by accountants. However, there still remain some doubts as to whether the software meets the needs of users for particular aspects of taxation such as tax planning.

14.2 THE SMALL- AND MEDIUM-SIZED PRACTICE

In general the arguments for using a computer for the calculation of taxation liabilities are convincing. However, the question arises: is this application appropriate for small- to medium-sized practices? In order to justify the cost of a particular taxation package, there clearly must be enough relevant tax work. It is unrealistic to expect one package to cater for all the needs of the practice in respect of the variations in taxation.

It is therefore extremely important for the practice, before purchasing any tax software, to identify the types of taxation work that are carried out and the associated client profiles. It is likely, for example, that this type of practice will have a heavy proportion of personal taxation work compared with corporation tax. Clients may be subject to differing rules within tax legislation; for example, there can be varying capital allowances for different types of businesses. It may be that a particular package cannot cope with these variations; the software selected should be capable of producing the entire computation for an acceptable proportion of clients.

The majority of the tax software has been designed so that unqualified staff are capable of preparing computations. This will give the practice the opportunity to free qualified personnel for other tasks. This is not to say that senior staff should not themselves be capable of using the software, as they would be required to supervise and manage the processing of taxation in the practice. The policy of using unqualified staff in this function could be an economical way of managing the resources of the practice.

Another aspect to consider is the relationship between tax software and other software used in the practice. It may be possible to integrate or link tax software with other software used for another application, for example the preparation of clients' accounts. This could also result in additional cost savings.

The use of computers for taxation purposes could also be used to extend the practice's fee earning capacity, through the extension of services to potential new customers. For example, one company is currently marketing a report service through a questionnaire which provides details of income, personal status and other relevant data. From this information the firm produces an income tax report which highlights personal tax aspects, such as whether a man and a wife should be taxed separately. Presumably, this may lead to a more formal tax consultation. The report service is relatively cheap and is aimed at the working population who do not currently consult with a tax advisor, but who may benefit from a review of their tax position. Whilst this service has been criticized by one well-known commentator*, it nevertheless serves as a good illustration of the way in which a practice could extend its services.

14.3 INCOME TAX SOFTWARE

Personal taxation, in particular income tax, is likely to represent the major proportion of a small- to medium-sized practice's tax portfolio. Software firms in association with practising accountants have spent a considerable amount of time in developing software for this purpose. This software is probably the most well used of all the tax software and in recent years the number of users has dramatically increased.

The following are the main features normally offered with this type of software:

1. *Clients records*, including personal details in respect of the client

---

*Phillip Hardman (9th July 1987) *Accountancy Age*; 'This will give a mismatch of information. Half of it will be wrong. That's why you pay an accountant.'

and spouse, address, sources of income earned and unearned, allowances, e.g. capital allowances.

2. *Tax computations* for income arising for Schedules A, B, D and E and taxed investment income. The output, in the form of reports, would normally show the computations and the tax liability for each schedule and in total. The relevant dates for payment will also be shown.

3. *Wife's earnings election,* detailing if such an election would be beneficial.

4. *Tax returns* — the production of substitute tax returns for completion of the standard Inland Revenue form. It should be noted that at present the Inland Revenue will not accept a substitute tax return; however, as previously mentioned, there is a possibility that such substitutes may be acceptable in the future.

5. *An analysis of taxable income* required under Inland Revenue Form 930, showing income under the varying tax bands. Figure 14.1 shows an example of the analysis produced by Taxpoint, a personal tax system marketed by Datasolve Ltd.

6. *A tax diary* that aids the practice in management and progress chasing. This includes records of letters to clients and the Inland Revenue, the state of work-in-progress, and relevant dates such as appeals.

7. *Standard letters* can be generated for clients and the Inland Revenue.

8. *Tax planning* — the ability to consider scenarios in respect of tax liabilities relating to the current period and the future. For example, whether the election now of wife's earnings will prejudice the tax position in the future. Tax commentators generally seem to feel that such facilities are useful but rather limited at present; they anticipate, however, that much more will be developed in the future.

Taxpoint, the system referred to above, and Taxman, a system marketed by CSM Ltd, are two packages that offer such facilities and are used by a reasonable number of practices.

There are two particular problems of concern to most users related to income tax software:

1. *Maintenance support.* It is essential with the constant changes in taxation that the software is updated regularly.

2. *Disk space.* Requirements for disk space may be very heavy if the records of clients go back a number of years. A system of archiving will probably be needed, to allow the user to archive records for previous years on to back-up disk or tape in a form that can be

```
                            Lindsay Bennett
                 Allocation of Allowances and Rate Bands
                       Year Ended 5th April 1988

              Domiciled, Resident and Ordinarily Resident in UK

Source        Amount   Ded'ns   Pers    Amount    27%     40%    45%    50%    55%    60%
                                rels    Taxable
------        ------   ------   ----    -------   -----   ----   ----   ----   ----   ----
               £        £        £        £        £       £      £      £      £      £

Schedule E    17475    9040     5160     3275     3275

Sch.D
Earned         7130    3000               4130     4130

Sch.D
Invest.       12015                      12015    10495   1520

Taxed
Income         1317                       1317             980    337

              ------   ------   ----    -------   -----   ----   ----   ----   ----   ----
Total         37937    12040    5160     20737    17900   2500    337
              ------    ----            -------   -----   ----   ----   ----   ----   ----
Less
----
Deductions    (12040)

Pers.
Reliefs        (5160)
              -------
Taxable
Income         20737
              -------


Tax Charged
-----------

B.R. Expansion                   £
£8200 @     27%                2214.00
-----------------
£17900 @    27%                4833.00
£2500  @    40%                1000.00
£337   @    45%                 151.65
------                         -------
20737                          8198.65
------                         -------

Tax Assessed
------------
Schedule E.               3098.25
Schedule D. earned        1115.10
Schedule D. Invest        3441.65
Taxed Income               543.65
                          -------
Total Tax                 8198.65
                          -------
```

Figure 14.1 Taxpoint: analysis of personal tax. Reproduced courtesy of Datasolve Ltd.

easily retrieved if necessary. Current records will, of course, be kept accessible on hard disk.

14.4 OTHER TAX SOFTWARE

Corporation tax software in recent years has been developed and sold by a number of firms. This software tends to be used in the main by the larger practices which are advising large companies. These systems are fairly comprehensive in their coverage, but a number of the features probably would not be relevant to the smaller companies who are likely to be the clients of medium and small practices. A careful evaluation of the workload of the practice is important, but a medium or small practice may well conclude that the purchase of this software is not justified.

Other software has been designed to compute capital gains tax and dividend costs for securities. Typically, it is only necessary to input sales and acquisitions, and the program does the rest. On the other hand, the calculations involved are relatively simple; it is not difficult to write a computer model for this type of computation using a spreadsheet. Whether this is a better alternative than buying a package will depend on the computing skills of the practice.

14.5 CONCLUSIONS

The evidence suggests that the use of tax software can create major cost savings. In the case of small- and medium-sized practices, these savings will only be realized if the practice matches its client profile with a relevant tax package. The potential for practices to open up new markets is particularly interesting. Tax services can be offered at reasonable fees using taxation software, which could result in a larger client base and a greater fee income.

The activity in the software market in respect of tax software is buoyant and competitive; this would imply that software firms see a growing profitable market. Tax software is still being developed and it is likely that the facilities offered will improve further to meet user's needs. This will offer further opportunities for practising accountants.

15 Concluding observations

We have considered in this book a range of activities in the professional accounting practice for which a microcomputer might be used. We started the research for this book with a relatively open mind, but our view has now become clear: in our opinion, any professional practice, however small, should be making substantial use of computers. A number of reasons have already been given in discussing particular applications, but they can be summarized as cost saving, extending services and better management information.

The cost savings are difficult to measure precisely, but there is no question that they exist. We have spoken to many professional accountants who are using microcomputers, and all felt that they were realizing substantial benefits in respect of cost saving. Although we have found occasional cases of microcomputers not being implemented successfully, the reasons appeared to be either software that did not perform up to expectation or, more commonly, a lack of resolution to see the matter through on the part of the user.

The introduction of microcomputers to a practice can create considerable opportunities to extend the fee-earning services of the practice, particularly in the area of planning and control.

The benefits of better management information are difficult to define in any tangible sense, but in many ways this aspect may be more important than the cost savings. Adopting new technology is often an article of faith, and most research studies on companies which adopt new technology have shown the difficulties of measuring benefits, even after the event. However, the post-war history of British industry shows numerous instances of companies which have gone out of business, because of a failure to adopt new technology. The

same economic logic will undoubtedly apply, perhaps less dramatically, to professional accounting practices. Practices that use microcomputers, and manage and market themselves professionally, will
tend to expand; those that do not get involved and continue to work
in the old way will tend to contract. Many clients, even one-person
operations, now use microcomputers to run their businesses; the
professional accountant who does not use microcomputers will
increasingly be regarded as an anachronism.

The aim of this chapter is to summarize briefly the factors to
consider in selecting a microcomputer, and to discuss the implications
for the accounting practice of adopting a microcomputer strategy,
including both the organizational and the audit implications.

15.1 BUYING ADVICE

Enough professional accountants have made bad decisions to
convince us that it is worth offering some brief advice here. Buying a
microcomputer is no longer a new and risky matter, and there should
not be major problems provided that some common sense is applied.
Some essential points to consider are as follows:

Define responsibility, and be committed
Unless the partners are clearly seen to be committed to implementing
a computer system, then development is likely to have low priority,
and the system will be under-used. It is also essential that one
committed partner (or other senior member of staff) is made responsible for selecting and purchasing the system, and for overseeing
implementation; otherwise, nothing may well happen.

Understand before you buy
Computer salesmen often try to impress by an air of mystique, which
may be a smokescreen for their own ignorance of accounting details.
Be prepared to ask boring, niggling questions until you are sure that
the system does exactly what is needed.

Talk to other users
Professional accountants can often make useful contacts through local
accounting societies. Alternatively, one may ask dealers for an introduction to current users of their systems, although such users may
sometimes be 'over-friendly' with the dealer. Discussions with current
users gives a useful insight into practicalities, which can never be
gained from a salesman to the same extent.

Find the right dealer

Even selling standard book-keeping software requires considerable specialist expertise, which the average high street dealer will lack; software for use in an accounting practice is even more specialist. Consequently, companies that market professional accounting software usually either sell directly to customers, or franchise a small number of carefully selected dealers. It is essential to buy from a dealer with a genuine experience and understanding of the work of the professional accountant. Networks also require very specific expertise that many dealers do not possess; it is worth asking dealers for a list of customers for whom they have installed networks if you are considering purchasing one.

Buy from one dealer

It may be possible to buy hardware and software at a discount from different sources, but this is unwise unless you know exactly what you are doing. Where software fails to perform, this may be a software problem, a hardware problem, or a problem of communication between hardware and software; unless everything is purchased from one dealer, it will be impossible to locate responsibility. Moreover, in the initial stages of implementation, one is likely to need considerable help and advice from the dealer; this will be far more forthcoming if the dealer sees you as a committed customer from whom he is making an adequate profit.

Buy software, not hardware

Hardware from different manufacturers is fairly comparable, in the main, if varying slightly in price and performance. The major consideration must always be the software: choose carefully both operating software (for networks or multi-user systems) and applications software (for accounting and office automation), to meet your requirements.

Get it in writing

If you have any doubts about whether the system can perform up to requirements, get the dealer to make a statement in writing; if they are unwilling to do so, it is probably because they lack confidence. This approach is particularly useful where one is concerned about possible response times on a network or multi-user system. A statement such as this can form the basis of a legal action if the system does not meet expectations. There have been a number of cases won against computer companies for not meeting promises, and it is quite possible to sue on this basis. However, this will probably not be necessary if the right dealer has been chosen in the first place.

Take independent professional advice
This is likely to be expensive; computer consultants charge upwards of £250 per day. On the other hand, taking advice can often avoid unnecessary expenditure and can avoid extremely expensive mistakes. On a large system, it is probably worth allocating 5–10% of the total budget for independent advice.

If you do not know of an appropriate computer consultant, most polytechnics and some universities offer consultancy services. Alternatively, the Association of Independent Computer Consultants is a useful point of contact.

There are a number of texts which offer useful advice on buying computers, which may be referred to for more detailed advice. Some of these are included in the list of references at the end of this book.

15.2 TYPE OF COMPUTER TO CHOOSE

In terms of hardware, the practice has three main choices:

1. stand-alone microcomputers
2. microcomputers in a local area network (LAN)
3. multi-user microcomputer or minicomputer.

Stand-alone microcomputers probably represent the cheapest solution, and are certainly simpler to implement. This may be a sensible choice initially for a practice with no experience of computers in order to gain experience on a small scale before implementing full-scale use of computers. It may also be the only viable choice for a small practice, and can yield significant benefits.

For any but the smallest practices, as we have indicated previously, it is worth considering buying a network or a multi-user system; the full benefits of improved management information and management control over the practice cannot be realized with stand-alone microcomputers. Which system should be selected depends on the type of workload processed by the practice; this is an area where independent advice from a computer consultant can often be useful. Another major factor is likely to be the availability of software; some software runs only under MSDOS or OS/2, and will not run under multi-user operating systems such as UNIX. On the other hand, some manufacturers of multi-user computers market their own software which will only run on their own equipment; this has the disadvantage of probably 'locking' the user to that supplier in respect of future purposes.

It should be emphasized that for most small- to medium-sized practices either a network or a multi-user system can provide an effective solution. Many examples can now be found of successful installations of either type of system in small- to medium-sized practices.

15.3 IMPLEMENTATION

Some practices will choose initially to purchase one or two single-user microcomputers to gain experience, and the problems of implementation will be much less than with a more complex operation. On the other hand, some practices will already have experience of microcomputers, and it will simply be a question of transferring files across to a new computer.

Here, we consider the most difficult case: where a practice with little or no experience of computers has decided to install a network of microcomputers or a multi-user system. In this case, it is essential to draw up an implementation schedule with the dealer supplying the hardware and software, who should have experience of similar operations for other practices. The points to be considered in this are as follows:

Installation of hardware

This will involve significant expense, and some inconvenience for a day or two, for computer cabling; any competent dealer could advise as to the likely cost. Obviously, space will need to be made for both microcomputers and for any central processors or file servers.

Purchase of furniture

New additional desks will probably be needed; cupboards and filing systems for computer printouts may well be necessary. An accounting office, which needs to be well organized and have a high degree of security, may require a substantial budget for related furniture. Practices are sometimes, mistakenly, unwilling to spend money in this way.

Training of staff

Some training courses are essential for the staff who are going to use the software; many courses are available from commercial training organizations for popular accounting packages such as Pegasus and Sage. With more specialist professional accounting software, or more obscure packages, it may be more difficult; a recent survey by the National Computing Centre (NCC) showed over one thousand microcomputer accounting packages on the market, while courses were available for only sixty-six of these. Admittedly, training is often available from suppliers on a 'one-off' basis.

Training on the job is even more important; the best way to learn to use a system is to use it with 'dummy' data, and to gain experience and confidence in a situation where mistakes do not matter. From the point of view of the practice, this does mean budgeting for a certain amount of unproductive time; even when the employee moves on to live data, they are likely to work slowly initially.

Data conversion

Data conversion usually entails typing details from manual records into the computer, although it may involve conversion of existing computer records to a new data format. For an accounting practice, the records will relate to clients and to employees; this should not be a massive task, but will require a significant amount of effort in the short term. For some clients, who may have several thousand customers on their sales ledger, data conversion can be a very major task.

Live implementation

This can only begin when staff are adequately trained, and when the necessary records are on the computer. Implementation should be a stage-by-stage process: for example, one section of the practice at a time, and one application at a time. Where possible, implementation should be scheduled for when the practice is less busy; the more pressurized staff are, the more mistakes will be made in the initial stages.

15.4 ORGANIZATIONAL IMPLICATIONS

As has been pointed out at various times in this book, the organizational implications on the practice of using a computer will be considerable, if effective use is to be made of it. The ability of the organization to market itself will be considerably enhanced, leading in the short term to greater profitability and in the longer term to likely expansion; profitability will also be aided by better credit control.

The work of staff within the practice is likely to change at the same time; much of the tedious figure work will be eliminated, enabling staff savings to be made or an increased workload to be undertaken by the same number of staff. Careful planning of work will be needed to ensure that staff are used in the most efficient way possible; for example, it is undesirable for a partner or accounts senior to type whole pages of notes to accounts which could be typed much more cheaply by a typist. However, planning of work is not a new concept in accounting practices, and replanning work to use a computer effectively is not difficult, given a moderate degree of common sense.

15.5 AUDITING IMPLICATIONS

For the clients of small to medium practices the formal requirement of an audit under the 1985 *Companies Act* will often not be relevant. In the main, the clients of this size of practice will be unincorporated businesses. However, in some cases such businesses, for other reasons, may still require an audit. For example, in the case of a partnership, the agreement between partners may stipulate the requirement for the annual accounts to be audited.

Where an audit is required and the accounts are maintained and prepared using microcomputer software, the audit implications are significant. The focus of the audit will differ depending upon whether the client maintains his own records and prepares the accounts using software such as that described in Chapter 8, or the practice prepares the client's accounts on software such as that described in Chapter 7.

In the latter case, if the client's records are in a relatively incomplete state, the system of control will probably be dependent upon the close involvement of the owners of the firm. In such a case it will therefore be appropriate to apply the small business audit qualification. On the other hand, if reasonable controls do exist, the focus of the audit will be on the controls of the client's recording system prior to the practice processing the data input. Although the practice will be responsible for the controls relating to the software and data input, it is still important that the software has an adequate audit trail, thus enabling the practice to trace source documents.

The major concern of the accounting profession, in respect of auditing microcomputer systems, is when clients maintain and prepare their own accounts. The main implications of the audit, in such cases, were detailed in Chapter 8. Bhasker and Williams (1986) have identified a number of different approaches to the audit in these circumstances. The majority of these approaches do require the auditor to possess a good working knowledge of microcomputer hardware and software. This knowledge is of growing importance as more and more small businesses introduce microcomputer systems into the accounting function of their firms.

References and further reading

Auditing Guideline 407 (June 1984) *Auditing in a Computer Environment*, ICAEW, London.

Berry, A., Citron, D. and Jarvis, R. (1987) The information needs of bankers dealing with large and small companies, *Certified Research Report 7*, Certified Accountants Publications Ltd, London.

Bhaskar, K.N., and Williams, B.C. (1986) The impact of microprocessors on small accounting practices, *Research Studies in Accounting*, Prentice-Hall in association with ICAEW, London.

Bradley, J. (1987) *Data Base Management in Business* 2nd edn, Holt, Rinehart and Winston.

Byers, R.A. (1985) *Everyman's Data Base Primer with dBASE3*, Ashton-Tate, Milton Keynes.

Jenkins, B., Perry, R. and Cooke, P. (1986) *An Audit Approach to Computers*, Chartac (ICAEW), London.

Person, R. (1987) *1-2-3 Business Formula Handbook*, QUE.

Waller, D. (1987) *Book-keeping with Pegasus*, Paradigm.

(1987) *Countering Computer Fraud*, Chartac (ICAEW), London.

(1987) *Workpack on Microcomputers*, 2nd edn, Chartac (ICAEW), London.

Index